The Abortionist

The Abortionist

A WOMAN AGAINST THE LAW

Rickie Solinger

University of California Press
Berkeley   Los Angeles   London

University of California Press
Berkeley and Los Angeles, California

University of California Press, Ltd.
London, England

Published by arrangement with The Free Press, a
Division of Macmillan, Inc.

First paperback printing 1996

Library of Congress Cataloging-in-Publication Data

Solinger, Rickie
    The abortionist : a woman against the law /
Rickie Solinger.
        p.   cm.
    Originally published: New York : Free Press ;
Toronto : Maxwell Macmillan Canada ; New
York : Maxwell Macmillan International,
©1994. With new addition to pref.
    Includes bibliographical references.
    ISBN 0-520-20402-6   (pbk : alk. paper)
    1. Barnett, Ruth.   2. Abortion—Oregon—
Portland—Case studies.   3. Pregnant women—
Oregon—Portland—Social conditions—Case
studies.
HQ767.5.U5S7326   1996
363.4'6'09795—dc20   95-38874
                                              CIP

Printed in the United States of America

9 8 7 6 5 4 3 2 1

The paper used in this publication meets the minimum requirements of American National Standard
for Information Sciences—Permanence of Paper
for Printed Library Materials, ANSI Z39.48-1984.

For Lee and Amy

CONTENTS

PREFACE

For the past one hundred and fifty years in the United States, when abortion has been discussed in public, the context has almost always been legal: we need laws to stamp out abortion. We need to liberalize the laws. We need to give women a legal right to choice. We need to restrict or recriminalize the practice. While these discussions have proceeded across the decades of the nineteenth and twentieth centuries—when abortion was a crime, and when it was not—girls and women have found abortion practitioners to terminate pregnancies they were unable to manage. Our history shows us that neither criminal statutes nor censorious public attitudes were ever sufficient to stop women determined to decide for themselves whether and when to become a mother.

Nobody knows for sure how many illegal abortions were performed each year in the decades before *Roe v. Wade*, the 1973 Supreme Court decision that legalized abortion. Law enforcement officials and public health experts often estimated the annual number of abortions at one million, with only ten thousand of those conducted in hospitals as medically sanctioned therapeutic abortions. In 1953, when abortion was most emphatically a crime, Alfred Kinsey's pathbreaking study, *Sexual Behavior and the Human Female*, reported that more than one out of every five women in the United States who had sexual relations — whether inside or outside of marriage — had had an abortion. The experts generally agreed that most illegal abortions were performed on married women, not surprisingly, since more married than single women engaged in sexual relations. But an enormous number of girls and women in both groups found abortionists to take care of them in the illegal era.

We have no reliable numbers to attach to illegal abortions, nor do we have a thorough profile of abortion practitioners. Many were able to conduct their business without exposure. Like many people who operate outside of the law, a number left no evidence of their illegal activities. We do know that in a great many cities and towns, medical doctors in the illegal era did sneak in an abortion case every now and then, often as a favor to a long-time patient who made her desperation and her determination frighteningly plain. In many regions of the country, there was at least one full-time physician-abortionist, such as the well-known Dr. Robert Spencer in Ashland, Pennsylvania. A steady stream of unwillingly pregnant girls and women from New York, New Jersey, Ohio, and farther away than that heard about Dr. Spencer and made their way to his office between 1923 and 1967.

Some practitioners were not physicians, but were nevertheless highly skilled and experienced. Some were midwives, others nurses, chiropractors, naturopaths. The vast majority of illegal abortions were performed by individuals—doctors and others—who knew what they were doing because they provided their services day in and day out, year after year, for decades at a time with the tacit consent of law enforcement.

Others who performed abortions in the illegal era were not trained or skilled. These were the notorious back-alley butchers, the car mechanics, the hairdressers, the proprietors of hardware stores, the housewives who saw that the law, together with women's need to control their fertility, created lucrative opportunities for a person with the stomach to try his or her luck at scraping wombs. These types performed a relatively small share of the abortions carried out in the illegal era. Their careers generally did not last long. They made mistakes, and they were arrested at once. The terrible consequences of their work, and the highly public fate of these abortionists—their arrests and trials and incarcerations—guaranteed them an enduring place in our historical memory of the illegal era, despite their brief and limited practices.

People who saw the results of anti-abortion laws firsthand in the illegal era—the physicians and public health officials who kept tabs on emergency room traffic—were well aware that it was not the physician-abortionist, nor the midwife or chiropractor or even the car mechanic, who caused abortion-seeking girls and women the most physical damage before Roe v. Wade. By far, the lion's share of the damage was at the hands of the unwillingly pregnant woman herself, so desperate and resourceless, so shamed and determined, that she'd take up a hideous array of herbs and implements, despite the spectre of damage and death from self-styled abortions that haunted every woman in those days. Dr. Kinsey and his colleagues in the 1950s estimated that seventy-five to eighty-five percent of septic abortions were self-induced. An obstetrician in Washington, D.C., observed in 1958 that attempts to suppress abortion simply raised the self-induced abortion rate and consequently the death rate.

This book addresses even broader sources of danger to women in the United States during the illegal era: the law itself and the cultural and political context in which the law was sometimes enforced, sometimes not. To address these sources of danger, I have reconstructed the career of one abortionist, Ruth Barnett, who practiced in Portland, Oregon, from 1918 until 1968. This woman's life and work make a very strong case that it was not the practitioner who created the danger for women before *Roe v. Wade*, it was the law—which was never effective in stamping out abortion, but nevertheless always pressed dangerously on the lives of women in this country. Whether the anti-abortion statutes were rarely enforced, as in the 1930s, or often enforced, as in the 1950s, the fact that these laws were on the books created opportunities for individuals—sleazy entrepreneurs and ambitious politicians—who did not perform abortions, but positioned themselves to benefit from women's desperation, at women's expense. The story of the illegal era provides a glaring example of how, when an activity is simultaneously illegal, culturally taboo, and perceived as one of life's necessities by women, the opportunities abound for exploiting women while enhancing the power of men.

The truth is, when the state seized the right to govern women's bodies, anti-abortion statutes put all women in danger, even though the statutes never came close to stamping out abortion. Today, anti-choice legislators and a minority of our citizenry are determined to use the law again to mandate "counselling" and waiting periods, to require parental and spousal notification, to deny insurance coverage for abortion, to prohibit certain kinds of procedures, and ultimately to outlaw altogether the right of women to control their own fertility. The effect of these efforts, where they prevail, will be to mandate the degradation of unwillingly pregnant girls and women and to further entrench a tiered system of access to abortion services that will hurt poor women first.

The history of our recent past teaches that anti-abortion statutes have had and would again have an additional malign effort—degrading the law itself. Although the law never did and never will stop millions of women from determining their own reproductive lives, it has in the past, as Ruth Barnett's story shows, provided a wealth of opportunities for police corruption, politically corrupt selective enforcement, and politically timed sensational and salacious exposés, all of which endangered and damaged women.

Anti-abortion statutes have never stopped abortion in part because these laws have always been at odds with public opinion. That fact may be difficult to remember in the midst of today's noisy, sometimes violent anti-choice rhetoric and legislative grandstanding. But in the depths of the illegal era, legal experts and law enforcement officials regularly pointed out that the majority of Americans were not opposed to abortion because, then as now, too many of our wives, mothers, sisters, aunts, girlfriends—too many of us—have been caught by unmanageable pregnancies. Yet, in the absence of a feminist movement that linked abortion rights and women's rights, public tolerance of abortion in the illegal era meant that most Americans passively accepted laws against abortion and quietly sanctioned massive, secretive, individual resistance. But today the public cannot afford to be passive about the right to abortion because a desperate segment of the opposition has turned violent and murderous. This opposition and its far-right supporters are determined to have the state control women's bodies and fertility once again.

Ruth Barnett and her colleagues in the illegal era lived and worked under constant threat of arrest and imprisonment. Their lives were infused with the anxiety that came from never knowing when politicians and law enforcement would find it politically remunerative to stage sex-drenched raids and trials. But today practitioners live and work in the darker, far more life-threatening shadow of harassment, violence, and death. Even from her jail cell, Ruth Barnett would have found it hard to believe that physicians carrying on her work have been shot down in cold blood, and many others wear bulletproof vests, fear for their staffs and families, and sustain fanatical threats and poisonous public preachments from clinic blockaders, movement spokespeople, and anti-choice lawmakers.

Barnett and her mid-century colleagues would be shocked and disheartened by the new dangers that define abortion practitioners' lives and work. But sadly, the old-timers would not be surprised that their counterparts today remain desperately vulnerable. The malignantly false epithet—"the back-alley butcher"—under which Ruth Barnett and her many highly skilled colleagues labored in our recent past lives on today in the dangerously scurrilous attacks on contemporary providers.

It is my hope that bringing Ruth Barnett's life and work out of the shadows after all these years will not only do honor to her courage and commitment to women but will also inspire readers to honor and support abortion providers across this country, who are once again targeted and reviled as they perform the difficult and crucial work that so few others are willing or able to do. For hundreds of thousands of women each year, these practitioners are agents of deliverance and dignity. The fact is, the fate of women and of their access of full citizenship rights are tightly bound to the fate of abortion providers in the United States. Anti-abortion fanatics build their strategies on this tenet. So must the pro-choice majority.

Rickie Solinger
Boulder, Colorado
September 1995

Chapter One

DANGER

*I*t is 1965. She is twenty-three, new in San Francisco. After nineteen applications and one interview, she has her first job after college. She is a junior high school home ec teacher. A few weeks after school starts, her college boyfriend flies down from Portland to San Francisco, more for old time's sake than for love. The two of them go to the movies, go to the ocean, go back to her place and have sex. He flies back to Portland. She misses her period.

All grown up and scared to death, she sees a doctor on November 30th who confirms, yes, she is pregnant. Suzanne Tyler—we will call her—talks to her sister and to her sister's fiance. She talks on the phone to Bill Holbrook, the young man in Portland. Bill says he has contacts. He knows a guy who knows a person. . . . Suzanne goes to school and teaches fourteen seventh grade girls how to make macaroni and cheese. As the fourteen girls slide fourteen half-quart casseroles into the oven, Suzanne decides to have an abortion.

Suzanne makes this decision, but she isn't prepared for it. Gazing at her seventh grade pupils, she realizes she isn't prepared for any of this. That night she talks to Bill on the phone again. Later she says about this conversation, "The only decision that we came to was that something had to be done. We weren't going to get married, and he wanted to see what I could do down in San Francisco and he was going to see what he could do up in Oregon."

By now Suzanne Tyler is seven weeks pregnant. She doesn't know any abortionists in San Francisco, or anywhere else. She knows the other teachers in her junior high school. And she knows her roommate, also a home ec teacher, a Catholic girl from Milwaukee. All unsuitable confidantes. Suzanne calls up Bill and tells him she will fly to Portland next week on Tuesday, December 7, 1965. Bill agrees to set everything up.

Suzanne tells the junior high school principal something about a family emergency, and that Tuesday evening, she flies to Portland. Her plane arrives long after dark. The young home economics teacher and Bill, a half-time instructor, half-time student at Oregon State University, check into a motel in downtown Portland as Mr. and Mrs. William Holbrook. Later, when the mayor of Portland has reason to reflect on this event, he points out that when the girl, on her way to an abortion, and her boyfriend registered in unit No. 35 of the Jamaica Motor Court as a married couple, even though they were not, it was "very probably a violation of the hotel ordinance in the City."

Bill's route to a solution for Suzanne's problem was attenuated. As it turned out, he knew a guy who knew another guy who knew how to find an abortionist. Wednesday morning the parts of the scheme began clicking into place. The couple left the Jamaica Motor Court, Bill driving and Suzanne huddled up against the passenger's window, grim-faced. They drove in Bill's El Camino truck to the edge of Portland's Southwest Hills, and pulled into the parking lot of Henry Thiele's Diner at 10:00. Bill remembered the details. "Well, I parked in the parking lot for awhile," he said, "and didn't see anybody, and then pretty soon a blue '62 Chevy drove up and this man got out and went in the door of the diner. I figured this was Don Rogers."

Bill watched as Don walked through the door of the diner and back out. Then Bill caught the other fellow's eye. "He said, 'Bill?' and I said, 'Yes.'" Bill motioned to his truck, where Suzanne hadn't moved and looked to be asleep, and then, he remembered, "I just took a walk down the street."

Don strolled over to the El Camino. He tapped on the window and Suzanne opened her eyes. She rolled down the window. For the next few minutes, as Suzanne tells it, "I was inside the car and he stood by the open window and talked with me. We were waiting for this person to come."

During this conversation Suzanne found out for the first time that they were waiting for a woman abortionist. She was sure that Bill had told her it would be a man. Suzanne, very scared already, did not take this well. Don tried to assure her that it was good—possibly much better—that the abortionist was a woman. "He said that sometimes men take advantage of girls that they—that they give these abortions to, and that I wouldn't have to worry about anything like that because it was going to be a woman."

While they talked—it was mostly Don who did the talking—both of them darted looks across the parking lot. Don started a short, nervous pacing from the window to the front of the truck and back, to the front of the truck and back again. But there was still no sign of his contact. He told Suzanne he was going into the restaurant to make a call and that she should watch out for a maroon Lincoln Continental while he was gone.

Instead of watching, Suzanne closed her eyes again. She imagined her vagina, her tissue, her blood. She imagined her hands and her thighs covered with blood. She started, and opened her eyes. Don had come back. He was standing by the truck window saying that the wires had crossed, there had been a little mix-up, but everything was straightened out now. The person would be there in a minute or two.

And then almost at once the maroon Lincoln pulled into the parking lot. Don signaled to the woman driving the car as he opened the door of the truck for Suzanne. The girl, feeling helpless and already bloody, left the El Camino and got into the abortionist's car. "I got inside the car and I was just—I was extremely nervous, and she drove me to her home. I was extremely nervous. I asked her exactly what the procedure was, exactly what she was going to do. She said it was going to be a simple curette and that I would be in and out of her house in no time.

"We drove up into the Southwest Hills, to Champlain Drive. It was a brown house, brick, and it didn't have much of a front yard. She drove into the driveway. I got out of her car and went inside of her house. Into her living room, and I laid my coat down on a chair."

The telephone rang just then, and the abortionist answered it. She sat down on the couch, and she spoke into the receiver, "Well, tell me about yourself." It was a short conversation because the woman said she was busy right now; the caller should try her again later. Suzanne stood by during the call, passive, waiting, scared.

The abortionist told Suzanne to go downstairs, to the bedroom, and she said, "Take off all your clothes except for your slip and your bra." She said that when Suzanne was ready, she should come into the other room.

Suzanne noticed that her legs were shaking, but she did as she was told. After undressing, she found the other room, down the hall. It was an L-shaped laundry room with a big tub-type sink and a washer and dryer. It wasn't the setup Suzanne had expected, but she was relieved to see that everything looked clean and orderly and ready for her.

The abortionist was standing near the washing machine when Suzanne came in. "She ushered me up on this washer and dryer. It had a brown rubber pad on it, and a raised toilet seat, or something that looked like a toilet seat, a rubber thing, and I sat on it. She said, 'Lie back now, honey,' and she got me situated on this thing.

"She gave me a shot in the arm and she told me it was for contractions of the uterus. And then she put this instrument inside of me. I felt a lot of pain, but she patted my hand once or twice and said I should relax. She said that girls were always scared and there was usually a little pain, but really, there was nothing to it."

Ruth Barnett was an old woman when Don Rogers arranged for her to take care of Suzanne Tyler's problem. Over seventy, her body was riddled with cancer, her joints racked by arthritis. Despite her physical condition, she continued to respond to the pleas of girls and women desperate to end pregnancies they could not manage. But by 1965, when Ruth Barnett operated out of her house in the Southwest Hills of Portland, the number of women she was able to help had fallen to a "relative trickle." She described how much things had changed. "My practice, once a well-organized clinical affair had been reduced by my arrests to a 'backstairs' sort of clientele. Ironically, I was forced to adopt tactics of which I would have once been ashamed. Now I pick up cases—and only the most desperate ones—and drive them to my own home where I do the examinations and operations. Quantitatively, my practice is only a shadow of the once busy round I knew at my clinic."

For fifty years, Ruth held herself leagues apart from and above the so-called "back-alley" practitioners whose services continued to be in demand in the 1960s. She thought of these others as lowlifes, and called them "those contemptible back-alley abortionists who prey on women, taking advantage of the reluctance of professional doctors to perform abortions—the characters who use instruments and techniques far beyond their competence and under filthy conditions. I have," she added, "nothing but contempt for them."

Her contempt was aroused as well by the way the culture in general, and Hollywood in particular, demonized the typical abortionist and insisted on the client's being a pathetic victim. "In the movies, they always depict the fallen woman sneaking up a dirty, rickety stairway to a dismal room—or making her way, furtively, into a dark alley that leads to a decrepit shack where some alcoholic doctor or untutored butcher performs the operation." Ruth was emphatic about the ways her own practice differed from those of the butchers—real and celluloid. As an old woman, she remembered the good old days, when her place of business was undisturbed by the stakeouts and frame-ups that would push her work into the shadows in later years: "A clinic such as mine was not that way at all. It was a bright, cheerful place where women's problems were handled quickly, efficiently, and with dignity, no matter what the circumstances of the patient."

In her heyday, and an uncommonly lengthy heyday it was, Ruth Barnett was the queen of abortionists in the Pacific Northwest, possibly anywhere. The state laws criminalizing abortion in Oregon had been on the books since 1854, but they were rarely invoked. In fact, Ruth estimated that between 1918 and 1968, she performed forty thousand abortions, and she never lost a client. But Ruth was more than a proficient technician. She was also the glamorous queen of Portland's demimonde: she draped herself in diamonds and furs, she cuddled lapdogs. She entertained politicians and whores, newspapermen and gamblers, businessmen and pimps in her lavish house in the Southwest Hills. She poured stiff drinks for everyone, belted bar songs, and unfailingly went to work the next morning, helping women.

For a half a century, Ruth took care of desperate women. Incest victims, rape victims, jilted girls, careless teenagers, adulterous wives, battered wives, pari-menopausal women, exhausted mothers, mistresses. For years she invited all of these women into her clinic and provided them with expert service.

Ruth's pride in her work was the pride of a woman who had apprenticed under the old masters. In the first decades of the twentieth century, when Ruth set out on her career, abortion was every bit as illegal as it was fifty years later, when the abortionist was sneaking around picking girls up in parking lots. But until the years after World War II, the crime of abortion, like the crimes of gambling and prostitution, had a protected status.

In 1910, Portland, Oregon, was home to a number of abortion-ists who had offices in prominent, downtown office buildings. Many were doctors, reasonably respectable and well-paid for their work. They had big, long-established practices and a number had medical training. So, unhappily pregnant women in Portland who had the money to pay could feel safe and confident about their decision to visit an abortionist. Indeed, Ruth Barnett herself was initiated into the world of abortion practice by her own unintend-ed pregnancy and her determination to end it.

Ruth got pregnant as a teenager in 1911, soon after her family had moved to Portland from Hood River, a tiny town in western Oregon where her father was the village's first grocer. To begin with, Ruth—who was living at home with her parents at the time and working at her first job, as a dental assistant—was panicked. "When I realized I was pregnant, that the boy responsible for my pregnancy was of no help to me, I thought vaguely of suicide, of hurling myself from the office window, of the deep cold waters of the Willamette River under the Morrison Bridge and of the vials of medicine in the office with the red letters spelling POISON."

But quickly enough, Ruth found a solution to her problem. She simply asked the first likely-looking girl she saw, a prostitute who'd come to get her teeth cleaned in the dentist's office where Ruth worked. Jane Allen, an elegant, chatty prostitute, clucked sympa-thetically at young Ruth's awkward attempt to get help, and with-out batting an eye, Jane referred the girl to Dr. George Watts, a fix-ture in the venerable Oregonian Building downtown.

At the time, Watts was in his late forties, a sweet, earnest doc-tor who not only helped Ruth early in her life, but also taught her a great deal during the five years she worked with him doing abor-tions in the 1930s. Years later, Ruth described the career of Watts as altruistic and heroic. He was, she said, "a highly skilled physi-cian and surgeon with a general practice in the city's leading hos-pitals. His change to abortion surgery—at first occasionally, and then exclusively—was prompted by a desire to be of help to woe-begone women." He was a godsend to sixteen-year-old Ruth Barnett, receiving her kindly, taking care of her "smoothly and painlessly," charging her eighty-five dollars (a sum Ruth found overwhelming but managed to collect, by hook and crook), and sending her on her way.

Ruth was getting her first taste of the mixed blessings of city life, and of the casual sex and abortions city people seemed to take for granted. She walked away from the Oregonian Building ready to heap more experience on her plate, possibly more experience with sex, but also deeply relieved to have been spared the shame that, in her day, inevitably came to a young unmarried girl who gave birth to an illegitimate child. Even greater than her relief, though, was a certainty Ruth took with her from Dr. Watts's office that day. It was a conviction about what she'd done that stayed with her the rest of her life. "One of mankind's man-made laws had been thwarted. But I was unable to perceive any crime in what either I or the doctor had done." Years later she remarked, "Today, I am more than fifty years older and, presumably, a great deal wiser. But I still cannot see the wrong in abortion."

Not long after her abortion, Ruth married Harry Cohen, a travelling salesman from Seattle whom the eighteen-year-old girl saw, first of all, as a vehicle for escape from her demanding, critical, and sexually importuning boss, the dentist. Apparently the dentist had figured out that his young, attractive assistant had had an abortion, and was enormously turned on by the idea, so much so that until Ruth quit to get married, he plagued her with salacious innuendoes and groping hands at every turn.

Ruth was grateful that Harry Cohen had rescued her, but the marriage was brief. According to Ruth's daughter Maggie, it was not only a dull and disappointing experience, it was also a tissue of lies. The wedding, however, turned out to be a crucial moment in Ruth's life because one of the guests was Dr. Alys Bixby Griff, who was married to a friend of Harry Cohen's. She was a woman with whom Ruth would have a long, intense, and engaging relationship much more enduring than her marriage to Harry.

Alys Griff was a pioneer. When she graduated from the University of Oregon Medical School in 1902, she became one of the first woman doctors in the Pacific Northwest. For a decade her practice in Portland focussed on "women's diseases," and she did well.

Ruth looked at Alys that night at her wedding reception and saw the sort of woman she wanted to be: vivacious, stylish, and smart, striking in a way that had little to do with conventional beauty, and a lot to do with personal power. "She handled herself with charm and confidence in a room crowded with happy, relaxed, laughing people. I was most impressed by her eyes. They were the first cold brown eyes I had ever seen." Ruth was compelled by the older woman.

Over the next few years, whenever she could, Ruth took time off from her not very happy married life and travelled from Seattle— where her husband was a sales representative for Can't Bust-'Em overalls and Argonaut workshirts—down to Portland. Maggie's birth probably made it indelibly clear to Ruth that she was not cut out to be the conventional, stay-at-home wife of a travelling sales- man. The fact was, Harry Cohen was not Maggie's father, a piece of information that Ruth probably told no one for nearly thirty years until, under extraordinary circumstances, she revealed the truth to her daughter. Maggie's father was Harry's much classier older brother Arthur, who became a very successful and prominent cor- porate lawyer in later years. In 1915 Arthur slept with his brother's wife, but he would not marry her. Ruth was hurt and sorry and now fatally tired of her husband. Her spirit, however, was intact, and she continued to look to Portland and her friend Alys Griff for a sense of adventure and a sense of purpose.

Every time Ruth came down to Portland, she told Harry she was going home to visit with her mother and father. In truth she came to see Alys. The fact was, Ruth's restlessness, her intellect, and her belief in her own capabilities were aroused by the trips down to Alys. And Alys was welcoming. "I was still a youngish thing and the doctor seemed to like my company. She would take me along on her house calls and to Good Samaritan Hospital where we would visit the maternity wards. I would sit up in the gallery above the operat- ing room and watch her perform appendectomies, hysterectomies, and Caesareans. She was a jolly, wonderful woman and I enjoyed her company."

Alys Griff was deciding to specialize as an abortionist at about the time that Ruth's visits began. Such a large number of Alys's patients came begging her to end their pregnancies that she began to devote herself to performing abortions full-time. Business was fairly booming: the United States had entered the Great War and as young men left for Europe, unhappily pregnant girlfriends and wives found Alys Griff. Ruth came down from Seattle often enough and displayed her devotion to Alys clearly enough that when the abortionist needed a companion *cum* confidante, she turned to

Ruth. The younger woman was thrilled to hear about Alys's life, and especially about her work, and found herself fully willing to spend evenings sitting for hours at the feet of the person who was becoming her mentor, listening. "It seemed to me to be the most wonderful work in the world. The subconscious urge to make this my life's work must have been growing fast." As Ruth stepped further and further away from Harry, she began to dream of becoming an abortionist herself. "The thought that I might actually be of help to women in this way began to obsess me."

By 1918, five years after she met Alys, Ruth was divorced and in a position to realize her intentions. In fact, she packed up her things and Maggie's, and came back to Portland. Soon she was working in Alys's office, earning the considerable wage of fifty dollars a week. Ruth learned quickly. In addition to abortion technique, she learned "not to be shocked at the sordid, not to be surprised at the ludicrous." After only a few weeks of training, Alys allowed her to stand by during the operations and then, to Ruth's pleasure, she was permitted to complete procedures begun by the doctor. Ruth Barnett had found her life's work.

In retrospect—and in light of the faith anti-choice Americans have in the law as a powerful deterrent to abortion — it is surprising that decades after the Oregon state legislature criminalized abortion in 1854 and then strengthened the code ten years later, abortionists were prominent professionals whose businesses flourished undisturbed in the state's largest city. What's more, a smart, attractive, resourceful, young woman—the daughter of old-stock pioneers, salt-of-the-earth, God-fearing parents who had travelled by covered wagon across the plains to Oregon in the 1880s—had her heart set on becoming an abortionist herself.

When Ruth embarked on her career, she was not, apparently, deterred by Section 14-208 of the Oregon Code, the language of which defined her as an outlaw and prescribed a dim future for her kind. It read: "If any person shall administer to any woman pregnant with a child any medicine, drug or substance whatever, or shall use or employ any instrument or other means, with intent thereby to destroy such child, unless the same shall be necessary to preserve the life of such mother, such person shall, in the case of the death of such child or mother be thereby produced, be deemed guilty of manslaughter."

In an odd show of ambivalence about the severity of the crime, the legislators gave judges wide latitude in setting the punishment for aborting "the child": "one to fifteen years and a fine of not more than five thousand dollars." Oregon lawmakers, however, declared the life of the woman equivalent to the life of the fetus; judges were allowed the same unusually broad parameters in punishing an abortionist who caused the death of a pregnant woman. As Ruth Barnett undertook her apprenticeship, however, the life of an abortionist did not feel like a dangerous life. The explicit character of the law notwithstanding, the Portland careers of Alys Griff and George Watts, and of their protégée who practiced as an abortionist unimpeded by the law until 1951, are convincing proof that the law is not necessarily an effective way to control behavior.

The truth was, the degree to which anti-abortion statutes were flouted in Portland, and across the country, was extraordinary. In Ruth's early years as an abortionist, she not only trained with seasoned old-timers whose lives had not been touched by the law, she also knew and respected the competition: other doctors in town who had thriving practices. They were all successors to old Dr. Albert Littlefield, Portland's first professional abortionist who had set up his office in 1890 above a hardware store on Front Street. In Ruth's day, Dr. Maude Van Alstyne and Dr. Ed Stewart both ran large clinics in the Broadway Building, Ruth's headquarters, for many years. In time, both these doctors recognized Ruth as the most promising of Portland's second-generation abortionists, and both sold their sizeable practices to her when they retired. It is no wonder that law enforcement officials, doctors, and other social commentators repeatedly observed that abortion—along with prostitution and gambling—was the least prosecuted crime in the country.

The law enforcement officials charged with upholding the law in the 1910s, '20s, and '30s routinely looked the other way, even though doctors across the country had been extremely successful between 1860 and 1880 in convincing state legislators that outlawing abortion was a prerequisite of modern, professional, doctor-controlled health care. In fact, historian James Mohr has called the doctors' campaign against abortion "the first and ultimately one of the most successful public policy crusades ever undertaken" by the then-fledgling American Medical Association. The doctors' crusade did not end until the last years of the nineteenth century, when every state in the country had enacted an anti-abortion law.

It would not be accurate to say that the lack of abortion prosecutions was a sign that medical men and their champions had lost their taste for activist roles once they completed the campaign to outlaw abortion. It would be closer to the truth to say that the generals simply shifted the battleground to a terrain where they could count on the support of law enforcement. Having won the abortion battle so decisively—and with so little opposition—they now trained their forces on the emergent birth control movement. In Portland in 1916, just before Ruth teamed up with Alys Griff, Margaret Sanger stopped to give a speech and distribute copies of her infamous, clandestinely circulated pamphlet, *Family Limitation*, which explained various methods of contraception and encouraged women to "learn to know their own bodies." She was promptly jailed. It is an ironic image: the advocate of pessaries and shields behind bars, while the city teems with abortionists and their satisfied clients. The irony was, of course, that the cops on the street, and those who set their priorities, daily tolerated, and thus sanctioned, the private, secret, and criminal practice of ending pregnancy, but could not bear a public figure or a public policy that countenanced prevention.

More influential than this hypocrisy, however, was the fact that in the early decades of the twentieth century, doctors and law enforcement officials had not established an effective partnership regarding the treatment of abortionists. Doctors may have been able to lobby legislators successfully in the second half of the nineteenth century, but they were not able to convince district attorneys or police chiefs to enforce the laws they'd hammered out in state capitals.

Maybe the most powerful factor undermining an effective medical-legal partnership to thwart abortionists was tradition. Modern doctors insisted that abortionists—both medical men and lay practitioners—violated the physician's professional prerogatives to minister to and monitor pregnant women. But thousands of women themselves were certain that the relatively new anti-abortion laws violated *their* traditional right to make decisions about their own pregnancies before the fetus "quickened."

The notion of quickening was a venerable, woman-centered concept, long embedded in the common law. It allowed that a pregnancy could not be confirmed until the woman felt the fetus move within her body. In the days before drugstore pregnancy kits, sonograms and rabbit tests, and all the other modern methods of verifying pregnancy, the woman herself was the definitive expert. Doctors and midwives agreed that menstrual irregularity—in fact, all the symptoms of pregnancy—*could* be associated with conditions other than pregnancy. So traditionally, it was not until the woman reported the sensation of fetal movement that she could be declared pregnant. Consequently, an abortion in the early months of pregnancy—often treated as an operation to restore the woman's menstrual flow by removing a "blockage"—was not considered a crime. During all of the eighteenth century and the first half of the nineteenth century, the quickening doctrine governed abortion law in the North American English colonies, and then in the United States.

Even after doctors had prevailed on legislators to make abortion a crime, many states retained the quickening doctrine by criminalizing abortion only after the woman reported movement. Oregon's first anti-abortion statute was based on this premise. The concept of quickening was so enduring that as late as the 1930s, seven states still incorporated it into the statutory language by specifically outlawing procedures on a woman "pregnant with a quick child."

Sometimes the issue of quickening made for enormously complicated abortion prosecutions. In the early decades of the twentieth century, for example, the state of Wisconsin had one anti-abortion statute with two distinct sections. One section made it an "offense against Chastity, Morality and Decency" to produce a miscarriage by destroying embryonic life. An individual who caused such a miscarriage was not considered to have committed an offense against a *person*, since an embryo—before quickening—did not have the legal status of personhood. The law indicated that the individual who caused an early miscarriage committed merely a considerably lesser offense against *morality*.

The second section of the statute dealt with abortion as an "Offense Against Lives and Persons." Legislators intended for this section to be used to prosecute abortionists who caused a miscarriage in a woman carrying a "quick child." This crime was unequivocally an act of homicide, specifically, manslaughter in the second degree.

The distinction between the two sections of Wisconsin's anti-abortion statute was tested in 1923 by a Racine man, a Mr. A.M. Foster, who was gratified to find out that the quickening doctrine was still intact and meaningful in his state. Foster was initially convicted of manslaughter by abortion. But a year later he was able to get the judgment overturned because, he argued, there was evidence that the woman he aborted was only about seven weeks pregnant. Consequently, he had been charged under the wrong section of the statute. He had, at worse, he said, committed a crime against morality, but not one against a person.

In the end, the Wisconsin Supreme Court agreed and expressed itself this way: "Neither in popular nor in scientific language is the embryo in its early stages called a human being. Popularly it is regarded as such, for some purposes, only after it has become 'quick' which does not occur until four of five months of pregnancy have elapsed. It is obvious that no death of a child can be produced when there is no living child. A two month embryo is not a human being in the eyes of the law, and therefore, its destruction is an offense against morality and not against lives and persons." Perhaps the most interesting aspect of the finding was the state Supreme Court's semi-veiled admonition of those who wanted to do away with the idea of quickening altogether. The Court wrote, "The law for obvious reasons cannot in its classifications follow the latest or ultimate declarations of science. It must for purposes of practical efficiency proceed upon more everyday and popular conceptions" when it defines the nature of crime. Most men, it concluded, can surely distinguish between a quick and a non-quick pregnancy.

The language chosen by legislators in Tennessee—a state that had, by the 1930s, revised its code to eliminate women's traditional right to abortion before quickening—made it clear how necessary it was to address the quickening issue explicitly and with absolute clarity. That state's law began, "Every person who shall administer to any woman pregnant with child, whether such child be quick or not. . . ." But the evidence is plain that women continued to avail themselves of their traditional rights, however these anti-abortion statutes were phrased and however the courts interpreted them.

When abortion did become the subject of a trial in the early decades of the twentieth century, lawyers representing the accused abortionist routinely used the issue of quickening—that is, the absence of proof that the woman had recognized fetal life—to try to undermine the prosecutor's case. If there were no proof of fetal life, there was no provable pregnancy and, therefore, no provable abortion. In many states, when lawyers carried these old, traditional claims into the twentieth-century courtroom, prosecutors and judges who knew the law inside out cringed and responded testily that such matters were irrelevant. But it was not uncommon for jurors—ordinary people who respected tradition—to take note. The typical district attorney knew all about these problems. He also knew all the other potential difficulties involved in proving that a criminal abortion had taken place. For instance, he had probably never met a woman who was looking for an opportunity to walk into a courtroom and testify about her criminal abortion. Few D.A.'s, therefore, wanted to get involved in abortion prosecution.

For years, Ruth Barnett, her predecessors, and her competitors in Portland had what Ruth called an "unwritten agreement" with the cops that set a very broad limit on how and where and by whom the abortion clinics were run: no prosecution unless there was a death. This is not to say that abortionists were never arrested unless a woman died. It was always the case that a woman lying in the city hospital, suffering the effects of a botched abortion, caught the attention of law enforcement officials. If the policemen called to her bedside by the hospital staff had reason to believe that the criminal abortion was the work of a lay practitioner, their eagerness to make an arrest might be quite keen. Some observers of the behavior of law enforcement in these years pointed out that police were especially eager to arrest a female abortionist, whether or not she had a death on her hands.

A medical man who performed abortions—on the side or for a living—was not so endangered. Certainly he was less likely to be arrested for being a known abortionist. After all, a doctor had the skills that came with medical training, so a district attorney, not eager for abortion prosecutions anyway, could reason that a doctor's abortion work didn't really hurt the community or put women's lives in danger. A seasoned D.A. knew for sure that any abortion conviction was hard enough to win, and a doctor-defendant only made matters worse. For one thing, just about any doctor in town had respectable, pillar-of-the-community colleagues to stand up for him in court and claim the abortion was a medical necessity, no doubt about it. One famous story involved an Ohio physician-abortionist who pleaded guilty to having performed three hundred abortions a year between 1934 and 1956 for fees in excess of one million dollars, yet his sentence was merely five years probation. It was clear that even if city officials decided to enforce anti-abortion laws, not all abortionists were equally vulnerable.

But there *was* a leveller, a device police frequently used against abortion providers whether they were physicians or not, male or female. As one observer in Ruth Barnett's day put it, "It was to be expected that the abortionists could not ply their trade in security without insuring that law enforcement agencies would keep their eyes fixed in the opposite direction." Many abortionists dutifully paid the insurance premium directly to the cops. Throughout the illegal decades and across the country, law enforcement officials who did not want to get involved in abortion busts understood that extortion was a remunerative alternative to arrest. In most towns it was common knowledge that wherever there were abortionists, there were cops being paid off. One reporter, snooping around among abortionists in California, came away convinced of this. He wrote, "In big cities an abortionist who operates openly in a downtown office building must be assumed to have purchased immunity, for the constant stream of women to his office would quickly attract attention." It was not unusual that a high-level investigator looking into the goings-on in these downtown buildings would end up with more extortion- than abortion-related indictments. In the real world, the anti-abortion laws created more problems than they solved.

For thirty-three years, though, the law seemed irrelevant to Ruth Barnett. Neither the district attorney nor the cops on the beat in Portland showed any interest in the way she earned her living, from the time Alys Griff began to teach her the ropes in 1918 until Ruth's ultimate arrest in 1951. Judging from this record, abortion was simply tolerated in Portland. It is indisputable that women requiring the services of an abortionist had a number of reputable practitioners to choose from. Many people believed that Ruth Barnett was the best. She was clean and careful and very highly skilled.

Business flourished, the money rolled in, and everything was so out in the open that it was probably hard sometimes for Ruth to remember that she was a criminal. As she described it, "There was nothing secret about my clinic in the Broadway Building. We had no locks on any of the doors except the one leading to a hall, which we locked at night. The majority of our cases were referrals from licensed physicians and surgeons." Even prominent Catholic doctors in town sent women to Ruth's offices. And for the clients, there was no sneaking around in those days, no strange parking lots, no dark basements. "Women came and went in my clinic," she said, "with scarcely any more fuss than there would be in keeping an appointment at a beauty salon. Many girls came to me during their lunch hour and returned to work the same afternoon with no distress."

In those years, Ruth was confident of her safety and of the safety of her clients. She knew that some of her colleagues were asked for what she called "hush money," but she was left alone. Her confidence was bolstered by the simple fact that everybody who was anybody knew about Ruth Barnett and her clinic. Ruth explained, "The duly elected officers of the law, members of the medical profession and state medical board knew we were in business. Trying to conceal the clinic, or its purpose, would have been as impossible as hiding an elephant in the parlor. Thousands of women had passed through our doors, of all colors, races, and creeds and from various walks of life." As far as Ruth could see, the anti-abortion law might as well not have existed and was treated as if it didn't. She was convinced—and with good reason—that no one even considered invoking the "archaic" laws against her.

Over the years, Ruth became so accustomed to working as an abortionist in this kind of permissive climate that when the weather changed—and it did change drastically—she was taken completely by surprise. Police and politicians in Portland, and in cities all over the country, began to violate the venerable "unwritten agreement" they'd had with abortionists for as long as most of them could remember. In some cities beginning in the 1940s, and in Portland starting in 1951, a woman's death was no longer a necessary condition for arresting an abortionist. From the early postwar years until the legalization of abortion in 1973, nobody involved ever again quite knew the rules. Anti-abortion statutes were invoked in what seemed like an utterly random way.

In the middle 1960s, when Suzanne Tyler, the home ec teacher, found her way to Ruth Barnett's basement, illegal abortions were, as always, an everyday event in cities and towns across the United States. But, paradoxically, anti-abortion laws were not ineffectual, despite the fact that they did not stop girls and women from ending their pregnancies. These laws remained powerful even when they were not enforced, because they constructed the back alley and forced Suzanne and Ruth down into the basement. These two conducted their business in the dreadful shadows because state lawmakers denied them the use of a well-lighted, sterile facility and didn't mind composing statutes that denied women the right to control their fertility. What's more, politicians and policemen, over time, were able to choose politically expedient moments to enforce these statutes. By now, among pro-choice advocates, Ruth and Suzanne in the L-shaped furnace room—and others like them— have become emblems of the power of the law to constrain and endanger women's lives.

But on December 8, 1965, Suzanne Tyler was no emblem. She was flesh and blood. After awhile she did sit up, barely, on the edge of the washing machine, and Ruth brought her a sanitary pad and belt. Suzanne remembered feeling awful. "I sat there and I felt like I was just going to die. I was just having all these cramps in my stomach, and I told her this and she said, 'Don't worry, that is what is supposed to happen.'" Suzanne was afraid that she wouldn't be able to stand up or walk or get back down to Henry Thiele's Diner and meet Bill, who was waiting to take her back to the airport. She was terribly afraid that she would miss her plane. But Ruth said that Suzanne would be okay, of course she would make it, and she began to help the girl get herself together and get out.

While Suzanne was dressing, Ruth got a phone call and when she hung up, the abortionist let the girl know that another client was waiting to be picked up. Suzanne dragged herself, somehow, up the stairs into the living room. She picked up her coat from where she had left it on a chair twenty minutes earlier. She concentrated what little energy she had on getting through the front door and across the lawn to the door of Ruth's Lincoln without letting her legs fail her.

It was difficult, but all this was done, and Suzanne thought that she should feel almost free now. But the pain in her groin was too sharp to associate with freedom. Everything about her was blurry and moving in slow motion at the same time, as Ruth helped her into the passenger seat of the car. The girl closed her eyes, squeezed them shut to squeeze out the pain, and a wave of nausea replaced the shooting stabs for a moment. Suzanne was so deep into the course of her pain that even with time slowed down, Ruth's car stopped before the girl expected it to. They were back in the parking lot of the diner. Right away Suzanne saw Bill and Don leaning against the El Camino, looking very buddy-buddy, like a couple of guys.

Somehow, without looking at Bill who had moved to her side, Suzanne got into the truck. The one thing she knew was that she couldn't sit up straight. It was too hard. She wanted Bill to know that it was too hard. As soon as Bill got into the driver's seat, she let her body fall over. She let her head fall onto his right leg. Bill said, "You're all fixed up now, and it's only 11:15. We have plenty of time to get you on the plane." Suzanne moaned, and Bill pulled out of the parking lot.

Suzanne made her plane to San Francisco that day at 12:30. And by mid-afternoon, she was back home in her own bed. But that was not the end of her ordeal. Unbeknownst to Suzanne, the citizens of Multnomah County, Oregon, had recently elected a new district attorney, a young, politically ambitious man, the sort of officeholder Ruth Barnett had always associated with abortion prosecutions. Indeed, the new D.A., aware that the old abortionist was still practicing, had arranged early in his tenure for the abortionist's house to be watched. On December 8, 1965, Ruth Barnett's house was under the surveillance of two members of the Portland Police Department. The two men, sitting in an unmarked car parked several houses below Ruth's on Champlain Drive, had carefully noted the time when the young woman and Ruth pulled into the driveway. They had watched Ruth and her client go into the house and then, less than an hour later, come back out. They had followed Ruth's Lincoln down the hill to the diner at 11:10. Then the officers had tailed Bill Holbrook's El Camino to the airport and watched Suzanne board the 12:30 flight to San Francisco. The next day, the airlines had cooperated with the D.A.'s office by providing the names of the thirty-two passengers who had been on board. It had not been difficult for the investigators to single out the one young woman who had travelled alone down the coast on that lunchtime flight.

On the evening of December 15th, a Portland detective paid a call on Suzanne in her San Francisco apartment. At first Suzanne refused to answer the detective's questions. She was shocked and terrified that this man was standing in her home, telling her he knew such a thing about her life. He also let her know that he was aware that Suzanne was a teacher. He told her that under the circumstances, she'd best cooperate. Indeed, the man was a skilled interrogator, and it was not long before Suzanne capitulated. After the detective collected all the details, he said that Suzanne should expect to hear from his office again, when they set the date for Ruth Barnett's trial. It would be in the spring, he said.

In the weeks that followed, Suzanne felt very odd looking into the faces of her seventh-grade pupils. She felt uneasy teaching them how to become creative and efficient homemakers. But it was a distraction to go to school every morning and put on her teacher's apron and assemble all the materials for that day's project. Suzanne required a great many distractions that winter and spring because she had received a letter from the Multnomah County District Attorney's office in late January informing her that the *State of Oregon v. Ruth Barnett* would be heard in the Circuit Court of Multnomah County on April 27, 1966.

Once in February, while Suzanne was teaching the girls how to make tuna casserole, and once in April, while the whole class was laying out jumper patterns across yards of corduroy on the floor of the home ec room, she saw herself in the witness box and began to shake. Sometimes at night, while she was sitting across the dinner table from her roommate, she could not get mind-bending interrogation images from "The Manchurian Candidate" out of her mind, and she would stop eating. When she was alone, she tried to prepare herself for appearing in public and telling the story they would make her tell. The problem was that the idea of telling a room full of strangers about her abortion was an impossible one. There were simply no useful thoughts or plans or strategies she could think of in preparation, because the whole prospect was just unthinkable. On an everyday basis, Suzanne experienced appetite loss, restless sleep, jumpiness, irritability, and a gnawing uneasiness.

The day that Suzanne took the witness stand to testify about her criminal abortion was unremittingly horrible. When she had tried to prepare herself for the ordeal, she had always attempted to focus on words, on what would come out when she opened her mouth and began to speak, on what she could make her voice sound like. When the day came and Suzanne was there in the courtroom, telling about Bill and the motel and about Henry Thiele's Diner and Ruth's basement, she was shocked to discover that the horror of being there had very little to do with her words. The shock was that her body—her naked body—filled up the courtroom and was projected onto the minds of everyone there.

Suzanne had seen herself that morning in the mirror at home, small, slim, looking ordinary and trim in a navy blue suit. She had thought she looked unremarkable and respectable, and that looking that way would help. But here, in the courtroom, she saw right away that something truly frightening had happened: her unclothed, sexual body, in fact her private, sexual parts, had become public business. The judge and the jury, the lawyers, Dr. Gold, the gyne-cologist she'd consulted in San Francisco, were talking about her body. They were drawing pictures of her parts on the chalkboard next to the witness box, so that the jury would be perfectly clear about what her body looked like.

They asked her if she was married, and they asked why she and Bill had registered at the motel as a married couple if they were not. When Bill took the stand, Suzanne could see the spectators watch-ing, in their minds' eye, the two of them having sex. When Dr. Gold testified, he very carefully explained about Suzanne's body. He did not shrink from the details. He drew a picture, and then he placed his index finger on the drawing. He said, "Assume we are looking straight on into the vagina. . . ." He was talking about *her* vagina.

The year 1966 was not a good one for Ruth Barnett. She was 72 years old, and only occasionally now did she feel her characteristic zest for life. For the past two years, she had known that she had melanoma, and the prognosis was not good. But Ruth had never been a quitter, so she regularly drove herself the three hundred and fifty miles round-trip to Seattle to get experimental treatments at the Swedish Hospital there. Some days, it seemed as if the treat-ments were helping, other days she dragged around, feeling old and tired.

On the days when she was feeling good, and on the days when she wasn't, she made herself elegant—with rings and pins and beautifully tailored dresses with fur-collared jackets in winter, and always an elegantly coiffed wig, nail polish, and a full makeup job. Every now and then she still had parties in the evening, entertaining, as always, a bizarre mix of guests in her living room filled with lacquered *objets* and gilded *chinoiserie* and the grand piano she played to accompany her bawdy bar songs. These were hilarious, hard-drinking gatherings, and Ruth still loved them. The drinking and the laughing made her feel better. She needed cheering up sometimes because she was sick and because she recently had lost a sweetheart she'd liked more than many who'd come around these past years.

The man was Charlie Marshall, a captain in the Portland Police Department. He wasn't Ruth's first boyfriend in the force, nor was he, despite her age and ill health, the last man who courted her. But he was sweet and she liked him. Even after all these years of living the criminal life, Ruth never thought it peculiar that a woman like herself should have a cop for a sweetheart. In fact, she thought it was natural. Everywhere she'd ever been, cops and criminals tended to hang together in their time off.

Ruth's daughter Maggie, who knows quite a lot about men herself, and about love and breaking up, feels bittersweet about Ruth's affair with Marshall. She says, "Mother had known him for years, and he took to dropping up to the house and as time wore on, lingering longer and staying a few days at a time. His police car—unmarked to the layman but known to other policemen—was always parked in front. He'd wait in the breakfast nook if she had to operate on someone in the downstairs apartment. She became rather dependent on him." When Marshall stopped coming by, Maggie had a hard time finding out why. "Finally," she said, "I got the story out of Mother that other police patrolling the neighborhood had been turning in reports to the Chief of Police about Charlie's car being parked on Champlain Drive in front of that abortionist's house. And dear old Charlie, who was only a few years away from retirement, put his pension before Mother and agreed not to see her anymore rather than be kicked off the force."

In 1966, Maggie, who only rarely seemed to notice the complexities of her mother's life, was not the least of Ruth's worries. At fifty-one, Maggie was still careening around at an astonishing pace between boyfriends and husbands, each of whom seemed to require thousands of dollars to back his business ambitions. For more than twenty years, Ruth had said yes to Maggie and to each of Maggie's paramours. She had laid out thirty-five thousand for a bar here, fifty thousand for a recording studio there. For all those years, she had supported Maggie's household, her children as well as her husbands, her maids, her furs and redecorating schemes. And even now, Maggie didn't seem to be able to settle down to middle age. She was an expensive daughter, and she never let Ruth forget that a lot of people were depending on her earnings.

So even when Ruth was feeling ill, she continued to do what she had always done. She continued to do abortions even after the beginning of 1965, when the new district attorney took office. Still, she took some heart from the fact that a handful of state legislators and judges across the country were beginning to consider liberalizing abortion laws. She followed the news from New York and Colorado and California, where abortion reformers were making progress. But her age and the illness and the pressure of her worries were exhausting. Ruth was not the crackerjack practitioner she used to be. She knew it, and sometimes she admitted to herself what she was risking each time she pulled out of the driveway and headed down the hill to pick up a client. But for her, there seemed not to be a choice. After almost five decades as an abortionist, she was as devoted as ever to her chosen career. Even after she was found guilty in the case of Suzanne Tyler, she said that she would not stop doing abortions, because "her big fat sympathetic nerve" claimed a far larger piece of her heart than her fear of prison.

But now her personal responses, her financial needs, and even the force of habit became, in a way, less important than an even stronger source of staying power for Ruth. For like the women's libbers in New York and California agitating for legalization, Ruth, in her old age, had become political. She began to express herself in the parlance of the day, insisting that women needed to "rise up and demand their rights," especially their right to decide whether and when to become mothers.

Ruth Barnett was sentenced to eighteen months in state prison for the crime of manslaughter by abortion. On February 5, 1968, at the age of seventy-three, Ruth turned her wigs over to the prison matron, and her walking cane. She gracefully accepted the prison-issue shoes that reminded her of her father's old hammertoe

clodhoppers, and a nightie, the likes of which she hadn't seen since
she left Hood River. She was glad that the room they gave her was
air-conditioned, and that there were clean blankets and pillows on
the bed. There were no bars on the windows. They had let her stop
by the prison library before locking her in, and Ruth had chosen her
volume, a tale of medieval Moorish Spain by Frank Yerby. It was
called *An Odor of Sanctity*.

Even in prison Ruth's spirit was intact. She made friends with
the young female guards, and entertained the other inmates with
bawdy stories and jokes. She listened to them. She spent considerable time figuring out how to procure cosmetics and how to fix her
hair, now that her wigs were gone. She enjoyed the food and the
rest. "Boy," she wrote in her cell, "if I was one of those poor mis-
guided devils they put in here—I would break the law the minute I
got out so I could get back to this beautiful place. I paid a couple
of thousand dollars at a place in California for my daughter to take
fifty pounds off her, and this place makes that place look like it's
warmed over."

In fact, Ruth was relieved. It was a cruel irony that, once again
in her lifetime, abortion had become a real crime in Portland, and
an abortionist had become a real criminal. This time Ruth was old
and too ill to feel confident, day after day, that she could live up to
her standards under the terrible conditions the law created. "The
days fly past," she wrote in prison. "Time doesn't bother me a bit.
I'm sort of tired, what with attorneys and the phone ringing day
and night. This is just okay—if my arthritis, my knees, my arm that
has developed a reaction, and my calcium in my neck will just let
me sleep nights, everything will be Jake."

Chapter Two

THE LIFE OF CRIME

Ruth Hanna Cohen Bush Barnett was born in Hood River, Oregon, in 1895. From the time she was a young woman until the day she died, she was a subversive, a woman against the law. Like other subversives in the Pacific Northwest in her day, she was the home-grown sort. Her parents were American-born, pioneers who travelled slowly across the country, starting their journey in West Virginia, stopping somewhere on the Great Plains for a year or two, moving on, out West.

Ruth's daughter Maggie is sure she knows where Ruth's independent, contrarious spirit came from. "You want to know where it came from. It came from the people who came across in a wagon—Land Ho!—and lived in a sod house and had two children behind a cheesecloth curtain. Grandma had her first two, a girl, Florence, and a boy, Marc, in the sod house. They cut the sod bricks actually out of the ground. They cut them out of the hard, solid earth and built the house. And Grandma said they just had two rooms with a cheesecloth curtain between. Later they pioneered into Hood River to have Ruth, my mother."

Margaret Belle Hanna, Ruth's mother, was a quiet, serious, hardworking woman. She was careful, too. She controlled her fertility by sticking a gob of beef lard up into her vagina before she allowed her husband to touch her. In this way, all three of her children were expected when they came. James Ellsworth Hanna was a "black" Irishman, a timberman, a purveyor of cordwood, a horse trader, a balladeer. He was wry and sinewy and tough, like the legendary men who built towns and villages on the frontier.

When Ruth was a girl, her parents were reserved in the way of small-town folks. They worked hard every day. They didn't socialize much, or gossip, or loiter on the steps of the Hanna grocery on High Street. Years later, Ruth described her mother's temperament. "She lived her life in the center of the hurricane that was frontier life, never rebelling, but never quite coming to terms with life either." Ruth spent a childhood she called "as smooth as glass" by the side of this placid soul, and emerged, for some reason, a rebel, a defiant, independent young woman who chose to ride not the eye of the storm, but its tail. When the time came for her to leave her mother's side and step out on her own, she was, she said, "a pretty brash kid."

Her sister, Florence, and her brother, Marc, drew lots of a much more conventional, turn-of-the-century sort. Coming along before Ruth, they fished and hunted and tramped through the Hood River woods, as she did. But when they settled down, they wanted family and security. Both sought, with success, a comforting balance of social status and anonymity. Both found a place in the community that was only ever threatened by the outrageous profession of their baby sister.

Indeed, Florence married an insurance man from Seattle, a man who sold quite enough policies for his family to live what looked to the more flamboyant relatives down in Portland like a snooty and uppity life, with a debut for the girl and medical school for the boy. When Maggie visited up in Seattle, her cousin Virginia and Virginia's sorority sisters whispered about her, *sotto voce*, "She's Ruth's daughter." None of them, Florence included, liked what Ruth did for a living one bit. Among the family, only Florence ever spoke her mind.

Ruth's brother Marc was a pleasant, heavy-set man. He seemed ordinary to everyone, a shopkeeper type who didn't mind a handout from Ruth to help his business or an elegant dinner with Florence in Seattle's affluent district. Most like his mother, his temperament was gentle and sweet.

Maggie's certainty notwithstanding, the particulars of Ruth's family background do not precisely explain how it was that she emerged from life in the Hanna household first a brash kid, and then a young woman who set her heart on becoming an abortionist. Whatever mix of Irish fire and gentle love and steadiness and delight in the good life this youngest child incorporated, the fact was that in Portland, when she was just over twenty years old, Ruth threw in her lot with a clutch of strong female doctors who shaped the course of her life, including Alys Griff and her friend Marie Equi, a socialist-feminist-lesbian physician-abortionist-rabble-rouser.

It is interesting to speculate about what Ruth might have done with her life had she not taken on the work of criminal abortion, if, let's say, anything at all were possible for a smart, high-spirited girl in Portland in those years. But when Ruth became a divorcee with a small daughter in 1918, it was clear to her that not everything was possible. Among the choices that did present themselves was working again in a dull dental office, this time for a lackluster dentist, many of whose clients were old trappers and fishermen with atrocious, rotting mouths. The better choice, by far, was to associate with hard-driving, elegant, and passionate doctors whose commitment to helping women was strong, but whose everyday work put them on the wrong side of the law. This, Ruth figured, was not an unreasonable place for a woman like herself, a pioneer daughter who'd seen enough of frontier life to be more impressed by the hypocrisy of the law than its sanctity. And so far as she could tell, the other side of the law was the place where some very interesting, independent-minded women in Portland seemed to be. Most of all, Ruth was a woman who needed to earn a living, and doctoring seemed a gratifying way to do that. She was impressed with a practice that concentrated on women. She decided that it made sense to apprentice herself to Dr. Griff.

For eleven years Ruth held her position as apprentice to Dr. Griff. She learned the abortion business well, and by the end of her association with Griff, she was doing it all, including the most difficult cases. From 1918 through 1929, the abortion office was a busy place. Ruth described the period that spanned the last year of the Great War and the Roaring Twenties as a time of working hard, and playing hard, too. It was not uncommon for the office to be packed to capacity, with three or four girls waiting in the reception area and an equal number in the inside offices.

For some of those years, Ruth and Alys and Marie Equi lived in three side-by-side suites on the second floor of the old Oregon Hotel in downtown Portland. The relationship between the three woman extended beyond professional life. "After work we would whoop it up till all hours in the morning. Night after night we'd go to parties. Those were Prohibition days and we'd drink all kinds of things. We'd go out to the roadhouses—Twelve Mile or the Clackamas Tavern. The doctor always had a big car, either a Winton or a Pierce Arrow. We had some great times. When you work hard, you appreciate the laughs, the big dinners and the booze." Other nights, Ruth worked late, going out into the community, often to one of the Japanese hotels, where she'd heard that a girl who knew no English and had no money needed help. Eleven years was a long association. Never once did Alys and Ruth lose a patient. Never once did the law come rapping on their door. During this period, Marie Equi was sent to jail for her radical politics, but in Portland, abortion was a lesser crime.

Eventually, in 1929, Ruth and Alys came to a parting of the ways. It was not an easy separation; Ruth knew she owed a great deal to the older woman. But increasingly in the late twenties, Alys's health and temperament became unpredictable. Over time the two women had begun to argue—about men, for one thing— and on a personal level the working conditions deteriorated. Ruth recognized that she was too good to be an apprentice-level employee, and yet she was still nominally in that role. She was restless.

When Ruth left Alys and struck out on her own, she had two goals. First, she wanted to maximize her independence. And second, she wanted women clients. Ruth opened a "darling little beauty shop" in 1929, but the project was a fiasco. It failed not because she lacked the business sense to make a go of it. The problem was there were too many men customers, too many men who squeezed her knee under the table as she worked on their nails. It was the dentist's office all over again, and Ruth couldn't tolerate it. It only required a few lusty squeezes for her to decide that this kind of independence wasn't worth so much after all. Several months after opening the shop, Ruth closed it and found a way back into the abortion business where, no way around it, the clientele was female.

This time she teamed up with her old benefactor, Dr. Watts, who'd taken care of her so kindly when she was a pregnant teenager. Always confident and convincing, she walked into Watts's office, now in the Broadway Building, and said, "You just *have* to hire me. I can fix this office up and I can help you with your patients." Selling her woman skills to a man who'd been in the business for forty years, she added, "You don't want the job of telling women how to take care of themselves after they go home from here and that sort of thing. You need a nurse to take care of them." She also convinced Watts that her skills were diverse: she could beautify his office, handle the appointments, and manage the cash.

Dr. Watts took Ruth on, and once again she was an apprentice to a master abortionist, but this time it was an apprenticeship with a future. Watts taught her his own sophisticated techniques, a primitive form of vacuum aspiration, for example. He also convinced her that she ought to get herself a professional credential, the kind that would allow her to be known as Dr. Barnett, the kind, in fact, that might come in handy if the law wanted to know.

It only took a little push from Watts because this advice made sense to Ruth. She enrolled as soon as she could in a two-year evening program at the Pacific States Chiropractic College, where the curriculum included training in naturopathy, a form of medical treatment that had been popular in the nineteenth century and persisted as a credentialed profession into the twentieth, even as the ever more dominant American Medical Association promoted scorn for all "irregular" branches of medicine.

As a student at the college, Ruth "looked out of the window" during the chiropractic lessons, but mastered the course in naturopathy. She was completely comfortable with the naturopathic emphasis on "assisting nature." She understood the herbal treatments and the bodily manipulations. She also understood that she could pursue her chosen profession while honoring the fundamental dictum that treatment had to be administered through the body's natural orifices. At the end of the program, Ruth had her state-recognized credentials and her license in hand. Now she was Dr. Barnett, a title that signified the end of her fourteen-year apprenticeship.

Ruth spent five years working under Watts. During this time, she learned her trade so well that in the early 1930s, when Maude Van Alstyne, another long-time abortionist in the Broadway Building, retired she sold her business to Ruth. Then George Watts himself gave up business in Portland, and he too left much of his business to Ruth. Finally, in the mid-forties, the last old-timer in the Broadway Building, Dr. Ed Stewart, a great practitioner and philanthropist who had inherited the abortion practice of old Dr. Littlefield above the hardware store, decided to pack it in as well. Ruth called Stewart's thriving and highly professional business "the most elaborate on the Pacific coast," and she was thrilled when Dr. Stewart agreed to let her buy him out.

By this time, Ruth was working up to twelve hours a day taking care of a score of women or more, each of whom paid a fee based

on the number of weeks pregnant she was. The cost for an abortion
had been in the thirty- to fifty-dollar range during the Depression,
but by the mid-forties, the average fee was several hundred dollars.
Consequently, Ruth had the money to pay Stewart the one hundred and fifty thousand dollars he asked for his equipment, for the
rights to call her office the Stewart Clinic, and for the right to step
into his shoes. She was the only abortionist left in the building, and
she was ready to assume all the business and all the responsibility.

Now that the eighth floor of the Broadway Building was all hers,
Ruth set out to sustain—and extend—the reputation of the
Stewart Clinic. She was determined to create an abortion empori-
um of utmost professionalism and surpassing beauty. Not the least
of Ruth's attention went to decor. The offices that had belonged to
Ed Stewart became her headquarters. The reception area and treatment rooms were decorated in a thoroughly modern style. She
wanted the premises to look tasteful and professional, and also
indistinguishable from the offices of the successful and respectable
gynecologists in town. Dorothy Taylor, Ruth's nurse in the clinic for
many years, described the rooms where the operations were done as
spotlessly antiseptic. "They were as clean, if not cleaner, than a hospital surgery, because she insisted on it and that was the one reason
she didn't have any trouble."

In the back, behind the rooms where the abortions were performed and behind the cubicles where patients lay to recover,
Ruth indulged her love of luxury and elegance. Here, the space
resembled the reception area of an opulent home: comfortable
lounges, plants, antiques, a massive painting of Shangri-la, other
expensive oils by nineteenth-century naturalists, oriental rugs, and
elaborate filigreed floor lamps fitted with seductive red lights.
Ruth's private lavatory was equally grand, with its Italian marble
sink and gold-plated fixtures. "One needn't think," said Maggie,
"this was a little grubby back-hall abortionist's office. This looked
like a Cecil B. De Mille extravaganza. That little girl that was born
over a grocery store in Hood River, Oregon, was living pretty high
on the hog."

The traffic through the reception area and the treatment rooms
was extraordinary. Twenty, sometimes thirty, girls and women a day
came up to the eighth floor, paid their money, and got well taken
care of. But as much as Ruth adored her clinic and loved the money

that flowed in every day, she never restricted her business to the office, or to clients who could pay. She did not scorn the ones who needed her help but were afraid or ignorant about going to a big downtown office building where, they'd heard, the furniture was fancy, and the clientele respectable. According to Maggie, "She would go anywhere," just as she had in her days as Alys's apprentice. "If a girl was down in Skid Row, a prostitute, down there in a hole in the wall, where women would fear to tread, Mother would take a cab down there, to a dirty old hotel room, and take care of someone. She did everything. No person was ever in any position that Ruth Barnett wouldn't take care of her."

In the office, it was the receptionist's job to set the fee and collect the money. The receptionist dealt firmly with all the stories and prodded girls to figure out how to come up with the cash: can't you hock your ring? Can't you get your boyfriend to pay? What about your mother and dad? *She* was tough. Few passed by her desk, into the back, without coming up with the required amount. But if a girl could get directly to the boss, and if her story was good enough, Ruth would take care of her even if she couldn't pay. At least in the early days of her proprietorship, Ruth did as many abortions for free as she did for paying customers. She did, however, cover costs by employing the Robin Hood principle: the women who didn't come in crying about the money subsidized those who did.

By the 1940s Ruth Barnett's reputation was everything she wanted it to be. She was a sought-after abortionist, and not by the police. Women in trouble found her when they needed her. In these years, Ruth and her third husband, Earl Bush, took long weekends at their horse ranch in eastern Oregon, but it wasn't uncommon for Ruth's time away from the office to be broken by an imploring phone call. Dorothy remembered a weekend when she and Ruth went up to the ranch for a much-needed rest. They were having a splendid evening after a long drive until, at dinner, the cook rushed in with a message. Ruth, who had steadfastly resisted having a telephone installed in the house, was to go immediately to the little grocery-post office on the highway, where an emergency call had just come in for her. Dorothy and Ruth left their steaks and salad half-eaten on the plate and raced down to the store, Ruth frantic that something terrible had happened to Maggie. But the call, it turned out, had been placed by a Portland doctor whose eldest daughter was unmarried and pregnant. He wanted Ruth to take care of her, and quick. Ruth spoke at some length to the distraught man, assuring him that she would take care of everything, in good time. As Dorothy put it, "She just came out of that call laughing. We got back in the car, and she turned toward me and said in a high, dramatic tone, 'No matter what I do, no matter how hard I try to relax, no matter what anything, they find me.'" Years later, Maggie echoed her mother, "God knows how people found her, but they always did. Word of mouth, somebody knew. Somebody knew somebody who knew somebody."

The Portland doctor's call was not an unusual event for Ruth. In Portland, as elsewhere, few licensed physicians would perform abortions themselves, but many were quite willing to refer their patients to Ruth's office. A California district attorney at mid-century assessed the behavior of doctors in his city in this way: "While an extremely small number of physicians are believed to be engaged in the performance of illegal abortions, a good many refer patients to illegal abortionists indirectly, and some directly, even in writing. Although the majority of physicians probably have a reasonably tolerant attitude toward this practice, most of them scrupulously refuse even to discuss abortion with their patients. This undoubtedly results in many troubled women having no one but the criminal abortionist to whom they may turn for advice and relief."

Many Portland doctors referred unhappily pregnant patients to the eighth floor of the Broadway Building, and Ruth always called herself, with good reason, a "doctor's doctor." In any given year, seventy-five to eighty-five percent of her business came by way of a physician's referral. She was enormously proud of her reputation and her expertise. Yet, according to Dorothy, Ruth could be withering in her assessment of the doctors who sent clients to her. "So often a doctor would call up and make an appointment for one of his patients, and he would say, 'She's only two months along,' or 'six weeks along.' And then we'd get them up on the table and they'd be three and a half to four months gone. Terrible. She'd look at me and say, 'You know, I don't know anything from the waist up, but from the waist down, I do.' She said, 'I oughta teach some of these doctors how to do an exam.'"

Indeed, by the mid-1930s, Ruth could have written the book on abortion technique. Maggie, who climbed up on the table quite a few times herself, gave personal testimony concerning her mother's competence. She said, "Whoever wanted to learn about abortions should have put a halo around her head and had her teach them. No one had her touch. I had abortions off her. It didn't take any more than five or ten minutes. And the last time, there wasn't one drop of blood. Her dexterity, her touch, after fifty years, she could find that little cluster of cells, no matter where it was hiding, in what little fold. I used to ask her, 'How could you tell where that is?' She said, 'Because when you're inside the cervix, it's corrugated and a little rough,' and then she said, a 'You come across a little patch that's slippery and that little patch that you take away, that little tiny fourth of a teaspoon, that little cluster of slippery little cells, that's what you feel for.'

"She knew exactly what she was doing. Even if a woman might have a double-walled cervix or an odd-shaped whatever. Nobody could operate like her. With the least pain, and as quickly. She was as deft and as fast as lightning. She was in there and out. Pat 'em on the ass and that was it."

Ruth herself was never willing to divulge the secrets of her technique. She claimed she was fearful that, were she to write her methods down, some "desperate and foolish couple" might take it upon themselves to follow the recipe. But Maggie, whose behavior was rarely governed by compunction, has recorded the process Ruth employed. Using her own abortion as an example, she describes her mother's unique procedure. "My legs were placed in the stirrups on the operating table. She was always a great believer in lots of hot, soapy water and strong disinfectants, so first, soothing warm water ran over me and down the Kelly pad and into the catch bucket below. The hot sterile instruments were removed from the sterilizer into a flat basin of warm water holding two pink cyanide tablets. She adjusted a bright spotlight on 'the scene of the action' and gently slipped the speculum into place. After swabbing my vagina and cervical opening with a cotton saturated with water and a mild antiseptic solution, she fastened an instrument called a tenaculum onto the lower lip of my cervix. This instrument hung down and out and held the cervical opening in view and also in place.

"Mama's instruments were irreplaceable delicate copies from German artisans, World War I vintage. Some she designed and had made, others she curved to suit herself. She always began by inserting a sound—a long, slender instrument with a rounded end—to gauge the womb depth and character of the interior. The sound would also remove any little 'plug' in the cervical aperture. Then, with various size curettes, she swiftly scraped a few teaspoons or more of clustered cells from the mucous membrane walls of my uterus.

"When all materials were loosened to her satisfaction, a hollow tube was inserted, with a small slit opening on the side of the far end, and this was attached to a small hose, to a hollow metal and rubber open-ended cylinder, which was forced onto the water facuet. When the water rushed through, it created a suction that would remove any particles that she couldn't remove manually. Thus, the aspirator was one of her most important instruments. Then, with one more quick internal examination of the womb, to be sure all remaining tissue and residue had been aspirated, she swabbed inside the womb, cauterizing it with a dilution of strong Churchill's iodine. She did all this through the natural cervical opening, without dilation. The strong fingers of her left hand would press and knead the pubic area to contract the uterus as she slipped the tenaculum and speculum out, and then again the comforting hot, soapy water flushed a very nervous vagina."

All the while that Ruth was doing this delicate, concentrated work of abortions, one after the other, day after day, she was surrounded by a remarkably devoted staff of women. Most of them stayed with her for years. Dorothy Taylor, now a very old woman, has never forgotten her years with Ruth. Nor has she withdrawn her loyalty, even devotion, to the woman with whom, in the 1950s, she once went to jail.

Dorothy was a year ahead of Maggie in school, and they started to pal around together as teenagers, in 1929. "After we were friends for awhile, I met Mag's mother. I knew all about Ruth's business. Most of Mag's Portland friends knew about Ruth. For years we stayed friends. I married my dancing instructor. He and Mag's first husband were great friends, so the four of us were very close, too. Then, after we both divorced, Mag and I still went around together a lot. About 1943, during the war, we were up in Ruth's office one day, and she said to me, `Would you come to work for me?' One thing was, I knew how to keep my mouth shut. I think that was the main thing, and to this day, I've kept my mouth shut.

"I worked with her there at the Stewart Clinic. She had such a business, she had to add help. There was myself and Bea, her girl in the front office, who had been with her for many, many years. In fact, Bea had been Dr. Van Alstyne's receptionist for years. When Van Alstyne retired, Bea made an arrangement with Ruth, and she just stayed on. Then she had Helen and Irene. She did have a large business in those years.

"I took care of the incoming patient. I gave her the medication. Ruth had trained me. I took care of the patient personally, if you know what I mean. Calmed her as much as possible. The treatment that they received there was a red-carpet treatment. It was a gorgeous, beautiful place—the whole top floor of the Broadway Building."

No other practitioner in Portland offered the service that Ruth made integral to a visit to the Stewart Clinic. Despite the fact that timeliness was crucial and women moved through the clinic in fairly astounding numbers, the place always ran like a clock. A nurse prepped the patient, and Ruth stayed in her office until the girl's feet were in the stirrups. There would be several other girls in the waiting room, maybe one or two in recovery getting a cup of hot tea, or maybe if one was hungry, the nurse would fix her a little something to eat. According to Maggie, "There was a hoity-toity service kind of thing. It wasn't like a hospital. It was like going up to a very nice atmosphere where people waited on you hand and foot: can I get you a cup of coffee? Can I get you a hot tea? How do you feel, dearie? She called everyone dearie. There were always people coming in. It was always getting this one ready, getting this one down, getting this one up."

Unhappily pregnant women—desperate and determined to make their own decisions about motherhood during the illegal era—knew the law. Most had heard stories about the back alley. Most knew that putting themselves in the hands of a criminal abortionist was supposed to be a dangerous proposition. And yet, as the numbers show, hundreds of thousands decided that the back alley couldn't be worse than an unwanted pregnancy. So the clinic on the eighth floor of the Broadway Building was a very special place, indeed. And Ruth Barnett, whose style and skill were well-known in Portland, filled a vitally important niche in that city.

In 1951, *Ebony* magazine published an exposé the editors entitled "The Abortion Menace." The article was at least partly calculated to warn its readers of criminal abortionists. The author drew on the stereotyped image of back-alley abortionists and cautioned the public that "each year nearly 700,000 abortions are performed on unfortunate, desperate women by quack surgeons and disreputable physicians whose criminal and unethical methods annually claim the lives of about eight thousand victims." Indeed, *Ebony*'s black readership had special reason to pay attention to this warning since, in grossly disproportionate numbers, black women were among the fatalities. A study of abortion-related deaths in Detroit from 1950 to 1965 found that of the one hundred thirty-eight fatalities at issue, all involved poor women, most of them black. (Somewhat later, in a two-year period in the middle sixties, Detroit General Hospital received twelve women suffering from post-abortion septic shock. Eleven were black; one Mexican.)

Law enforcement officers during Ruth's heyday judged that a private house, one not too close to a police station or a church, was the most attractive place for an abortionist to set up headquarters. Especially attractive was a house in an extremely busy neighborhood, "wherein the stream of women entering and leaving at regular intervals would not arouse comment." The problem with sites such as the downtown office building where Ruth worked, they determined, was that doormen and elevator operators were too apt to recognize what type of work was going on. Such people could too easily inform the police or become blackmailers.

These experts clearly never considered the possibility of an abortionist like Ruth, with her capacity to run a smooth organization and inspire loyalty in everyone around her. In fact, in the Broadway Building, the elevator operators became Ruth's assistants, letting girls in when they arrived so early for appointments that the office door was locked, warning the staff if they heard unpleasant rumors about impending trouble with the cops. Throughout the 1930s and '40s, Ruth's offices were the ideal place for women who wanted to end pregnancies, and Ruth herself was the ideal abortionist. She was meticulous, caring, personable, and she had what it took to work on the other side of the law, as the best criminal abortionist around.

There were, of course, substantial rewards for a woman of this status, although the nature of these rewards was more complicated for Ruth than many could imagine. Common wisdom and common sense said it was simply a matter of money, lots of it, collected hand over fist by get-rich-quick quacks who preyed on desperate women. One observer put it this way: "Working out of cheap hotels and back-room offices, abortionists are only interested in fat fees and getting the patient off their hands as quickly as possible."

Psychiatrists who got into the act of diagnosing abortionists at mid-century found the female variety "an unethical type, punishing, domineering, and even sadistic toward her own sex." And according to these experts, at the heart of the woman's motivation was the dollar. Two experts who were more willing than some to allow that an abortionist *could* work for reasons other than a desire to amass cash found the species pretty unredeemed, nonetheless: "Although there may be, and probably are, some abortionists who are motivated in their practice by other than monetary considerations, not one of the cases we examined concerned an abortionist who consistently displayed any real kindness, understanding, patience or delicacy in handling their patients." The abortionist's alleged love of money and her cruelty inevitably went hand in hand.

If Ruth Barnett was not concerned about the Oregon statute that criminalized abortion when she took on the work, neither was she concerned about what people thought of abortionists. Nor did she organize her life in such a way as to dispel the townspeople's suspicions that she was one of those criminal practitioners who was in it for the money. People who saw her sumptuous offices, or heard about them, or who saw the woman herself, decked out in designer suits with all the trimmings, could easily assume that Ruth fit the stereotype to a tee.

Indeed, it was a fact that Ruth made millions of dollars over the course of her career, some say seventeen million. Maggie, who can get pretty nostalgic reminiscing about the money nowadays, estimates that she herself pried two million out of Ruth. She says that Ruth made so much money, they couldn't spend it fast enough. "She kept it in her closet, stuffed in different hatboxes or shoe boxes."

But despite the thousands stashed and the thousands spent, and despite the experts' diagnoses and the onlookers' suspicions, money never did seem to be the heart of the matter for Ruth. When she spoke for herself, she described her intentions in the dangerous arena of criminal abortion in quite different terms. "I am the instrument," is the way she put it, "the means by which the abortion is accomplished, quickly and safely and without pain. I see those tears dried and the smiles appear; those who had feared disgrace walk out of the office with heads held high, unafraid to face the world."

There is no question that, when the choice was hers, Ruth defined herself as a rather selfless godsend to desperate women. And surely it is difficult to know today exactly how essential the money was to Ruth. According to Maggie, the cash was a kick. "We had it and we spent it. Clothes for everybody. Jewelry, expensive bric-a-brac, minks; how many do you want? Everybody in the pool, just help yourself. Buy yourself a man, a husband, a lover. What can't money buy?" But even Maggie, who stinted herself nothing while the cash flowed ("I was the spendthrift, the ne'er-do-well, the leach, I left no stone unturned."), concluded in retrospect that for herself and for Ruth, "money was like toilet paper and the value the same."

"People tried to say she did her business for money, but money was just happenstance," says Maggie. "It was wonderful to have the money, but if it wasn't there, it didn't really change anything. It was just part of the package. It was not the inspiration at all."

It would have been difficult to convince anyone who disapproved of abortion and abortionists in those days—maybe anyone fortunate enough never to have needed their services—that money was not Ruth's inspiration. Even today, people don't like to think of legal abortion practitioners making a living saving women from the consequences of their sexual misadventures or their carelessness, which some imagine are the only factors leading to an unwanted pregnancy. Sometimes the thinking goes this way: it is immoral for anyone to benefit from the irresponsible sexual behavior of a woman. Indeed, such a woman must pay for valuing sex and devaluing maternity, but the only valid payment is atonement. A person who transacts to relieve such a woman for money is likened to a mercenary, or even a seducer.

Even people who believe women must have the right to control their own fertility can get squeamish over the subject of what

Maggie wryly calls "abortion gold." It sounds like filthy lucre, tainted money. Apparently, discomfort with the subject of cash has little to do with whether or not abortion is a crime, since abortionists of the illegal era and legitimate abortion providers today have both been charged with perverse economic interests. It is an enduring accusation, especially against women practitioners who, as "economic women," are charged with violating their feminity, as well.

It is a fact that during abortion trials in the 1950s, prosecutors and judges across the country singled out the economic motive as particularly disgusting, especially in a woman. In Sacramento, California, for example, Geraldine Rhoades, an abortionist, was pilloried in court for what the prosecutor implied were her perverse economic interests. She was accused of performing abortions so she could buy diamond rings and fancy cars and other luxurious accoutrements. The prosecutor dwelt on the image of Rhoades wantonly enjoying her ill-gotten money and asked the jury to convict her because she was greedy and lacked the caring nature of a real woman. At length he described the plight of unhappily pregnant women who "submitted to that operation by reason of social condition, the fear of a lifetime of shame and a lifetime of embarrassment and because of economic conditions that made it impossible to carry the pregnancy. Their minds were full of horror and fear and they did not think reasonably, but Geraldine Rhoades," he argued, "was not activated by fear and horror and shame, and her mind was as clear as crystal." The prosecutor pointed his finger and announced in the courtroom that Geraldine Rhoades performed abortions because she had an unnatural love of money.

The theme appeared over and over again in scores of abortion trials. It took several different forms. But at its center was always the conviction that a woman who took money to scrape the womb of another woman was some kind of pervert. Mary Paige, an abortionist in the early 1950s in Cincinnati, stood before the judge as he pronounced her guilt in 1953. The judge found a great deal about Paige's life "exemplary." But her work as an abortionist made her abnormal and defined her, finally, as less than a woman. "She has," he said, "performed abortions for the purpose of lining her pocket with money. So far as I know there is little evidence here that she performed an act that may be inspired by sympathy." It was upon this assessment of Mary Paige that the Cincinnati judge determined her jail sentence. One wonders on what basis the judge would have sentenced an abortionist who operated for free. State abortion statutes, after all, contained no language that addressed the issue of money.

As an old woman, Ruth Barnett knew that her enemies invariably put the millions she was paid as an abortionist at the top of the list of her sins. Certainly the Multnomah County district attorneys who had dragged her into court a number of times after 1951 always placed her fees at the center of the charges against her. Just before she died, Ruth addressed the issue of her earnings. The most important thing to remember, she said, was that "I have never, in fifty years of practice, ever solicited a case. The women who wished operations came to me. I did my work well and I charged what I believe was a fair price for the operation. And I've also done a lot of operations without a fee. The laborer is worthy of his hire and so it is with each professional service that is rendered in the marketplace. Not long ago I paid a surgeon $2,500 to excise a malignant mole from my leg. I did not carp or criticize his fee. That is his profession and he is entitled to charge for his skill and knowledge."

Characteristically, Ruth defended herself with confidence and dignity and deep conviction. She considered herself an expert and a professional. She asserted her rights as a professional to make a good living, just like her medical colleagues who sent so much business her way. That was the essence of her defense.

The judges and the prosecutors and jurors harped on the heinous relationship between the abortionist and her ill-gotten riches, but for Ruth money was often—though not always—a simple joy. By all accounts, she simply got a tremendous kick out of extravagance, out of dressing, always, in the height of fashion—as Maggie puts it, "to the teeth." Maggie recalls that when the money rolled in, "We wore Adrian, Dior, suits and long evening clothes, beaded dresses, sequined dresses, five or six or seven hundred dollars each."

Ruth loved to shop, and Maggie remembers their trips downtown, to the fancy stores, with a special clarity. "Believe me, when we walked into a store, the red carpet was out. Everybody knew us. They knew we were there to spend. They took us right away to a private room and we would sit down and the buyer and the salesperson would bring things in to us for our approval or disapproval. We were both heavyset and most of the time we would buy anything that we could get over our heads. I'd say, 'Hell, if it's a size twenty, I'll take it.' We really looked nice. Once when we were in New York together, at the Waldorf, a very nice-looking lady stopped us in front of the elevator, wanting to know where we got our clothes, we looked that nice.

"I wasn't too flashy. I was conservative. But Ruth was flashier, a little more toward the Gypsy Rose Lee type, silkier and shinier, flashier. She liked flowery things a lot. She was smashing. God knows she had the most gorgeous fur coats, always had one draped over her shoulders when she came strolling in the room. We had about four or five fur coats apiece. Short ones and mid-length ones and full-length ones. Silver mink and ranch mink and black."

Clothes *and* jewels. Ruth aimed for glamour, and around Portland, she passed for glamour. "She always looked beautiful," says Maggie. "She loved jewelry. She had some gorgeous pieces. A canary diamond, about five carats, with jaguar and square-cut diamonds on the side—white, but flames of ultraviolet in them. You could even catch a flicker of red. The finest diamond in the world." During the day, at work, Ruth was all business, no fancy clothes, no diamonds. But when she dressed for the evening, it was an event. "She put her jewels on right and left, big sparkling pins, the biggest, brightest, sparkliest things you ever laid your eyes on—diamonds, sapphires, rubies. Big sprays."

When Ruth Barnett strutted her personal extravagance through Portland's supper clubs and its lesser nightspots, she looked to be emblematic of the wages of sin. The good citizens who tagged her as they would a whorehouse madam assumed that abortion money and a generous spirit were mutually exclusive. If someone had told them that Dr. Ruth loved her money most because having it allowed her to give lots away, they never would have believed it.

Starting with her parents, who never asked about where she got the cash, Ruth took care of her family, her staff, stray friends, associates, and strangers, including unwed mothers and other stranded females. She wanted to help. She helped without being asked. "My mother went across town every week to see her parents," Maggie remembers about the 1920s and '30s, "to make sure they had everything they wanted. The house they lived in was paid for, but she always made sure they had enough money for groceries and good

clothes after grandpa went blind and retired. In the end, she supported them all the way. They didn't want to hear about her business, she knew that. They didn't even like drinking and smoking. So
she didn't talk about it. But she did take care of them, paid all their
bills, right up to the nth degree." The fact was, Maggie adds, "she
took care of lots of people that had a bad luck story. She would help
them. She never had any regrets, either, when people would tell her
she was a mark, that people were working her for her money."

Because she was an abortionist, bad luck stories came to Ruth
by the bushel-full. The stories poured out in the office, and sometimes on her doorstep at home, as well. It was not unusual for a forlorn young woman to be sitting huddled by the front door when
Ruth got home, late at night, after an evening on the town. The girl
was broke, she was crying, she was alone and ashamed. She
implored Ruth to help. According to people who knew her, Ruth
didn't turn these girls away. They say she cried with them, and she
told them when to meet her downtown.

Sometimes, she convinced a woman to go ahead and have the
baby. Ruth was proud of an encounter that she felt proved what
kind of a woman she was. One day in the late 1940s, a young married woman travelled from one of the tiny beach villages on the
coast to Portland, to beg Dr. Barnett to end her pregnancy because
she and her husband couldn't afford a baby, but, as Ruth told it, "I
talked her out of it. I knew she and her husband loved each other
and I begged and pleaded and finally bribed her—that if she would
go ahead and have her baby, I would give her twenty-five dollars to
start her confinement fee and later, I told her, I would send her the
most beautiful complete layette any little girl would want. Which
I did, and today she has the sweetest little blond daughter who is
the delight of everyone around her."

Sometimes the girl on the doorstep was too far gone, too many
months pregnant to get an abortion. In some cases, Ruth gave
these girls too, enough money for the layette, and every now and
then she arranged for one of her friends or a doctor she knew to
adopt the baby out. Ruth remembered one such arrangement vividly. "A girl came to me sometime around 1949, after the war. She was
in such distress, she couldn't talk to me for crying. She had just
learned that it was possible for a girl to be helped if she got pregnant and didn't want to be a mother. But the poor dear learned too

late. She was about five months pregnant. I told her she would have to have her baby. I tried to explain that she could hide out away somewhere that she wasn't known, and that there were good people who would be glad to pay the doctor and hospital bill in exchange for the baby. She seemed so desperate. She just didn't want to leave me and my office. We fixed her a cup of hot tea and sandwich and all the time I kept explaining that it wasn't the end of the world for her. She was a good-looking little blonde, and I could just think of a dozen of my own personal friends who would be glad to get her baby. I told her not to give up hope and to remember that when she thought it over she could come back to me and I would see that she had perfect care." The young woman did not return, but one morning about four months after the little blonde cried her heart out in the Stewart Clinic, the staff and two early-morning clients found a tiny infant, a three-day-old girl, rolled up into a torn corner of a wool bed blanket tucked carefully into the down cushions of the davenport in the clinic's waiting room. The baby was wrapped in the blanket but was otherwise naked. "The little umbilical cord was still attached," remembered Ruth. "The laundry mark on the blanket had been burned off," so that no clues to the child's origins remained.

Maggie, who had recently given birth to her first child, a girl named Ruthie after her doting grandmother, was called into service at once. "My daughter came on the run with a quick stop at a furniture store to order a baby crib to be sent to her apartment. She brought a bottle of her own baby's formula, diapers, shirt, and nightdress. My daughter kept the little girl nine months. Every day I looked at that baby and saw the poor, bewildered young woman who had been in my office a few months before. When Maggie knew that she herself was pregnant again, she felt three little ones so close together was too much to handle, so my dearest girlfriend, who had never had children and wanted the baby desperately, took that sweet little girl and legally adopted her. What a joy and a pleasure my friend has had from that child."

Unlike many abortionists, Ruth didn't make baby placements a big money-making sideline. She simply found homes for babies on occasion, mostly with her friends, when an unwed mother—too far gone for an abortion and especially desperate—begged for her help. Ruth had no interest in running the kind of abortion/adoption operation that Grace Schauner, a sometime abortionist, sometime baby broker, ran in Wichita, or that Louise Malanowski ran in Alabama, Faye Wasserman ran in New Jersey, and many others across the country ran in those years. It was not at all uncommon for an abortionist to take on baby selling as a lucrative sideline in the decades before *Roe v. Wade*. Combining businesses made good sense at a time when illegitimacy rates were rising, and "single mother" was still far from a viable status for women in the United States. But many citizens thought that an abortionist who also sold babies on the black market was particularly depraved. Ernie Warden, for one, a crusading reporter who worked for the *Wichita Beacon* in the early 1950s, was disgusted by these activities that he felt exploited the sexual misadventures of unfortunate females, and he didn't like living in a city where they were tolerated. With outrage he targeted Grace Schauner, and wrote about Wichita as a "reception center for midwestern girls who want illegal operations." The city was also, according to Warden, "the delivery center for babies who are put on the auction block." The reporter made it his personal business to halt the "manipulations of the baby killers and the baby sellers who exact a toll of a million dollars annually from expectant mothers and married couples who are willing to pay a high price for a child."

Grace Schauner's business was particularly lucrative and partic- ularly grim, although as she saw it, she was simply responding to a new postwar opportunity. In those years, when unmarried girls who got pregnant were expected to give their babies up for adoption and couples who could not conceive children were eager to adopt new- borns, Schauner developed a strategy for helping both groups real- ize their goals. Routinely, she sent unhappily pregnant girls and women who came to her after the safe period for an abortion had passed to the house of a woman the Kansas press came to know as "Mrs. T." In the basement of this house, unmarried pregnant girls and women were warehoused, six or seven at a time, to wait out their pregnancies. "Mrs. T. would have them on cots for prospective adoptive parents who would come in and she would take them downstairs, and she would point to the girls and say, 'Point out the girl that you want to be the mother of your child.'" Schauner and Mrs. T. worked with lawyers and other local black-market baby bro- kers who sold infants for as much as fifteen hundred dollars cash.

As another Wichita reporter put it, "The vendors' price scale for babies runs from $800 to $1500, from the least expensive to the more choice infant. Prices average just like beef over the meat counter. And the filet mignon on the black market is the new-born youngster."

Ruth Barnett was not against helping the individual girl whose family insisted that she could not bring her bastard child home. She was not against harboring such a girl in her own home. In the mid-1950s, she took in one girl, "a poor unfortunate girl who I've put in my own home, at our ranch." Ruth could see the good in this kind of an arrangement. The girl, she said, "is waiting for the time to come in a month when she will come back to Portland and have her baby by one of the best obstetricians in town. And then she will return to her home and friends, who will be none the wiser. She can start life anew, and in the meantime, she will be making another childless home happy."

But Ruth saw what she felt was the horror of the arrangement even more clearly, and she summoned it up to justify her work as an abortionist. "Now, hiding out and giving your baby away is all very well for a girl to do when there is no other solution. And if a girl wants or needs to adopt her baby out, that is her business. But not me. Never, never, never would I have a child and then turn it out into the world and never know where that baby was." Presciently expressing the feelings of so many unwed mothers of this era who were pressured into relinquishing their babies, Ruth added, "I could not sleep nights as long as I lived. I know I would wake up haunted at night and think, 'Where is my baby tonight? Is someone treating it kindly? How much better for girls to know when they get into trouble that they shouldn't put off dealing with the problem. They should come at once to a reliable, kind doctor who can gently remove a few little bloodclots and cells—and let the girl learn by her experience to be careful and not trust the men when they start their persuasive ways."

Ruth went to work every day with a sympathetic understanding of girls and women in trouble. She positioned herself between the legs of unhappily pregnant females day after day because their plight was real to her, in large part, she said, because of her own teenage abortion. Ever since she was a girl in Portland, she had thought a great deal about these issues—pregnancy and motherhood—and had come to believe that sometimes it was wonderful to be pregnant and other times it was not. She had come to believe, like the pioneer that she was, that women—so often the easy targets of persuasive men—must be stubborn about forging their own way in this terrain. Women must finally claim their own destinies, she thought, even if they'd given in to importuning husbands and boyfriends earlier, and even if claiming their destinies meant breaking the law.

In Ruth's heyday there was no feminist movement in Portland and no feminist parlance in which to frame her convictions. She was deeply, instinctively attached to her work as an abortionist and completely committed to it, some said irrationally committed. The money was the fun part, the part that made life a sport. But the job she had to do was serious.

Yet, as simply dedicated as Ruth was to her work, its criminal aspect created a very complicated state of affairs because doing abortions was not consistently an objectionable *métier* throughout her fifty-year career. She lived in a city where for years at a time, even for decades, the men in charge of deciding who was a criminal allowed her to work undisturbed, and during those periods she could do abortions under excellent conditions in her clinic. But sometimes the city fathers explicitly disapproved, or said they did for one or another political reason. Then Ruth had to hide out, move her office, work out of Maggie's house or her own basement under impossible conditions. Perhaps this kind of never knowing did not distinguish the abortionist so sharply from other people— draft resisters, for example—who have been willing to break the law to honor their convictions.

What *did* distinguish the abortionist from other conscientious objectors was her association with the stain of sex, and the fact that this association made her a rich woman. The profits of her profession supported her generosity and her elegance, and made her much less like other dissidents and much more like a criminal.

It was not only the fact that, from time to time, the city fathers, other disapproving citizens, and the law defined Ruth Barnett as a criminal. More to the point, Ruth herself lived in a morass composed of her rational choice to help desperate women, her determination to proceed at any cost, and the unstable context of a life of bounds in Portland. In the end, no matter how skillful Ruth was or how much integrity she had about her chosen path, she was a criminal. Her life was filled with the comfortable things that money could buy, but it was always out of bounds. It was the elegant life of crime, a difficult and even destructive way of life.

A woman like Ruth with a big spirit, a woman who loved her money, who loved to spend it and give it away, shaded into a woman of intemperate, grotesque expenditures as she dipped into the shoe boxes full of criminal cash. She couldn't report her earnings to the IRS. She couldn't keep bank accounts. So she peeled the bills from the wads of money she earned and spent them, in a wild show of defiance. The money became the only ballast for the abortionist living the criminal life.

The money that rolled in was important partly because it subsidized her defiance. Great sums of cash made it possible for Ruth to create herself as a woman of substance, to spite the genteel citizens who tagged and scorned her. From the earliest days of her work as an abortionist, she was tagged in town that way, and Maggie was tagged as the abortionist's daughter. Ruth instinctively knew how to hold her chin up and go about her business no matter what they said about her, but the ostracism damaged Maggie. It was hardest for her when she was a teenager, a beautiful young girl painfully vulnerable to the sting of disapproval and exclusion. Sometimes Ruth's plans for Maggie made it likely that her daughter would encounter just that.

The first time Maggie remembers suffering because of her mother's profession was when she was fifteen, about to enter her junior year in high school. This was in the early 1930s, and at that time Ruth was especially busy, doing abortions all day and going to chiropractic school at night. She had just separated from her second husband, Paul Barnett, an automobile mechanic when she met him and later an insurance salesman. She took a heartbroken Maggie from the family house that the girl had loved on Oak Street, and from her beloved Daddy Paul, to live in the Congress Hotel downtown. Knowing that she was too busy to look after Maggie—a task that never came first in the best of times—Ruth made the inexplicable decision to send her daughter to Catholic boarding school. Maybe she chose St. Mary's because by then she sensed the wild stuff that Maggie was made of and hoped the stern climate of parochial school would starch her up a bit. Maybe the Catholic boarding school was the only one close enough to permit Maggie to make visits home regularly. Maybe Ruth was making a particularly pointed effort to disassociate Maggie from her abortionist mother. At a Catholic boarding school, after all, Maggie would be trained to be a lady. Whatever the reason, the placement didn't last long.

Maggie imagines that sometime during Easter vacation, one of her classmate's mothers called up the Mother Superior and said indignantly, "Well! You've got Ruth Barnett's daughter in your school." Maggie imagines that the angry mother gave the nun a choice: either Maggie left the school, or everybody else would. It must have been like that, says Maggie, because for the first time, when she came back from the holidays, the other girls began to whisper, "She's Margaret Barnett, the abortionist's daughter."

No one, however, spoke such words to her face, and when she was asked to leave at the end of the year, "the excuse they used was trumped up," according to Maggie. "Clarice Feamster and I usually led the boarding school students around the block after dinner," she calls more than sixty years later. One night, in the spring, "Sister M. St. Claire brought me before the Mother Superior for expulsion, or rather for a neat 'Don't come back here next year!' They said I had made an obscene gesture at some boys across the street coming out of St. Andrew's. I don't know how obscene I could have been at fifteen." Maggie protested the charge to the Sister and to the Mother Superior. Her friend Clarice said that Maggie had done no such thing. But Maggie had been tarred with a school-girl version of sexual taint: making an obscene gesture was the sort of thing an abortionist's daughter might do, and she was expelled.

Maggie came home to Portland and finished high school in the spring of 1932. But her life during what she calls "the last year of my youth" was a most peculiar sort of school girl's idyll. Ruth was entering her heyday, money was plentiful. She and Maggie together were stars in the boozy, sexy nightlife of the city, the only "society" that admitted all comers, including the abortionist and her daughter. Maggie remembers that "it was 'party time' all the time. If it wasn't her gang of disreputables, it was my gang of ne'er-do-wells."

Every night was a bash. Ruth and Maggie got dressed up and made the scene. "There was the Press Club in the old Oregon Hotel. Billy and Teddy, two drinking gal pals of Mama's ran a pretty good 'bust out' joint. Crap tables with chippies and rounders, gamblers, pimps, whores, and a few wide-eyed squares. It was our hangout. Anybody who was anybody usually started there and drifted on to other hot spots. I remember Blondie and Sugar Keeting had a dive called the Milton Rooms down by the Hawthorne Bridge. Now, I know it was a whorehouse, but at that time, to me it was just a place to get a drink and sing some songs. Mama would rapturize about her kid's ability to hold her liquor and sing 'You're My Everything' and 'Once in A While.' And Mama—everybody liked her. She was just entertaining as hell. She'd throw her head back and laugh. I never knew anyone who didn't like her. We had a ball! If someone got a divorce, we celebrated. If someone got married, we celebrated. Whatever the occasion, we celebrated! Mama's group played harder than any group I've ever seen. Their hangovers were beauts.

"Sometimes we'd go over to colored town across the river and Spicers would roll out the New York steak and black-eyed peas anytime of the night or morning. Portland was pretty rough and jumping back then, before the newspapers and the politicians tried to make a lady out of her."

That summer, when Maggie was seventeen and due to go off on her own to the University of Oregon in Eugene, no one was trying to make a lady out of *her*. But sometimes Maggie herself imagined giving up life as the abortionist's daughter and trying on a life of prim, feminine respectability. It was a refreshing idea, especially that summer when she was feeling tarnished and tired and ready to get away from the pimps and whores and gamblers who made up the only social set she could really claim. The Catholic school episode two years before had shaken her, but the escape route she devised for herself this time was through what might have been, after the church, the most censorious institution she could have chosen. She decided to become a sorority girl.

Maggie was enormously excited to get to Eugene in the fall of 1932 and remake herself. It never occurred to her that "family background" or anything else could be an obstacle. She was pretty and high-spirited, ready to embrace life as a coed, and she came well-equipped. "Mother bought me everything a young girl could possibly want. There was a trunkload of clothes and my Aunt Lil went down to Eugene with me for rush week. I went to a tea at the Gamma House and I went to several others, wide-eyed and bushy-tailed, but as the week drew to a close, I was panicky because I hadn't had that final bid for the last Friday before the formal bid to a sorority."

Then on Thursday afternoon, a girl from Alpha Chi Omega called Maggie's room at the Eugene Hotel and asked her to lunch at the sorority house the next day. "This was it. Oh, how I dressed, so painstakingly. I was so deliciously nervous. This was really it; I was sure to be pledged. I was invited into their inner sanctum, the smoking room. They gave me a cute little gold safety pin with two colored ribbons, pink and yellow. I was in! All I had to do now was to pick up my bid at the Dean of Women's office at 8:00 the next morning and be ready to have my trunk and things moved over to the sorority house that same afternoon. I was in heaven.

"The next morning Aunt Lil and I were up early packing and chattering away. She was going back to Portland, her chaperoning over with and her mission accomplished. She was in the bathtub and in high spirits when the phone rang. I answered it, and I swear I had a premonition that something was going to happen to spoil my dream. It was the Dean of Women who told me not to come over to pick up the pledge because my bid had been withdrawn. I was speechless and crushed. The woman refused to tell me what was going on. She just told me to call up one of the girls at the sorority, who would explain everything to me. I was crying when I dialed the number the Dean gave me. I couldn't believe this was happening.

"The girl at Alpha Chi must have been sitting right by the phone waiting for my call because she answered on the first ring. I'm sure it was very painful for her to answer my questions. She explained to me that there had been a special Panhellenic meeting held in Portland the night before when all the names had been turned in. The meeting had been called, she said, solely to reject me. She told me she was sorry, but that they had rejected me because of my mother's profession."

An old woman now, the abortionist's daughter hasn't gotten over the rejection. "The parsimonious bastards, sixty years later my lesson in being unacceptable in Portland society still hurts. It's ridiculous, I know, but the seventeen-year-old girl that I was, fumbling around the threshold of adulthood, grasping at straws for right and wrong, I hadn't lost my idealism yet."

When Ruth heard what had happened to her child, she had one of her boyfriends drive her to the top of Council Crest, where she sat on the running board of the car, screaming and crying in rage. *Here* were the wages of sin. Maggie came back to Portland, once more, and Ruth told her, "Well, don't feel too bad, honey. For every fraternity ring or pin I take in off these girls trying to pay for their abortions, and for every sorority girl that comes in my office, you'll get a new dress!" Maggie recalls, "To say the least, I was the most fashionable and best outfitted girl at the university that season. And also the wildest, wickedest, drunkenest, most daring, and most promiscuous. I ran with the fastest crowd of seniors, tore around in a Model T3, drank out of flasks, in dismal bootleg shacks, lousy gin and moonshine rotgut so bad that we'd pour a package of baking soda into a gallon so we could keep it down. I stumbled into class so loaded I could hardly hit the seat, but if I didn't keep going, I knew I'd weep and I wanted my year of tears behind me and to hell with the future." If Maggie hadn't lost her idealism by the time she arrived in Eugene, the girls of Alpha Chi had washed the vestiges away. The fall of 1932 was the last time Maggie tried hard for a life of respectability for nearly forty years.

In the crisis, Ruth had reached for her wallet. Its contents were her only weapon against the Alpha Chi's and their ilk, and her only means of compensating Maggie for the hurt. Ruth's formulation was instinctively, pointedly vengeful: the sorority girls who snubbed their noses at her daughter would pay. Ruth would see to it that *their* secret shame—their abortions—paid Maggie back for the public humiliation of being blackballed. Ruth was determined to exact some retribution. In her mind, their abortions became Maggie's enviable wardrobe, a cruel revenge indeed.

Over time it became a predictable pattern—the money and Maggie, the money and revenge, the money and defiance. It was a painful pattern for a woman like Ruth—a woman of discipline and competence, of high style and wealth. Here she was, a pariah and a criminal except in her office, where she was an angel of mercy, and down at the Press Club or across the river at Spicers, among the lowlifes. Increasingly, Ruth was hemmed in by her outlaw profession, so that the money was her only weapon of self-defense, and increasingly, it was tipped with poison.

Maggie painfully remembers the grotesque part that money played in their lives, especially in later years when Ruth spent wild, uncontrolled sums in an effort to mimic proper family life. At

Christmas it was predictable. "We spent hours helping her decorate the house. We had waves of evergreen boughs, every nook and cranny had to be decorated. Everything had ribbons and holly and candles and we spent hours. She'd call us over, me and my daughters Ruthie and Nina, we spent hours. We *hated* Christmas. Every year we'd have to go over there and wrap these cockamamie presents for everybody she knew. Who in God's name wants eleven, twelve, thirteen presents. It was awful, just awful. I've never been able to have a Christmas since then.

"One year she gave me a diamond watch and a mink stole. One would have been enough. But not this overload. Eight, ten presents for each of my kids. All ripped open. It had no value, no value to the children. When she'd take a trip back East, she ordered all the Christmas stuff, in spring or summer. She bought a surrey with the fringe on top at F.A.O. Schwarz one year, covered with real pony skin. You pumped it and this little imitation pony pulled the surrey around. She never stopped at that. It went on and on. Maybe she spent four thousand dollars. God knows what."

Maggie hated Christmas, but she submitted. She always submitted when Ruth bought her furs and houses and another drink. She submitted when Ruth got drunk and turned on her and began to call her names, in public or on the way home from a night on the town. Maggie submitted partly because she had her own agenda. She needed Ruth's money for the kids, for her many husbands and their business ventures, for the cars and maids and everything else. Maggie reports, in fact, that in the 1940s and '50s it took five or six thousand dollars of Ruth's money to run her household every month, and an equal amount to support her shopping sprees. Maggie was skilled at getting to Ruth's money and managing her mother's temper. "If Mama tried to make me feel bad for using so much of her money, who cared? I'd just get more anyway. Her complaints just ran off of me. I didn't pay any attention to what she said. I knew just as soon as I came up with a good idea, she'd go for it anyway." On an everyday basis, Ruth and Maggie managed each other, but the project was corrosive. And Maggie bore the brunt of it.

For by this time, Maggie had become the site of Ruth's war against Portland society. The fact was, the abortionist's daughter paraded through town as the genuine product—and the emblem— of Ruth's criminal life. Maggie became, in time, her mother's most effective revenge. Ruth paid Maggie with pots of abortion gold to flout genteel conventions, to marry nine men, all deadbeats ("every man who asked me," says Maggie), and to live like a princess in Portland's best neighborhoods, never exchanging a word with her neighbors, never even knowing their names. Ruth paid Maggie to be sleek and fat and sexy and wild, to be a renegade spectacle, and to need her mother.

And this was the other way Ruth redressed the problem of her status through Maggie: Ruth paid Maggie to be helpless without her mother's money and without her mother bossing her around. Even far into Maggie's many marriages, Maggie never handled money and never knew how much there was. Ruth took care of everything, with cash. "She just came over sometime around the first of the month and paid all the bills, paid all the help. It was just a common occurrence. I never knew anything about those things. I only knew about buying clothes and jewels and drinks for everybody at the table."

In another time and place, Ruth—with her expertise and her success unsurpassed—could have earned a place of respect and dignity in the community. But as an outlaw abortionist, her earnings were never so straightforward. So Ruth gave Maggie the job of affirming her mother's value and her indisputable authority as no one else could. With her disordered dependence and helplessness, Maggie needed Ruth, and Ruth paid for that, too.

Ruth Barnett estimated that she earned nearly two hundred thousand dollars a year during her proprietorship of the Stewart Clinic from 1945 to 1952, the sort of money that tended to curtail the possibility that someone might pity the abortionist for her wild daughter, or for the persistent danger of arrest and imprisonment that dogged her for years. The people of Portland—especially those who had never gotten pregnant by mistake—typically condemned Ruth in terms like those Raymond A. Bruntrager used in 1951 when he prosecuted abortionist Sophie Miller in St. Louis. He said, "All she cared about was one thing—did you bring the money? If you got the money, sure I'll do it for you."

After *Roe v. Wade*, in Portland they would call Ruth Barnett "a woman before her time," and many would be willing then to give her the special, posthumous halo due a fearless heroine. But for decades before then, the abortionist was cast as the diabolical architect of the back alley, as if she had personally constructed all the danger and all the opportunity, all by herself. For her part, Ruth always knew that she and her clinics—she and her furnace room— were the creation of a law she reviled. Ruth knew that her life was fatally beleaguered because the criminal's billfold, the danger, and the fear were all the offspring of a law designed to govern women's bodies and their lives, but utterly unable to do so.

Ruth Barnett and Sophie Miller and all the other abortionists who weren't responsible for building the back alley, but who worked warily within it, would have agreed with Grace Schauner, the abortionist in Wichita, who was arrested during the same crackdown era that ultimately netted Ruth. She explained a few things in 1954 to the journalist trying to send her to jail, such as how defenseless women were often the victims of sexually demanding men, and how afterwards, these women had no choice but to bear the consequences. She didn't believe that was right. "Many of these girls who get into difficulty beat a path to my door for help," she told Ernie Warden. "I felt it was my duty to help these girls. I believe that in every community there must be someone to do the work that I have done." Grace Schauner was no saint, and neither was Ruth Barnett. But Ruth had a point when she said in the early fifties, before she was sent to jail, "God Almighty, what would my women do without me?"

Ruth Barnett's father's general store in Hood River, Oregon, at the turn of the century. Ruth was born in the second-story apartment in 1895.

A pioneer family, circa 1905. Ruth Hanna, first row, second from right. Margaret Belle Hanna, Ruth's mother, is at Ruth's right. Ruth's brother, Marc Hanna, is second from left, first row. James Hanna and Florence Hanna, Ruth's father and sister, are top row, right. Others are members of the extended Hanna family, all early settlers in the Pacific Northwest.

Ruth Hanna as a teenager, circa 1909, in a Hood River photography studio.

Ruth Hanna's high school class, Hood River, Oregon, circa 1910. Ruth is seated in first row, right.

Ruth Hanna and her high school basketball team, circa 1910.

Ruth Hanna in Portland, circa 1912, about the time she became pregnant and went to Dr. George Watts for an abortion.

Ruth Hanna Cohen as the young wife of a travelling salesman in Seattle, circa 1917, with her husband Harry's family. Ruth's daughter, Maggie, is at far right.

Ruth Hanna Cohen in Portland, circa 1920, after she left her husband to become an apprentice to Alys Griff, one of the first woman physicians in the Pacific Northwest. During World War I, Griff began to specialize in abortion services. By 1918, the demand for abortions in Portland was so high that she took on Ruth as a trainee-assistant. Once Ruth found her life's work as an abortionist, she immediately began to cultivate her life-long interest in the glamorous way of life her earnings made possible.

Ruth on holiday from her busy, Depression-era abortion practice, salmon fishing in 1932 with Fred West, a member of the Portland Police Department.

Ruth's daughter, Maggie, circa 1940. At this time, Maggie was in her twenties and living the wild, fairly dissolute life of a young woman constrained by her social status as "the abortionist's daughter."

William Byrne (left) and Reginald Rankin, master-
mind of a west coast abortion syndicate in the
1930s, just after the two men were ordered into
custody during the 1936 abortion trial in Los Angeles. Several witnesses for the prosecution had
accused both men of attempting to intimidate them.
(Copyright 1936, Los Angeles Times)

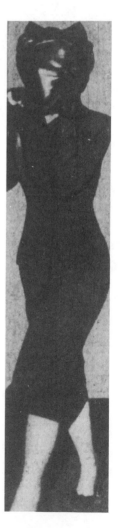

A woman hiding her face behind her pocketbook as
she left a San Diego courtroom after having been
forced to testify in the 1949 trial of abortionist
Laura Miner. During the postwar crackdown on
abortionists, Miner was accused of performing
what the newspapers called an "illegal operation"
on this "young mother in a smart hat." *(San Diego
Union, 2/22/49)*

Between about 1940 and 1951, with the retirement of the older generation of abortionists in Portland, Ruth Barnett's practice flourished undisturbed by the law. She often performed 20–30 abortions a day in her elegant downtown office, earning enough money to support her love of high style and glamour.

One of Ruth Barnett's series of Portland mansions, 1940s.

Ruth with her first grandchild, Maggie's daughter Ruthie, 1948.

Ruth and Earl Bush celebrate their first wedding anniversary at a Portland supper-club, 1949.

Ruth with one of her prize race horses at the Portland Meadows racetrack, 1950.

The heated coverage of the July 1951 abortion busts in Portland. The city's two dailies and each paper's star reporter vied with each other to produce the most sensational pictures and text of the "abortion nests" exposed.

Ruth Barnett in 1969, soon after she was released, as the oldest woman ever incarcerated by the State of Oregon, from her last jail sentence for performing abortions. This photograph was taken a few months before Ruth died of melanoma.

Chapter Three

A MAN'S WORLD

*I*n Portland, the winter of 1934 was the toughest season. The Great
Depression had settled down on the ordinary citizens and on cor-
ner-store merchants with a cold grimness. Everyone in town read
about it in the morning papers, as if they needed to: the city's relief
rolls, already swollen for three years, got bigger still that winter. But
Ruth Barnett did not suffer in 1934. She was quick to admit that
the circumstances bringing down her neighbors weren't half bad for
an abortionist.

The fact was, the sad demographics of the Depression heightened the demand for Ruth's services and for the services of abortionists everywhere. With one-quarter of American workers out of
a job, thousands of young couples felt pressed to put off marriage,
if not always sexual relations. Married men, mortified and degraded by unemployment, deserted their wives in record numbers in
the early thirties. Men and women with the resources to weather
grim times knew that one more baby could destabilize delicate
family strategies for survival.

In the depths of the Depression, a woman could get pretty desperate waiting for her period, all the more so because everybody
seemed to be pointing fingers censoriously in those days, at "relief
babies" who garnered state subsidies, and especially at their mothers, who should have known better. A young woman with a toddler
on one hip and an infant on the other could easily evoke disgust, or
resentment. People might whisper about her, calling her a slattern
or a sow. A woman with too many children and too little money
wore her poverty and her sexuality in public as twin failings.

Portland had just begun to notice the thawed response to birth
control that was seeping through some liberal Protestant churches
in the thirties, and that was taken up as a cause by well-heeled,
reform-minded women and fringe New Dealers. Those who came

to the Broadway Building looking for Ruth Barnett, though, were rarely victims of contraceptive failure in those days. Most of them had no contraception, except perhaps a crude device such as a pessary or some homemade business like the gob of lard that Ruth's mother used. But these women knew they had to do something to protect themselves from the finger pointers and to protect their other babies from hunger. Some knew they had to get rid of the pregnancy to stave off their husbands' wrath.

Like Alice Hawksworth, who felt forced to get three abortions between December 1934 and November 1935, these women were deeply distressed that they couldn't control their pregnancies, especially when times were so hard. Alice was beside herself the third time she had to go down to the abortionist's office. "I was in tears and I said I was back again and how miserable I felt and everything. And my little boy had a cold, and in fact both my little boys had colds and there wasn't nothing I could do for them. I told the doctor that I hated to have to come back for another operation, but I felt like I couldn't have another child right then. I had two little babies and not enough to go around and I had such trouble the time before, with the Caesarian."

Ruth was prepared to do her part for the Alice Hawksworths of Portland. Years later she described her sense of purpose in the Depression years. "There was plenty of work and I loved it. I was young and strong and my health was good. I liked the income, naturally. But most of all, I liked what I was doing. In spite of my patients' tears and anguish, I toiled in a happy climate because here, in my surgery, came the end of tears and anguish."

Three events helped set Ruth up particularly well in 1934. Early in the year was the purchase of Maude Van Alstyne's practice for two thousand dollars down, plus what Ruth considered to be reasonable monthly payments. Ruth now had her own office and her own clients after fourteen years as an apprentice. Equally important, she had her own official credentials, having completed the naturopathy course she had taken at Dr. Watts's urging.

The third event that shaped Ruth's life in 1934 was the arrival in Portland that summer of Reg Rankin, a California man with some very big ideas about setting up an abortion syndicate. The story of Mr. Rankin's role in the abortion business must move into the foreground here because it is so arcane and so revealing at once.

The syndicate that Rankin set out to create, and in fact did create between 1934 and 1936, is a classic artifact of the confluence of the Depression and the criminal status of abortion, and an emblem of how criminalization put women everywhere in danger.

As a man on the make, Rankin correctly perceived abortion to be a growth industry in the mid-thirties. He had a good understanding of how things were for women desperate not to be pregnant in hard times. He recognized, in addition, that one person's desperation was another's golden opportunity. Indeed, a man like himself was aware that when an illegal but unofficially tolerated service is in very high demand, there is a great deal of money to be made, with relatively little risk, by supplying that service. Rankin, who was a businessman, not an abortionist, determined that the opportunity was particularly attractive because the group he aimed to serve was enormous, it was exclusively female, and to one degree or another, every female seeking the service would be in a state of shame. This was a very appealing target population indeed for a shady dealer like Rankin. Since their own stake in keeping the abortion secret would be so high, his clients would not be likely to turn on him, or turn him in.

In sum, Reg Rankin had a very strong sense in 1934 that he could step into the abortion arena and use the plight of desperate women to his own considerable profit. From the beginning to the end of his adventures in the abortion trade, Rankin usually thought of himself as providing a quality service. But the details of his transactions—with abortionists, clients, and others who crossed his path, including Ruth Barnett—demonstrate above all that the laws criminalizing abortion created space for thugs to prey mercilessly on unwillingly pregnant and defenseless women.

In some ways, although he himself never performed an abortion, Rankin is more perfectly the product and personification of the illegal era than so-called back-alley practitioners like Ruth Barnett. Although for some the odor of illicit cash clung to Ruth, her heart was invested in helping, and her skill made this possible thousands of times over. Rankin, on the other hand, was a middle man, a crude opportunist who used the law and the circumstances of desperate women, in a time of economic dislocation, to slake his greed.

Rankin's story eclipses Ruth Barnett's for a time because throughout the mid-thirties, while Ruth quietly performed abortions day

after day and lived it up at night, Rankin was building an unsavory
abortion empire on terrain where women were not safe. At the end
of the decade, Rankin fulfilled his long-standing intention of
pulling Ruth Barnett into his employ, but when the entrepreneur
showed up in Portland in 1934, the person he came to town to see
was Ruth's Dr. Watts.

Watts had been performing abortions in Portland, only lately
with Ruth's help, for forty years. To the casual observer, the doctor
was like many abortionists of his era. A regular physician and married man with respectable roots in his community, he turned gradually to performing abortions when his lady patients showed up in
the office with steady regularity asking for the service, and other
doctors, eager for a colleague who would accept referrals, heard
through the grapevine that he was willing. But Albert Watts was
distinguished from the run-of-the-mill doctor-abortionists who
broke the law but remained within the profession in the decades
after the turn of the century. He was different from the others
because no one whispered around town that Dr. Watts was a drunk
or a pervert or a man with skeletons in his closet. More important,
Watts was special because he'd developed a highly effective vacuum aspiration technique for performing the operation, a way of
doing his business that left him, after thousands of abortions, with
an absolutely clean record of successes, and no unpleasant encoun-
ters with the law.

Rankin came up to Portland from Los Angeles looking for Watts
because his grandiose plans called for a medical man who knew
what he was doing. Rankin was the sort of operator who prided
himself on knowing where there was a buck waiting to be made,
and just now, Watts figured in his plans. Earlier, in the 1920s, when
fat wads of money were changing hands among land speculators
and builders, insurance agents, and surveyors of water rights in Los
Angeles, Rankin's particular niche had been second-guessing property assessors. He called himself a "tax factor," or, in more up-to-
date terms, an "evaluation engineer," and passed around brochures
describing himself as the director of a company known "for twenty
years in general property tax assessment appraisals and adjust-
ments." His special skill was helping taxpayers lighten their burden.

Rankin's enterprise was a fringey sort of effort, but there were
years when it produced a good income. It was the sort of business

that required Rankin to learn his way around town and become savvy about who was who. Over the years, the "evaluation engineer" became particularly skilled at determining who to pay off to clear a way for his profits. But when the Great Depression put a damper on assessed values and on most business opportunities in southern California, Rankin found he had had enough of scrounging up clients for his services in what he called the "tax racket."

By the early 1930s, he had a better idea, an idea that felt more up-to-date, a sure winner. He decided to go into the abortion business, to become a sort of abortion factor, as it were. Rankin was a married man and also a man-about-town who liked to have girls on the side. So he was well aware of what a continual and frustrating effort it was for the ladies to keep from getting pregnant. He was also aware that more women were trying harder than ever to keep from having babies as times stayed tough. Rankin figured that in hard times the abortionist made out, and the abortionist's handler could make out even better.

As a tax man, Rankin specialized in knowing the right bureaucrat to pay off. His acquaintances also included bookies, bootleggers, pimps, and abortionists, the kind of professionals who needed specialized help to prepare their tax returns. With characteristic bravado, Rankin once informed a high-placed California official that he handled the tax records of practically all the leading abortionists on the Pacific coast. That was how he met Dr. Watts in Portland.

Criminal abortionists tended to know each other in the 1930s. They knew who was good and whose botched cases they had to clean up after. When Rankin decided that abortion was the business for him, he tapped into the network, and all his sources spoke well of Watts, touting especially his method and his good sense. In the summer of 1934, Rankin travelled up to Portland to visit the seasoned practitioner. He wanted to talk to Watts about his big plans for a high-class abortion syndicate, with offices from Seattle to the Mexican border, each one staffed by a doctor who'd been trained under Watts. He wanted to see if the older man had a taste for going in with him.

That summer Dr. Watts was sixty-eight years old. He listened to Rankin and he was tempted. His colleague Dr. Van Alstyne, several years younger than he, had just given up her office. Van Alstyne herself had told Watts that it was time for the next generation to take over their work in Portland. She said she was well pleased that Ruth Barnett would succeed them. True, Ruth wasn't a doctor, but they both knew that the younger woman had extraordinary skill and the termperament to do the job, and after all, Watts had been her teacher. Maude Van Alstyne said that he knew better than anyone what Ruth could do.

Watts was surprised that Rankin's idea did not make him feel old and tired and ready to go home to bed. In fact, it was quite the opposite. Rankin made him feel important. He was pleased that abortionists down in San Francisco and even Los Angeles, and up in Seattle, had all said he was the man Rankin needed. Rankin told him that he had heard from other doctors that Watts knew more about doing abortions than the rest of them put together. He was the abortion king, the teacher, the expert. Rankin make Dr. Watts feel energetic and eager for the future.

Rankin was careful to let Watts know that he had all the right contacts and that he had already arranged for all the protection the syndicate needed. "There's no risk to speak of," said Rankin. The California man also talked a great deal about money, and Watts was attentive. Ruth heard some of this talk, and she didn't like it. One afternoon she joined the two men in Watt's office, and listened to Rankin spin his tales about the vast sums they would rake in. Watts had told Ruth that Rankin was a good man, a great humanitarian in fact, who believed that every woman had the right to an abortion. But Ruth formed her own opinion that day. She left the two men still talking, and went back to her office fearful for Watts. She saw her mentor under the influence of a man she considered "glib and smoothly aggressive." Ruth listened that afternoon for Rankin's sentiments about the plight of women, and she came away convinced that Watts read the man wrong. "He may have been a humanitarian," she concluded, "but all he talked about was money."

Rankin did not strike Watts this way. The doctor saw promise in the man's eyes, and admired his acumen and drive. Watts knew he couldn't work forever, and now was a good time, he thought, to bring in his last big bundle of cash before he called it a day.

In July 1934, Watts and Rankin made a verbal agreement to form a partnership, and later in the fall the two men drew up a contract representing their agreement. The contract provided that Rankin would receive fifty percent of the net profits from the business, in consideration for acting as Watts's "business, financial, accounting and tax agent in both his professional and private business."

Before Watts could leave Portland, though, and begin work on Rankin's project, the entrepreneur insisted that Watts find a replacement for himself in the Broadway Building. One didn't walk away from an established business, Rankin insisted, without taking one's profit. Watts's solution was to turn everything over to Ruth, outright and clear. He felt grateful for her assistance and her companionship, and he admired her skill. But Rankin was adamantly opposed. It wasn't that he didn't admire the woman, too. In fact, Ruth remembered later that Rankin flattered her repeatedly in 1934, as he was in the process of taking Watts away. Once Rankin was sitting up on the table in Watts's surgery, and he caught Ruth's arm as she crossed the room. He pulled her close and purred, "Dr. Watts tells me you've got the finest touch of anyone he knows. We want you in our organization, too, as soon as we begin to expand. We'll open a clinic for you that will make this one look like a broom closet." Ruth liked the compliment at the time, and she always remembered it. Despite herself, she responded to Rankin's touch and his big, bold images. But this time she looked away, and only said enough to let him know that she would stay where she was.

Rankin didn't want Ruth to handle Watts's office, because she wasn't a doctor. In his scheme, each of the offices he was aiming to set up had to be headed by a physician. His come-on to Ruth notwithstanding, this point was crucial and, for now, nonnegotiable. A doctor in the office, a doctor's name on the door, made everything safer, more legitimate looking. With a real doctor in charge of every office, there would be no problems, Rankin thought, in arranging for protection from both the medical standards people and the cops.

Dr. Watts was inclined to do things Rankin's way. And he felt satisfied that Ruth's practice was well set up for the present, now that she had Van Alstyne's clinic. He was convinced that Ruth would never hurt for clients; he knew that many of his former patients would seek her out the next time they wanted an abortion. They'd feel more comfortable with her than they would going to a new man in the building, even if he were a friend of Dr. Watts's.

By mid-summer of 1934, the old abortionist began to arrange his affairs in preparation for moving down to L.A. The first thing he did was write to two old friends, Dr. Harry Houston in Bandon, Oregon, and Dr. Jacob Hosch over in Bend. He explained that henceforth he would be involved in "certain practices" that would necessitate his presence in California "at least a large part of the time." He said that just for now, Ruth Barnett was taking care of his office, but that he was turning to his friends for a long-term solution.

Then Watts laid out his proposition. He wrote, "I am now desirous of getting someone to take hold of the Portland office on a permanent basis, and one which I believe should have a California license so that the offices can be operated on an interchangeable basis which would allow the respective parties a change and the possibility of vacation. It would be necessary for whomever took the office to come here for awhile and become familiar with a very special technique which has been developed. Owing to relations with you in the past and the fact that you are familiar with my activities, together with the further fact that you have a California license, it has occurred to me that you might be interested. I might add," wrote Watts in closing, "that the office will be operated under my name."

Watts didn't mention abortion, but the nature of his offer was unmistakable. Dr. Houston found the proposition interesting, and he communicated with Watts about various details over the summer and into the fall. By the end of October, the doctor declared himself ready to come to Portland.

For a short while in early November, by which time Rankin, back down in Los Angeles, was becoming most impatient to have Watts with him full-time, the plan seemed to be unravelling. Houston was having trouble, in the depths of the Depression, selling his pharmacy in Grant's Pass, and couldn't make a final commitment to Watts and Rankin before that was accomplished. In the meantime, however, he had been willing to come to Portland and place himself at Watts's elbow to learn the doctor's "very special technique." Watts had put Houston to work at once doing abortions, while he stood by to assess the man's competence. Houston watched the master at work for several days until he was ready, as Watts wrote Rankin, to be put in charge of an office at any time. In the meanwhile, however, Ed Stewart, who had for years run the biggest office of all the abortionists in the Broadway Building, was edgy about a new man moving in. Stewart let Watts and Rankin know that nothing could be finalized without his okay.

By November 15th, Stewart had extracted certain guarantees from Rankin, and Houston had closed a deal on his drugstore. Everything was ready to go, and before Thanksgiving of 1934, Watts and his wife Alice had packed up and moved over a thousand miles down the coast to Los Angeles. Ruth kissed her one-time savior goodbye with uneasiness in her heart. "I was sorry to see him go," she said. "He was a dedicated doctor as well as a good friend to me and I did not like his new associate. I could see trouble ahead for that sweet old man."

Ruth Barnett knew that Reg Rankin talked a big game. But she could not see, or even imagine at this point, the full scope of the abortion empire that he and Watts began to build in the fall of 1934. Ruth could not visualize the big picture in part because she was a small-time operator, the glamour and the worldly patina, the steady stream of customers and the steady flow of cash notwithstanding. She had learned her craft from solo practitioners, and she emulated their style of practice. Like Dr. Griffs and Dr. Equi and Dr. Watts, Ruth worked in a proper downtown office. She was known to her medical and her lay colleagues and looked to them, increasingly, as a source of business.

As a matter of course, she had highly personal relations with her clients. She saw Mrs. Robinson in the office one day and then at a nightclub or at the grocery store or in Zell Brothers Jewelry Store on Morrison the next. She did an abortion in 1933 for Marilyn Woods, for example, after that woman had twin boys one year and a tiny premature boy the next. And then she operated on Marilyn again three years later when Mac Woods lost his job as a carpenter. Mrs. Robinson and Mrs. Woods and the others knew where to find Ruth. They felt comfortable going to her office when they needed help. They had friends and relations who had sought out her services, as well. Ruth was familiar with her patients and she liked it that way. She thought that quality was near to the heart of being a good practitioner, and it made the work enjoyable, too. At the end of her life, Ruth remembered these days before the arrests and the danger, and she named the best part about being an abortionist: "I loved it when they put their arms around me, kissing me and thanking me."

The tradition and the sentiments that shaped Ruth Barnett's abortion practice couldn't have been more at odds with what Rankin had in mind, and with what, in fact, he was able to accomplish in the next few years. A law enforcement officer, looking for the words to describe Rankin's enterprise in 1936, used an apt figure; he called it "a chainstore business," a tag that captured a great many of the entrepreneurial intentions of its founder. It also captured the shift away from local owners and community ties that all sorts of businesses, legitimate and otherwise, were undergoing in that era. Indeed, by 1936, Rankin and Watts were running abortion offices in three states—Washington, Oregon, and California—and nine cities—Seattle, Portland, San Francisco, Oakland, San Jose, Los Angeles, Hollywood, Long Beach, and San Diego. The same law enforcement officer described Rankin himself as "the dominating and guiding arch-criminal" behind these offices. He might most aptly have called Rankin the arch-capitalist.

The fact was, the erstwhile "evaluation engineer" had spent years roaming the streets of L.A. in keen observation of modern business practices. Now he aimed to apply these up-to-date strategies in an effort to capitalize on the ever-growing demand for abortions.

In retrospect, Reg Rankin's enterprise of the 1930s was a parody of corporate expansionism as practiced in his day. Like the kingpins of bootleg liquor and narcotics operations, Rankin based his moves on what he thought of as the logic of capitalism, and for a while the logic yielded results. His idea was to concentrate the abortion business on the West Coast so that it took on the form and functions of an abortion corporation, with himself at the helm. Rankin's business plan was comprehensive. He intended to corner the market by creating a web of "companies," a string of offices that together would form a vast regional network. He aimed for monopoly.

Rankin figured that even if he couldn't get control of all the abortionists from San Diego to Seattle, he *would* have a say in who stayed in the business and who didn't. The message he began to send around was bold and threatening, and he meant it to be. If you play ball with Rankin, okay. If not, you're the competition, and Reg Rankin doesn't like competition.

Rankin had another group of principles, a set borrowed from Henry Ford: standardize, homogenize, rationalize. The way it

worked in his business was that all the abortion offices had to be as
nearly identical as possible. Rankin wanted the same layout, the
same furniture, the same surgical tools laid out in the same pattern
in all the surgeries. All the abortionists were to be doctors, all were
to be trained by Watts, and no matter which office any one of them
was assigned to, he would be able to find his way around and take
up the work in a minute. Every office followed the same procedures, medical and clerical. The receptionists were trained according to Rankin's method. Every aspect was to be uniform and interchangeable, including the doctors themselves.

The office Rankin controlled in San Diego, for example, was run
in the same way as all the others. Rankin himself trained the office
nurse. She was to greet women when they arrived, find out how far
along the pregnancy was, and set the price for the operation. The
fees were the same as Ruth Barnett's: for two months or under, the
standard price was thirty-five dollars, for two-and-a-half months,
forty dollars, and for three months, fifty dollars. As it worked in practice, the fee scale was merely for guidance. Nurses understood that
Rankin wanted them to get as much as they could for each case. They
also understood that their boss was very strict about the bot-
tom line: a minimum of twenty-five dollars for each procedure had
to be retained by the office. If a woman had been referred by a druggist or a doctor, he was due anywhere from thirty to fifty percent of
the amount the patient paid, a cost that had to be figured in.

The nurse was to collect the money and then have the woman
sign a consent form that read like this: "I hereby declare that I am
at this time freely and voluntarily applying to Dr.——for treatment.
I believe my condition demands immediate medical and surgical
attention and therefore give consent to such treatment as the doctor may determine in the premises; that I have read the above state-
ments and am fully aware of the contents thereof, and state that I
believe the same contains a true statement of my physical condition." Rankin was emphatic that under no circumstances should the
name of the doctor be filled in. One of his employees explained the
strategy: "In case there was any complaint, they would put some
other doctor's name in so that the patient couldn't testify."

It was also the nurse's job to take down the woman's name and
address on a white printed slip and fill in data about whoever
referred her to the office. Next, the nurse prepared the patient on

the operating table, and at the last minute, called in the doctor to perform the operation. Rankin counseled his doctors to proceed cautiously at this point. One doctor said, "Rankin told me never to take a case that had some semblance of infection. He told me never to operate on any woman who had been tampering with herself. He didn't want to have any trouble. He wanted all the cases to run smoothly. The point was, I should make sure nothing was wrong with the woman before I got started." Another of Rankin's doctors expressed the same principle more bluntly: "If a girl is in the least bit sour, just send her home."

If everything was in order, the doctor opened the woman's vagina with a speculum, administered a local anesthetic, and then dilated the cervix. Using a curette, the doctor scraped the woman's womb. The final step was Albert Watts's innovation. He trained all his men—as he had trained Ruth Barnett—to complete the abortion by using water suction to draw all the "residue" from the uterus. Each office was equipped with a hose running from a faucet in the surgery to the operating table. A metal catheter was attached to the hose and placed inside the uterus. Then water was run through the hose to create a vacuum, and all the remaining products of conception were suctioned out.

Once the abortion was completed, the office nurse in San Diego, just like all the other nurses, had additional duties. She was to keep all the money collected from patients in the office safe until the end of the day. When the office closed, she was to take the cash to the bank and deposit it in an account held in Rankin's name. She was also instructed to send duplicate deposit slips to Rankin's associate in Los Angeles, a banker named Joseph O. Shinn, along with the sheaf of personal data slips on all the women who had come in that day. Generally, the nurse and the doctor assigned to the San Diego office had little direct contact with Rankin. Paychecks came in the mail every week, always signed "R. Rankin by J.O. Shinn." In the normal course of things, Rankin came down from L.A. to inspect the office once or twice a month at most.

Up in Los Angeles, Shinn and Rankin made all the financial and strategic decisions for the business: typical business decisions about whom to hire, where to open the next office, how much to pay staff, how much to pay for protection. They worked well together, and in the summer of 1935, after Rankin realized that opportunity was once again knocking, the two men decided to branch out by establishing a credit arm of the business. Rankin told one of his doctors that summer, "At first I thought it would be fine to have a little office, a hole in the wall, down the hall or something from each of the abortion offices, where people could go to pawn their jewelry—watches, rings, like that—if they were short on cash. But now, I figure, we've gotten big. We can do better." Rankin's idea of doing better was a little scam operation he called the Medical Acceptance Corporation. He told a doctor in Seattle how it worked: "When a girl comes to the office and she doesn't have the cash, why, the first thing is to find out if she's working steady and what her salary is. Then if the operation she needs calls for fifty dollars, well, make it sixty and send her over to the M.A.C. office."

Hundreds of transactions later, the L.A. county prosecutor explained the workings of Rankin's Medical Acceptance Corporation more fully in open court. He said, "Let's take a case. A woman would come to one of the offices, we will say the Hollywood office in the Guaranty Building, seeking an abortion. She didn't have the cash. She would be sent by the office nurse to the Signal Oil Building where the Medical Acceptance Corporation maintained an office on the same floor and immediately adjoining the offices where the abortions were performed in that building. There this woman would be interviewed by some employee, usually Mr. Creeth, the manager. The nurse would give the woman who went there a card having upon it some symbol indicating the price agreed for the abortion. If the price was fifty dollars, Creeth, by the time he got through with the woman, would have a note from her for around seventy-five dollars. Creeth would lead the woman to believe that he was merely financing the bill; that he was sending the money to the doctor to take care of the bill and that the amount over and above the fifty dollars to be paid to the doctor represented the profit to the Medical Acceptance Corporation. But this was not true. The Medical Acceptance Corporation was merely an agency of this entire proceeding. No money changed hands by these transactions. Collateral would be taken by Creeth and then Creeth would telephone the office nurse, telling her everything was okay, to go ahead, and the woman would go ahead and have her abortion."

Rankin would not have argued with the prosecutor's characterization. He defined himself as a businessman, and he was clear-minded about the fact that profit was the name of the game. He never doubted that he shared the fundamental belief of other business-men that a good profit margin depended on the client's naiveté, and in this case, on the client's desperation as well.

Rankin also banked on the weak position of his staff. Most of his doctors and their female assistants were people squeezed particu-larly hard by the Depression. That was the reason most of the men and women around Rankin found themselves in the business of criminal abortion to begin with. And once they had begun scraping wombs in secret, they were in a position, of course, to be squeezed by the law. Rankin presented himself as the answer to their prob-lems: by allying with him, they could earn a good living. In the meantime, Rankin would take on the job of neutralizing the law. That was, in essence, all Rankin promised. He didn't review his business philosophy with the doctors and staff whom he set up in San Jose and Long Beach and the other offices. He just put them to work.

It is unknown whether Rankin was familiar with the notions of Frederick Taylor, the man who introduced "scientific management" to the business community in that era. But in retrospect, Rankin's methods of running his abortion clinics at least suggest that he planned his venture along the lines followed by the chainstore mag-nates and manufacturing tycoons whose workplaces were reshaped by Taylor's ideas in the 1920s. Taylor preached a few basic tenets; he expressed his cardinal principle this way: "The law is almost uni-versal—not entirely so, but nearly so—that the man who is fit to work at any particular trade is unable to understand the science of that trade without the kindly help and cooperation of men of a totally different type of education, men whose education is not necessarily higher but of a different type from his own." Taylor argued, most famously, that a man fit to make his living handling pig iron was by definition not fit to understand how best to handle pig iron. Rankin applied the essence of this axiom. From his point of view, he had the moxie to achieve something big, and the con-tacts to boot. He couldn't do an abortion himself. But neither could his abortionists on their own parlay their skills into an empire. Rankin aimed to supply what Taylor called "kindly help and cooperation." In Rankin's case, this meant "deskilling" the doctors. He collected their experience as diagnosticians and practitioners, their experience as small businessmen running medical offices, and replaced all that with standardized practices and interchangeable physicians. He transformed professionals into workers, and told the workers they would all profit from the transformation.

Rankin's twenty years as a "tax factor" left him with an appreciation of the need to prepare the ground for profit. He understood that this meant cultivating proper allies and arranging for protection. In the fall of 1934, while he was waiting for Watts to come down from Portland, Rankin began to look about for a well-placed collaborator, and he also began to boast. An L.A. pharmacist who ran into Rankin at the time described him as "a very bold and very busy man who knew what he was about." He remembered that Rankin came to see him and "he had no hesitation in bandying about the names of state and county officials. He had no hesitation in saying he dominated the narcotics division of the district attorney's office and the State Board of Medical Examiners and some other offices, too." A doctor whom Rankin called on during the same period recalled him boasting that it had cost him sixty thousand dollars in San Francisco and thirty thousand in L.A. to "fix things."

Rankin carried himself with *savoir faire* and, according to many of his contacts, he had charm. He projected know-how and success, and it wasn't long before his search for a strategically located partner was rewarded. The man he found was William Byrne, an employee of the California Board of Medical Examiners. Byrne had been a special investigator for the board for seven years when he ran into Rankin. By this time he was bored with earning his meager living by stalking misbehaving chiropractors, malfeasant osteopaths, careless abortionists, and other assorted practitioners accused of violating the state medical practice act. He was ready to step up his income, and when Rankin came to see him, Byrne let the entrepreneur know that he was for sale.

Beginning in the fall of 1934, Byrne began to perform services for Rankin. He first made himself useful by arranging to have murder charges dropped against an abortionist whom Rankin had picked to head one of his offices in southern California.

About the same time that Rankin began wooing Dr. Watts in Portland in July of 1934, he also started to pay a series of calls on one Paul De Gaston in his bungalow on Harold Way in Hollywood.

Rankin considered De Gaston an exotic specimen, but well qualified to join his enterprise. Indeed, De Gaston was an unusual type. He'd been raised in China, where he was born in 1892, by a Swiss mother and a French father who was a missionary doctor. In China Paul received what he called "private tuition," though his mother often took him on trips to England and Germany to further his education. After a prolonged trip to Leipzig in 1908, where Paul studied chemistry, his father determined that the young man was ready to begin his studies in medicine. To that end, he was sent to Paris in 1911. The ordinary course of study to obtain a medical degree from the Sorbonne in those days was nine years. But Paul De Gaston was bright and his courses abroad had prepared him to finish the program in only five. When he graduated in the spring of 1916, De Gaston later told Rankin, "I got ambitious at the first recruiting station I saw in April 1916, so I volunteered in the French army. I was in such a hurry that I left Paris without my diploma." Soon after the war was over, he came to the United States and over the next fifteen years pursued the main chance in a style that Rankin could recognize.

De Gaston lived in those years in Portland, Maine, and in San Francisco, Los Angeles, and points in between. He served briefly in the U.S. Army, tried briefly to become an executive in the steel business, attempted numerous sales ventures, and then arrived in Hollywood in 1925 with plans to become a movie star. His worldly flavor was initially interesting to several directors willing to cast him in bit parts to see what he could do. But apparently De Gaston could not do much in this line, and soon enough directors and would-be actor alike knew that he did not have a future in the entertainment business. Still, he stayed around on the fringes, occasionally getting jobs in musical stage plays or travelling with small acting troupes. During the fourteen years between 1916 and 1930, Paul De Gaston never practiced medicine. In fact, he never touched a surgical tool of any kind in all those years. Nevertheless, in order to support himself, he began in the early thirties to perform occasional abortions.

In June 1934, Rankin heard De Gaston's name from one of his many knowledgeable friends and went to see him, hoping the man would contribute in one way or another to the fledgling organization. As the doctor remembered it, Rankin told him that he knew

De Gaston was an abortionist. He said, "We are doing the same work. I have a proposition for you. Maybe you would like to take a little vacation from your business, and we will do your work. Then we will give you half of whatever comes in while you are away." De Gaston was not interested in this offer, but when Rankin came back the next month and offered him his own abortion office in Hollywood, with half the proceeds, De Gaston accepted. Rankin continued to visit periodically during the summer, until the deal for De Gaston to open up the Hollywood location was completed on August 8th.

Two days later, on August 10, 1934, Marion Eilert, a hairdresser, died at De Gaston's house after having an abortion. De Gaston was promptly arrested on three charges: murder, abortion, and practicing medicine without a license. Over the next eight months, De Gaston's crimes were aired in several courtrooms, but the man was never convicted of any crime, despite the fact that Louise Eldridge, the young woman who had brought Marion to the abortionist, testified to an excruciating set of details regarding the event.

De Gaston was exonerated despite the additional fact that William Byrne, in his capacity as investigator for the State Board of Medical Examiners, made a report on the death of Marion Eilert to the city attorney of Los Angeles. The report included the information that on the day of the woman's death, De Gaston called Louise Eldridge at her office after the abortion to allay her worries about Marion. He told her, reported Byrne, that the girl was all right and in good condition. He said she had been unwell the night before, after the abortion, but that she was back to normal now. Then De Gaston said something threatening to Louise that she didn't understand. After assuring her that everything was okay, he now seemed to be implying that the situation was far more complicated. He said, "She is all right, but if they hang me I will shoot you first."

While Byrne was preparing and presenting his report on Eilert's death, he was simultaneously getting rid of the evidence. As he explained later, Rankin told him that the best way to handle the situation was to make sure none of the state's witnesses (except Eldridge) wanted to appear in court. Rankin told Byrne, "Naturally, then they will have to dismiss the whole thing." Implementing Rankin's directive, Byrne set out to put the heat on the doctors and druggists who had sent cases to De Gaston, ensuring that no other state witness besides Eldridge appeared at the trial, and thus ensuring acquittal.

After De Gaston was, indeed, acquitted of the murder and abortion charges, he faced a second trial for practicing medicine without a license, a charge he wanted to fight. But Rankin advised him, with a surprising show of delicacy, that it would be "in poor taste" to fight the medical charge, and not to worry, he and Byrne could fix it up for a couple of hundred dollars. This time, he said, they would see that the case was postponed when it came up for trial, they would then get it postponed again the next time, and finally the case would be dismissed. Once again, Byrne took care of the details, and by mid-winter 1935, De Gaston was free to join Rankin's stable. The doctor lost no time making himself useful. Between February 20, 1935, and the end of that month, after Dr. Watts had observed and approved his technique, the man who had just lately caused Marion Eilert's death performed forty abortions in the Signal Oil Building at 811 West Seventh Street in downtown Los Angeles.

De Gaston's legal troubles had not bothered Rankin. Despite Marion Eilert's death, Rankin remained eager to employ De Gaston and, in fact, now saw the doctor's difficulties as an opportunity to create a special tie between himself and the abortionist. He figured that now he could buy De Gaston's services very cheaply, in exchange for the "legal assistance" he and Byrne had provided.

The fact was, Byrne's handling of De Gaston's case had been both savvy and timely from Rankin's point of view. Without Byrne's intervention, the foreign doctor may well have gone to jail. Yet in these years, it was standard practice for a physician-abortionist, even one with a death on his hands and no license, or with other problems equally troubling, to be given what may charitably be called the benefit of the doubt.

It was not only in Rankin's orbit that such things could be arranged, or only in California where opportunities were golden. All over the country in the illegal era, doctors could arrange for the intervention they required when abortion was involved. In Brooklyn, for example, one year after De Gaston was acquitted of all charges associated with Marion Eilert's death, another doctor who caused the death of a woman was charged with filing a false death certificate and forging hospital records in an effort to cover up his part in the fatality. The death certificate stated that the woman had died of "fibronyoma uterus contributory to vasomotor collapse."

The case against this doctor couldn't have been stronger. In the days before he was indicted, the doctor admitted to investigators that he had performed the abortion and had made out a false death certificate. At his trial, three gynecologists, including Dr. Charles Gordon, who at the time was Chairman of the Kings County Medical Association, and the Chairman of the County Committee on Maternal Welfare and the Director of Obstetrics and Gynecology at Kings County Hospital, all testified that the cause of the woman's death was a botched abortion. Nevertheless, this doctor too was acquitted at trial and resumed his abortion practice at once.

In addition to fixing the legal process, there was a second sort of service William Byrne was able to provide his partner as the abortion venture was getting off the ground. In 1934, he began to pay visits on small-time practitioners up and down the Pacific coast, to let them know that their practices were now a subject of interest to Mr. Rankin. When Byrne visited the offices of abortionists like Dr. Simon Parker who'd had a medical practice in Long Beach for twenty-three years, he reminded the doctor that he was an investigator for the California Board of Medical Examiners. He explained to Parker and all the doctors he called on that Reg Rankin and his associates had taken over the abortion business on the coast. He made it very clear that any doctor who intended to perform abortions in the region henceforth had best become one of Rankin's boys or be prepared to be put out of business.

Doctors like Simon Parker and John Folsom in Oakland were impressed with special agent Byrne's sincerity, and they agreed to become Rankin's employees. In fact, these abortion doctors were just a few of the many practitioners around the country in the Depression years who were subjected to these kinds of pressures.

In the illegal era, state anti-abortion statutes provided lucrative opportunities not only for a West Coast thug like Reg Rankin. On the contrary, opportunities flourished everywhere because abortion was illegal and in demand in all parts of the country. In New York

City, for example, an East Side dentist, Dr. Abraham Ditchik, performed a similar service in 1934 for State Assistant Attorney General Sol Ullman. Ullman was the Attorney General's designate to the New York State Committee on Medical Grievances, a group of ten doctors who heard and decided all charges of malpractice against physicians. Ullman sent Ditchik out to visit, threaten, and extort substantial sums of money from practicing abortionists around the state. A review of Ditchik's activities in the thirties included details of his meetings with many abortion doctors. One such doctor was Henry L. Blank, who met with the dentist in September 1934. Ditchik told Blank that a complaint had been lodged against him with the Medical Grievance Board and that he would take care of it for ten thousand dollars. Ditchik hinted strongly that he was on familiar terms with Sol Ullman. He also said that if Blank did not pay, he would lose his license. The abortionist was inclined to believe Ullman's emissary, so he agreed to pay sixty-five hundred dollars, two thousand down and the balance in monthly installments. Ditchik assured Blank that the money was going directly to Ullman and that sixty-five hundred dollars bought two years' protection. Any complaints brought against Blank for the next twenty-four months, he said, would be disposed of. In addition, the dentist agreed to advise the abortionist of the way the Medical Grievance Board worked and to warn him of impending visits by investigators. Over the next two years, Blank was visited by representatives of the Board several times, but no complaints were filed against him.

A report prepared in 1939 that detailed Ditchik's activities included testimony from eight doctors who claimed to have paid the dentist $35,150 since 1933. The doctors gave Ditchik money after being told that payment was necessary if they didn't want to be prosecuted by the Medical Grievance Committee for performing abortions. The report concluded that none of the doctors who paid was ever punished even though complaints had been filed against at least three of the eight. Two doctors who refused to pay up, however, were brought before the board and had their licenses suspended.

With the same climate prevailing on the West Coast, Rankin was emboldened to speak freely to the doctors he recruited, and to make both large demands and large promises. He told a doctor in

Los Angeles, for example, that since his chain of offices was operating with the knowledge of the Medical Board there was absolutely no danger of prosecution, and the doctor should feel completely safe in referring clients to them. To underscore his claims, Rankin sent Byrne to the doctor's office so he could hear it from the horse's mouth.

In Seattle, Norman Powers, a physician and surgeon for thirty years, received Rankin at his office in the summer of 1935. He remembered that Rankin was charming at first. "Mr. Rankin told me that he was from California and that he wished to see me about entering into an association of doctors that he represented in California. The doctors had offices in different cities. He said I had been recommended to him, and now he wanted to find out if I would care to join the association. He told me he would take me down to California and introduce me to the various men in the association, and after I had seen the men and the various offices, then if I cared to make up my mind to join them, he would be glad to have me, and if I didn't care to join, why I could consider the trip as a vacation, and he would take me down, pay my expenses and bring me back the same way. He said that if I did join, I would be paid a thousand dollars a month."

Powers was, indeed, interested in the proposition, and he pressed Rankin for more information. Like the other doctors, he wanted the money, but the risk was a big concern. As always, Rankin insisted there was no risk. He promised "ample protection" and told Powers he need only speak to the other doctors down in California to find out how safe they felt. "He said he would introduce me to all the men so that I could satisfy myself that there was protection for the doctors."

Rankin poured on the charm with Powers because he needed him right away in California, but other doctors in Seattle were not treated with such solicitude. On the same trip up north, Rankin saw a number of other practitioners. He chose one to be his man in Seattle, and put the heat on the rest to get out of the business or go elsewhere. The man he chose to run his operation was Eric R. Wilson, a doctor who had shared an office with Powers for some time.

Rankin's first order of business after muscling his way into control of the abortion scene in Seattle was to bring in De Gaston to train Powers and Wilson in what he called the "Watts method." De Gaston arrived in town in late June, still deeply beholden to Rankin and Byrne for having engineered his freedom. He was aware that paying back his debt entailed doing what they told him to do. It was less clear to him how long his bondage would last.

The first thing Rankin demanded when De Gaston arrived in Seattle was that he change his name. On the morning of June 26th, the two men met in the lobby of the Earl Hotel and Rankin told De Gaston to sit tight, right there in the lobby, and keep his mouth shut while Rankin went down to the King County Medical Society and checked up on what name was available for De Gaston to use in that city. De Gaston did as he was told, and later that day Rankin informed him that from now on his name was Dr. F.T. Read. As De Gaston remembered it later, Rankin said, "You are supposed to be from Glendale, California, and in case anybody asks you, you are a graduate from Bennett University in Chicago, a school that's out of business." Rankin added, "You don't look much like that fellow Read, but no one's going to know that around here."

As Dr. F.T. Read, De Gaston spent the summer training Powers and Wilson and making trips to Portland to train Ed Stewart, as well. By August 1935, Wilson and De Gaston were set up in a suite of offices on the sixth floor of the Security Building in downtown Seattle as Rankin's employees. Business was brisk, but none of the players was satisfied. Early on, Rankin sensed trouble from Wilson. He suspected him of fudging the numbers and holding back receipts. He also suspected that Wilson was undermining his control over De Gaston.

In September, Rankin and Byrne decided to take a trip up to Seattle to scope out the situation. Rankin wanted to find out if Wilson was a cheat, and Byrne had begun to think that maybe it was time to ease himself out of the medical investigator's office in L.A. Maybe there were some opportunities up in Washington. Specifically, it seemed a good time to take over the M.A.C. office in Seattle, and he made the trip an opportunity to talk to the Washington State Director of Licenses about going in with him. Byrne told De Gaston that fall that it was not "good policy" to openly pay off the Director of Licenses in cash, but that "if he could be induced to join the M.A.C., he could get his payoff that way and leave everybody alone."

Dr. Wilson, it turned out, was indeed not the sort of man Rankin considered a good soldier. With Powers out of the picture, Wilson's abortion business was flourishing, and he was beginning to wonder why he should serve as Rankin's man in Seattle when all the signs indicated he could do just fine on his own. During the September visit, Wilson complained about the paperwork, about Rankin's management style, and particularly about the fact that the Seattle M.A.C. was not forwarding cash to him properly. In general, he made it clear that, from his point of view, the arrangement was not working.

For the time being, Rankin took steps to placate Wilson, including allowing him to buy in as Rankin's partner for about nine thousand dollars. But even as a partner, Wilson continued to complain, writing to Rankin almost daily in Los Angeles. In November, Rankin suddenly agreed to sell Wilson the Seattle operation outright. On November 20th, Rankin and Wilson signed this bill of sale, representing Rankin's departure from the city: "For value received, the undersigned [Rankin] hereby grants, bargains, and sells to E.R. Wilson, all of his right, title, and interest in and to the business and professional practice conducted at 306 and 309 Securities Building, 1904 Third Avenue, Seattle, Washington, together with all of the furniture, equipment, instruments, and other things of value in said office. Also all equipment in the office formerly occupied by W. Norman Powers, excepting one Autoclave and two hot water boilers, situated in said premises." The transaction was officially witnessed by Paul De Gaston, whose name was not mentioned in the text of the bill of sale but whose services figured in the bargain. As De Gaston put it later, "I was sold with the office to Dr. Wilson."

Rankin was willing to sell out to Wilson late in 1935 because he was sick of the doctor's bellyaching and of the daily letters that made him "so damn sore" he wanted the man out of his life. Rankin was all-around testy that winter. He told an associate, "I can't take the aggravation anymore, and I am going to get out and sell all the offices to the various doctors as soon as I can." But the money was still good, and Rankin did not walk away from its source easily.

In fact, as soon as he sold the Seattle office to Wilson, he began to regret it. The very night he signed the bill of sale, Rankin summoned De Gaston to the Olympia Hotel in downtown Seattle and warned him that the deal was not quite as sewn up as it had looked earlier in the day. Sitting in the hotel lobby with De Gaston, he leaned close to the man he had just sold away to Wilson, so their foreheads almost touched. He said, "Now Mr. Wilson has bought the business and don't be surprised what will happen. I am going to pull you out of there, and I am going to get that office back with gravy on it." De Gaston was appropriately unsettled. He tried to find out just what Rankin meant and how he was going to accomplish it. He pressed Rankin and was rebuffed. "He told me not to ask any questions but not to be surprised as to what would happen."

Over the next couple of weeks, Rankin continued to toy with De Gaston. By now the entrepreneur wasn't so sure that he wanted to get out of the abortion business, and he felt the need to remind De Gaston and Wilson that, despite the sale, he was still a player. He wrote De Gaston letters frequently and fully expected him to show the contents to Wilson. Rankin used threatening, mobster-type language in the letters, calculated to keep his former employees on edge. In late December, Rankin warned Wilson through De Gaston that the doctor's show of independence was a bit much, and that he was "laying himself wide open for a good wallop." Rankin let De Gaston know that Wilson's efforts to go out on his own in Seattle and down in L.A. were dangerous and unacceptable. He wrote, "I know about what Wilson has in mind, and if I were you, I would egg him on to give me all the grief possible as it gives me all the more excuse to take a good crack at him." Feigning solicitude, Rankin warned De Gaston that he himself was not safe. While checking up on the Long Beach office, he penned a brief note to the unlicensed doctor in Seattle. "There is one thing, you must be very careful of yourself," he wrote. "You must keep completely out of the picture. I have a man watching every move you make." And he concluded, "It looks like there is going to be some real fun."

Six weeks after the sale, Rankin was still stewing about Wilson, about the profits going into Wilson's pockets, and about losing the fealty of the man whose neck he had saved a year earlier. In mid-January 1936, Rankin made another trip to Seattle, this time to finish off the Wilson business with a masterful stroke. Again he summoned De Gaston to the Olympia Hotel. Later De Gaston remembered, "He told me to hurry over. It was very important. I did not want to go, but Wilson said I must. I went up to his room and he was sitting on the bed with a girl next to him. The first thing he said when I walked in was, 'I am going to have you arrested.' He said he had been weeping tears ever since he sold the practice because he heard we were doing a land-office business. His hand was on the girl's thigh while he said this to me, and he was pinching her thigh with every word. He said that he hadn't received all the cash that was due him from that office, but I said he didn't have another dime coming to him. He kept on pinching the girl's thigh and then he said he had only one more thing to say to me and that was that he would have me arrested and he would have Dr. Wilson arrested, too. I asked him what for, but he didn't say. He just motioned for me to go."

Rankin was a man who liked to use a threat, and his threats were rarely idle. Indeed, De Gaston and Dr. Wilson were arrested the next day. The charge was conspiracy to perform an illegal operation. A week later, Rankin pulled Dr. Powers out of the Long Beach office where he'd been placed on August 1st, and sent him back to Seattle to resume his practice there. Rankin was in his element: pulling strings, shuffling doctors, playing with the law. By seeing to it that Wilson was removed from the playing field, Rankin was able to pocket everything Wilson had paid to buy him out. Plus, Rankin now had an office in Seattle again, staffed by a doctor who was in his employ.

All the while that Rankin was engineering maneuvers in Seattle, he was carrying on similar activities in San Diego, L.A., and the other cities where he had abortion offices. For example, Jesse Ross, an L.A. abortionist, sold his practice to Dr. Watts and Reg Rankin in September 1934 and became Rankin's employee. A month later, Rankin placed another physician-abortionist, Dr. James Beggs, in that office and kept him there until March 1935, when he moved Beggs over to the Oakland office that Rankin had just bought from Dr. John Folsom. When Beggs was shifted out of the L.A. office, Rankin brought in Dr. Houston, who had been running the San Diego clinic since Rankin had brought him down from Portland. This was how Rankin liked to run the business. He moved the practitioners around at unpredictable intervals, so the doctors understood that their salaries and their fates were tied to Rankin and to the syndicate, not to the community where they worked or to their clients or the clinic staff.

Rankin also thought it was a good idea for his doctors to maintain a low profile. No single doctor was associated for long with any
of Rankin's nine locations, and none of the nine offices had an
occupant-practitioner's real name painted on its glass door. It was
one of Rankin's many regulations that the sign on the office door
should read, "Dr. Watts's Medical Clinic." Unlike the patients who
particularly sought out Ruth Barnett in Portland, the women who
moved through Rankin's syndicate took whomever they got, and
the point was that they not know who that was.

Rankin was a busy man in 1934 and 1935, moving up and down
the coast between San Diego and Seattle, seeing to the staffing and
financial details of his empire. But he had tasks to attend to even
beyond these. Rankin had to make sure there was a steady flow of
women showing up at each clinic if his offices were to turn a
healthy profit. He had to make sure that word of his clinics got
around, and he did not believe in depending on the word-of-mouth
recommendations, passing from woman to woman, that many doctors relied on. Nor could he depend too heavily on the tradition of
doctor-to-doctor referrals that fueled the practices of many abortionists. After all, he moved his doctors around so often that a local
gynecologist might be leery about sending a woman to a stranger.
Instead, he mounted an extensive marketing scheme that incorporated a variety of approaches.

Most formally, Rankin pressed every abortionist whose business he
purchased to sign a contract that included a seller's vow to act as a
feeder. For example, when Watts and Rankin acquired Dr. Folsom's
office in Oakland on March 9, 1935, Folsom, as the "vendor," agreed
to the following: "The said vendor agrees that on the payment of the
residue of the said purchase money as hereinabove mentioned, he will
introduce and recommend the said purchaser to his patients, friends,
and others, as his successor, and will use the best endeavors to promote
and increase the prosperity of the said practice or business. To his end,
the vendor shall transfer all business to the purchaser and shall at all
times recommend the purchaser as capable." In addition, Dr. Folsom
was pressed into agreeing that he would desist from practicing "gynecological surgery" in eight specified cities for five years without the
written consent of Rankin. Finally, Folsom consented to "furnish the
purchaser with a list of names and addresses of all contacts or parties
which constituted a source of supply of prospective patients."

Rankin collected these promises from the abortionists he bought out and then put his people into the field to call in the referrals and to drum up more. In the spring of 1935, after De Gaston had completed his stint in the Signal Oil Building but before he was shipped up to Seattle, the boss sent him out on a mission to do what Rankin called "detailing doctors." In the past, De Gaston had had experience looking for abortion clients, but his efforts when he was in business for himself were strictly penny-ante. In those days, he simply went out on Hollywood Boulevard, and as he put it, "I passed the word along until I got one." In 1935, under Rankin's direction, his efforts were more comprehensive and more professional.

Now De Gaston was to call on scores of doctors in Marin County and as far south as Carmel, Salinas, and Santa Cruz, soliciting their "gynecological work" for the San Francisco office. In addition, he was to go to all of the Rankin-controlled offices in the Los Angeles and San Francisco areas to see that every abortion patient was provided with a referral card. Rankin explained, "Sometimes these girls travel and in case they go up and down the coast and need the same service again or their friends need the service, they will know where to go." The card De Gaston handed out listed offices in the Signal Oil Building in Los Angeles, the Guarantee Building on Hollywood Boulevard, the Ocean Center Building in San Francisco, the Tapscott Building in Oakland, and the Broadway Building in Portland. De Gaston worked hard and his efforts brought in business, but Rankin's system of soliciting business did not stop there.

In late 1936, a law enforcement officer described the syndicate's system of solicitation as "well planned and well-thought-out, careful and comprehensive." At the time, the officer was thinking particularly of the work of Beatrice Bole, a sometime office nurse, sometime solicitor employed by Rankin. Bole was assigned a vast territory in southern California where she visited doctors' offices "under the guise of selling medical instruments. She would secure entrance to a physician's office in a comparatively innocent manner and then she would propose to the physician that he send pregnant women to the nearest office. She would promise the physician a split or cut or commission of from fifteen to fifty percent of the amount ultimately secured."

Sometimes Beatrice Bole did not bother with the pretence of comparative innocence. There were certain practitioners she visited again and again, and with these men she was straightforward. Generally these visits were to chiropractors, osteopaths, and a physician or two, all of whom had run afoul of the law in the recent past. Beatrice felt this group was unlikely to be offended by her overtures. One such person was a Dr. H.N. Tatum, chiropractor, who described his work, in the parlance of the day, as that of a "drugless man." Tatum first met Beatrice Bole in 1935, when she picked his name off a list William Byrne had drawn up of chiropractors he had run in for practicing medicine without a license. Byrne had run Tatum in three times—in 1931, 1933, and just recently in 1935—for violating Section 17 of the State Medical Practice Act. In total, the chiropractor had spent forty-nine days in the state penitentiary for his offenses.

At first, Bole made brief visits to Tatum's office, merely leaving packets of advertising cards with the chiropractor and urging him to make the cards available to his patients. But over time, Bole became more persistent and pressed harder. When she visited Tatum at home in December 1935, the man was under indictment once again, and Bole implied that if Tatum was forthcoming with referrals, it would mean something to William Byrne, his accuser.

When Tatum had occasion to recall his final encounter with Beatrice Bole, the details remained vivid in his mind. He said, "Well, she came to the door and I opened the door and she spoke to me and I asked her in. The first thing she said to me was, 'Is there anybody here?' And my wife spoke up and said, 'One of my daughters is working and the other one is in school.' And Mrs. Bole said, 'Well, it doesn't make any difference who hears what I have to say. I am so well protected it doesn't make any difference.' I asked her to have a seat and she sat down and began by saying, 'Well, I am still on the mission of soliciting work for the same people.' She was telling me that I should send patients to Dr. Watts and the rest of them. She wanted me to see that they guaranteed no prosecution for me. And she told me they had their thumb on the district attorney's office, the sheriff's office, and the police department, and that those fellows didn't dare make a move.

"Mrs. Bole said that the prices range from fifty dollars to three hundred dollars." Then Tatum remembered that Bole made an effort to convince him of the high-quality care those sums purchased. "She said the long-term patients were sent to a home. There were graduate nurses there to take care of them, and physicians and surgeons, too. I asked her what she meant by long-term patients, and she said anyone who came in after three and a half months they sent to this home. Before that they were taken care of in the office. She was talking about seven and a half and eight months. So I says, 'Mrs. Bole, do you mean to say that such as that is going on?' And she says, 'Yes.' And I says, 'What in the world do they do with babies seven and a half or eight months old, they are livable babies?' And she says they have a way of doing away with them, running them through the sewer."

Dr. Tatum was not a young man when Beatrice Bole came to see him, and he viewed himself as a man of experience, a man who'd partaken of life. But this was hard to believe. He looked hard at his visitor and said, "How do you get away with such work as that?" Beatrice Bole was a cool as a cucumber. "We pay off the Medical Board," she said. Dr. Tatum remembered that he was thunderstruck. Byrne had come after him for some trivial little infraction, and here these people were flushing little babies down the sewer. He said, "Do you mean to tell me, Mrs. Bole, that you pay off such men as Dr. Pinkham and Mr. Will Maloney and those men, members of the California Medical Board?" And she said, "No, we pay off Bill Byrne." "And I says," Tatum recalled, "if you do that, you certainly have a lot of protection."

Beatrice Bole wound up her sales pitch that afternoon with a word to the wise, and she made herself plain. "If you will just send a few cases to us," she said, "we will assure you that *your* case will be squashed. I will talk to Bill for you, and you will be glad you met me, I can say that."

In the mid-1930s, the findings reported in an investigation of criminal abortionists in major cities in the United States confirmed Reg Rankin's sense that all his hard work and all the aggravation he endured would yield him a good return in the Depression years, such a good return, in fact, that only the captains of industry could provide a comparison. "Yearly incomes," the report stated, "would be in the same numerical brackets with earnings of heads of large corporations." Few clues remain to the annual earnings of Watts and Rankin and their professional staff in those years, but the

scraps of information that have survived verify the report's contention. A private accounting kept by Dr. Jesse Ross, the L.A. abortionist bought out by Rankin, shows earnings of $4,885 for 1935,
$3,400 of which he was paid by his boss. The rest he earned from
"private fees." As for Watts and Rankin, they did quite a bit better.
In both January and February of 1936, each of the men made profits of approximately twelve thousand dollars, earnings surely in a
league with those of the business tycoons Rankin had set out to
emulate. By contrast, the salary range of the average worker in the
U.S. in 1934 and 1935 was five hundred to fifteen hundred dollars
per annum.

For a time, Rankin directed the syndicate with a slick sense of
purpose. His three-man team did well for him, and for themselves.
Shinn managed the money, Byrne took care of the legal angle, and
Watts, of course, provided the medical expertise. They were loyal,
they were good at what they did, and Rankin was satisfied with this
part of the business. Throughout 1934 and 1935 and much of 1936,
as he bullied nurses, threatened doctors, and cajoled landlords into
leasing him prime space, Rankin was proud to be succeeding in a
tough man's world.

It was a fact that the tough man's world that Ruth Barnett had
caught a glimpse of back in the summer of 1934, when Rankin
lured Watts away from the relative simplicity of the Broadway
Building, had little in common with the world known by her or by
most female abortionists at the time. It was a world that turned on
the exercise of power and the willing use of the instruments of
power: know-how, money, and threat.

Rankin's worldly experience had prepped him for ruthlessness
and prepared him for business. He knew how to recruit the personnel he required and how to create a web of professionals. He understood the use of branch offices and how to move his human
resources around advantageously. Man-to-man, he could make
promises; he could seduce and intimidate doctors with an ease that
would have been surprising if it weren't for the hard times that
clouded lives in the early years of the Depression.

Rankin built conduits to well-placed bureaucrats and petty law
enforcement types. He wasn't fearful or uncertain when he dealt
with the law. He was brash and bold. He knew about the power of
contracts and forced everyone he served or who served him to sign

long, dense documents stipulating reciprocal obligations regarding patently criminal activities. Finally, he was not afraid of the "almighty dollar," and was neither too loose with it nor too tight. Unlike Ruth Barnett, for whom money was the fun part, for Rankin it was the power part. He understood the process of capitalization and understood what it yielded. He knew just how and when to buy people out and how to change them into wage earners and hirelings. He understood the value of credit and of the corporate form. He knew how to run a scam.

There was no sentimentality in Rankin's repertoire. He was motivated by enthusiasm for the main chance. As one might expect, Rankin's use of criminal abortion to pursue the main chance was no gift to women.

Chapter Four

A WOMAN'S HELL

Diane McDermott had two god-awful years, 1935 and 1936, when she found herself so cruelly entangled with Reg Rankin, his doctors, and the law that she often thought she would not survive the ordeal.

Early in 1935, Mrs. McDermott became pregnant for the fourth time in six years. Two of her children were still in diapers; the eldest was five years old. As the person who handled the family budget, she knew well that her husband's salesman salary was already stretched dangerously thin. Another baby would make things hard to bear. Another baby would probably make it hard to pay the rent. Throughout the month of February, Mrs. McDermott pleaded with her husband to ask the other men at work for the name of an abortionist. "Someone must know," she insisted day after day. But Dean McDermott did not approve of his wife's intention. Each time she brought the matter up, he said, "We'll get along. We always have." If God brought them a baby, he thought, it was their duty to be its parents. Besides, he was embarrassed to ask the other men. He didn't think of himself as the sort of fellow who brought his troubles or his sex life to the job.

But over the weeks that Diane nagged him, day after day, to find someone, Dean took notice of his wife's determination. He had never known her to insist like this, and finally he agreed to do what she asked. As it turned out, it was no trouble at all to find what he was looking for. He asked some men at lunch and two or three of them dug out little dog-eared slips of paper they'd tucked under flaps in their wallets. One man had McDermott copy down the name of George Watts and said Mrs. McDermott could just go down to his office in the Signal Oil Building and he'd take care of her real quick.

Diane McDermott was so relieved when her husband came home with the name and address that she cried, and she said she would go over there to Dr. Watts's office on Saturday morning. Dean liked the whole business now no better than he had, but when the time came, he took his three little children to a neighbor's and went with Diane to see the abortionist.

Later Diane described how the first person she saw in the doctor's office was a sweet-looking woman dressed like a nurse. The woman said her name was Miss Wilson. Diane said, "I told Miss Wilson I thought I was pregnant and I wanted to see the doctor. She asked me my name and address and how long I'd been married and how many children I had. She asked me if I wanted an operation. I told her I'd missed one month and, please, I needed help." Miss Wilson nodded and asked Diane to sign a paper and told her it would be thirty-five dollars for the procedure. Dean McDermott felt awkward and angry as he stood by Diane, and when the negotiation was complete, he went out in the hall for a smoke.

"I went into Dr. Watts's office," Diane remembered. "I got on the table and he examined me and told me I was pregnant. He put a sheet over me and he performed an operation on me that he called a curettement. After that, he put a rubber pad under me. Then he connected a rubber hose to the faucet and inserted the other end of it in my vagina. He said he was putting that hose in there to get anything out that might be left in. I think he hosed me out for about five minutes and then I got down from the table and went into the next room and laid down on the cot for maybe fifteen minutes."

Diane McDermott appreciated the care she was given that day. She said, "Miss Wilson was awful nice to me. She brought me some water and put a hot pad on my abdomen. She was very kind. I was surprised that it was all so quick, and easy too. By the time we got home, I was able to make my children's lunches and do the laundry. I felt fine."

If Diane's experience in the early part of 1935 had been the beginning and end of her contact with Dr. Watts, she would have been considerably better off. Unfortunately, within the year, she was pregnant again. This time, Diane knew how to find the abortionist herself, and she had the notion that she could just drive down to Seventh Street on her own, slip in and out of Dr. Watts's office, and no one would be the wiser. She was thinking of Dean, of course, who had never come to terms with the first abortion. She knew he was still mad, but the sad truth was, he hadn't learned a lesson from it, and here she was pregnant again, and just as poor.

Diane brought her little ones over to the neighbor's on a Tuesday morning in November. She planned it for Tuesday because that was the only day of the week Dean caught a lift to the Santa Monica Montgomery Ward's, and left her the car. By 9:00 she was on her way downtown. And by ten, she was discussing her situation with Nurse Wilson. Right away the nurse tried to console her about having to come back again. She said, "Well, after awhile you will get used to it and you won't mind anymore." Miss Wilson asked for fifty dollars this time, but she settled for the thirty-five Diane had brought with her. Diane signed the same kind of form she had the last time, but now she was crying because she felt so bad about having to come back. She remembered that the nurse patted her back kindly and tried to reassure her that she would be okay. She said, "There is nothing about this that is going to hurt you, Diane."

A few minutes later, just like before, Diane was up on the surgery table and Dr. Watts was standing at the end of the table, between her raised knees. The doctor saw that Diane had been crying, and he, too, made an effort to calm her fears. Diane recalled, "He said he didn't think it would hurt me at all. I was in good physical condition, he said, and it wouldn't even keep me laid up more than a day or two at most." But this time Nurse Wilson and Dr. Watts—who worked, like all medical practitioners in that era, without the benefit of antibiotics, and like all criminal abortion providers, without the benefit of hospital conditions—were wrong.

The second abortion was much more painful for Diane. "Afterwards," she said, "I was feeling very badly and I almost fainted before I got into the room where you rest. While I was lying on the cot, Dr. Watts gave me two aspirin. They were awful nice to me again. They put a hot pad on my abdomen and made me very comfortable." The nurse was particularly solicitous. "She came in two or three times and brought me a glass of water. She asked me if I felt like going, but I didn't. I asked if I could rest a while longer." After an hour, Diane thought she would be able to stand up and put her clothes on. She remembered, "When I got dressed and left, I didn't feel very good, but I had told Dr. Watts that I could make it all right. It was my fault, really. I told him I could go. I drove home but I was in no condition to drive the car. I felt dizzy and had very severe pains in my abdomen."

Diane felt even worse when she arrived home. "The doctor had told me to stay on my feet as much as possible, it would be better for me. I tried, but I had to lie down." Diane was terribly worried about what Dean would do to her, what he would say, if he found out what she'd done. At this point, she decided to pretend she had caught the grippe. Dean would believe that, and maybe she would feel allright by tomorrow. But on Wednesday, she continued to feel worse. "I had terrible pains in my abdomen and felt quite dizzy and uncomfortable all around. I took my children back over to Jennie Miles, the neighbor lady who minds them for me, and went home to bed. I put a hot-water bottle on me and took some aspirin tablets like they told me to do in case I did have any trouble. It didn't help me very much.

"Thursday afternoon when Dean went to his job, I called up Dr. Watts's office and talked to Miss Wilson. She told me to take some ergot [a rye fungus that, taken orally, promotes contractions of the uterus] and go to bed. I did stay in bed for several days. I think maybe till the weekend. Then suddenly I got very ill and started to hemorrhage very badly, so I called up the doctor again. Miss Wilson told me to come right down there and let the doctor see me.

"I told her I didn't feel like coming down, I was too weak. But she said that was the only thing to do. It was Saturday and Dean was at Ward's. So I brought the children over to Mrs. Miles again, and I took the streetcar downtown.

"When I got there, I told Miss Wilson how badly I felt and she sympathized with me very, very much. I was about to cry, and I thought she was, too. She felt so sorry for me. She said, 'You poor thing. I am so sorry. We'll have you fixed up in a little while. We'll do everything we can for you.'"

Miss Wilson took Diane by the hand and led her into the surgery. Instead of Dr. Watts, there was another man there, dressed in a doctor's coat. Miss Wilson didn't introduce the man to Diane. She just motioned for her to get up on the table. Then she turned around and left the room. The man curetted her again. He used the hose longer than Dr. Watts had done. He hardly spoke at all, but when he turned off the water, Diane remembered that he looked pleased with his work.

"I felt terrible. I told him that, but he said I would be allright. But I could tell right away that I was hemorrhaging, more so than ever. I was bleeding all over the floor. I wanted to get home, so I didn't even lie down this time, even though I was weak and bleeding.

When I got downstairs, in front of the building, I actually fainted and fell down on the sidewalk. I don't remember how I revived, but I do know that I was very ill on the bus, and when I got home, I felt even worse, very much worse. I went to bed, and do you know, I stayed in bed for five months after that.

"After three days or four days—I don't remember exactly—my condition was critical. I was unconscious most of the time and I had a fever of a hundred and four degrees. I guess I didn't feel very good. Dean just stayed away from me. I guess he'd figured out what happened, and he didn't mind if I died.

"Jennie Miles, the baby-sitter, she stayed by me, though. She called down to Dr. Watts's office, and that other man—now I know that his name is Valentine St. John—came up to the house. He said I would have to go to the hospital. He wouldn't tell me what hospital, but he said they wouldn't charge me any more than I could pay.

"I was weak and very, very upset, but I kept insisting that I couldn't go. I didn't have the money, and I couldn't leave my children. Mrs. Miles backed me up. She didn't want that man to take me. Especially since he wouldn't tell where it would be. But the doctor said it was the only way to save my life. He didn't like us arguing with him, and he asked us, 'Do you think I'm a crook?' Mrs. Miles tried to stand up to him then. She said, 'I want to be a mother to this girl. I want to know what you intend to do with her and where you intend to take her.'

"But I was too weak to argue with the doctor. I was pitifully weak. So he just picked me up out of the bed and brought me out to a car in front of my apartment building." According to Diane, the driver of the car was a man she had never seen before, a man she later learned was Reg Rankin. Mrs. Miles recalled, "We went out to the car. He called it an ambulance, but it was a car. They put her in the car and took her away. She got in the car and left me."

Later Dean McDermott remembered that he was showing an elderly couple some dinette furniture when St. John and Rankin walked into the Santa Monica Montgomery Ward's. "They told me my wife was outside in a car and that she wanted to see me. Then they told me she was very sick and had to be taken to the hospital." McDermott went with the men to their car. He got into the back seat next to Diane. "My wife told me she was losing a lot of blood.

She said these men made her come with them because her life was at stake. They said she wouldn't live if she didn't go to the hospital right away."

Dean McDermott expected that the men would drive to the nearby General Hospital. He did not understand that if Rankin and the others took his wife to the emergency room in the condition she was in, the first thing hospital personnel would have to do would be to call the police and report that the victim of a criminal abortion had arrived. The members of the syndicate were sharply aware of hospital procedures in these cases, so instead, they drove Diane to North Vermont Avenue and pulled up at an apartment building with an awning that stretched to the curb. In arcing letters on the front of the green canopy it read, Dryden Apartments. Dean carried his wife into the building, then into the elevator. He noticed that her clothes were soaked with blood.

Diane remembered that the men brought her to the fourth floor and put her to bed in a dark room. They left her alone with an old woman they told her to call Nurse Grady. For the two weeks that Diane stayed in the dark room, her attendant did not speak to her and did little for her, but Diane barely noticed because, she said, "I was never so ill in my life."

The morning after St. John and Rankin brought Diane to the Dryden, Dr. Houston—whom Rankin had recently transferred from Portland to L.A.—came to see her. He said he was her doctor now. He also said she had to be operated on again. "He did it on the kitchen table, even though I begged for something better. He said this was the best they could get. He wouldn't give me an anesthetic either, said it would smell too much. Afterwards I felt like I was going to die."

For two weeks, Diane languished at the Dryden Apartments, indeed near death. Dr. Houston came to see her from time to time. Otherwise, she was alone with her silent attendant. During this time, Diane was certain that she was not improving. She told Dr. Houston, "I am not getting any better. I am going to die if I don't get out of here and get some medical attention."

Diane was surprised that Dr. Houston agreed with her. None of them had paid attention before to what she said. But now the doctors arranged to take her to Benedict Hospital in Hollywood, where again she languished for two weeks, although this time people spoke to her, and the sunshine came into the ward. Diane felt safer in the hospital, and she regained a bit of her strength. But she did not rest easy. As she put it, "I improved there a little but I had to leave because my children were without anyone to take care of them. Mrs. Miles had gotten sick and my husband had just walked out. He was so disgusted about what I had done. The children were staying with friends and I was so worried about them. I knew I couldn't get well if I didn't get that worry off my mind."

Once again, Rankin and his men bundled Diane into a car. This time they brought her home, where one or another of the syndicate doctors looked in on her every day. They were solicitous but cool. Most days they told her she was doing fine, that she was looking better. These assessments did not comport with the way Diane felt, but the doctors seemed to have something else on their minds. One day, when Diane was feeling particularly ill and despairing, she called Dr. Watts at his office but, as she put it, "he wouldn't do anything for me."

Another day, William Byrne came to see her. By this time, Diane was positively begging for medical treatment, even if it meant leaving her children again. "I told him I was feeling very ill and that my own doctor, Dr. Smiley, had come to see me and he said I would never be well again if I didn't get the right operation, once and for all. And Byrne said, 'Well, I am Mr. Rankin's representative. I can give him any message. But you don't look sick to me.' And then he left." Diane added, "It was three days later that I had to go to the General Hospital in a dying condition."

Diane McDermott finally got the care that she needed at the General Hospital, and over the course of the next few months, her body began to heal. But the woman's encounter with the syndicate, and especially with Rankin's determination to protect his operation at all costs, had very nearly killed her. As she was mending, it became clear to her that—despite what Rankin's doctors had done to her—they were still in charge, and she was still at their mercy.

Diane began to realize that this was the case after her neighbor, Jennie Miles, went to the police with the story of what those men had done to her young friend. Jennie assured Diane that the police would do right by her. She was certain they would arrest Rankin and his gang. But after Jennie went to the station and told about the whole awful business to the man on the homicide detail, the one responsible for investigating abortion crimes, nothing happened.

She was surprised, since the policeman had appeared concerned about what Jennie had to say. He took down her words, and he told her that he would be out to see Mrs. McDermott. But then nothing happened.

What Jennie Miles did not know was that William Byrne had also paid a call that same day on the same man, Lieutenant Ted Brown of the Los Angeles Police Department. He came in his official capacity as investigator for the California State Board of Medical Examiners. He did not take the opportunity to tell the police officer that he was there as Rankin's representative. But he did encourage Lieutenant Brown to read him the notes he'd taken of Jennie Miles's gruesome account of Diane's abortion ordeal, from start to finish. He said that he was familiar with the case, as indeed he was.

After Byrne heard Lieutenant Brown's version of Jennie Miles's story, he told the policeman that the important issue here was that Dr. Watts and Dr. Houston were legitimate doctors. He said that the facts of the case were these: the doctors had performed an abortion on Mrs. McDermott to save her life. But now, he said, the two ladies, Mrs. Miles and Mrs. McDermott, were trying to shake these doctors down for some money. The ladies saw an opportunity, and that was all there was to it. He said there was nothing to investigate. Lieutenant Brown had no trouble believing a man in an official capacity like Byrne, or lending his goodwill to a couple of doctors. Nor was it hard for him to dismiss the ladies as a couple of questionable dames, if that would make Byrne happy. Consequently, he dropped the investigation that very afternoon.

Now that Rankin and Byrne were aware that Diane McDermott thought it was a good idea to bring her troubles to the authorities, they set out to convince her otherwise. Reg Rankin went to see Diane. He brought her magazines and candy and a hundred-dollar bill. He sat on the edge of her bed and he held her hand. And then he came right out and told her that she would regret bringing in the law because he, Rankin, had the law in his pocket. Then he said that she and her friend were liars. He said that she knew, and he knew, that Mrs. Miles had carried tales to the cops. He said if Diane wanted to reconsider her plans, Rankin would play ball with her. Next Rankin showed Diane that he knew how to improvise, how to make up a story that sounded true but was not. He said he would see that the cops never got wind of what he called her "little secret" that before she went to see George Watts, Dean had beaten her up. He had smashed her around and knocked her down, and that's why she had gone to see the doctor in the first place.

He said she wouldn't have much credibility after he and Byrne got through with her. He squeezed her hand and suggested that she consider whether she would like to go to court and tell the world how she had decided to kill her own babies. Or how she had driven her husband to the point of madness, how she had driven him out of the house. That was something to consider, Rankin said, before she got in touch with the police again, didn't she think? Rankin left Diane to mull over the situation. But just in case she needed a little more motivation to hold her tongue, he arranged for Creeth and several others in his employ to call Diane on the telephone every now and then, and remind her about what she didn't want to do.

By the middle of 1936, Diane McDermott's life bore little resemblance to what it had been a year and a half before. Her husband was gone. Her body was weak and she trembled at night. In exchange for what she'd lost, she had acquired a pack of gangsters in her life who first ripped her apart, then threatened to do worse if she showed her scars. The way Diane saw it now, Rankin, the law, her husband, and her own body had betrayed her. She had only meant to protect the babies she had. She had only meant to be a good mother, but she had hit the wall trying.

Reg Rankin did not restrict his exploitation of vulnerable women to the ones who were unhappily pregnant. Sometimes he preyed on other women too, when he had a good reason. When Laura Miner's life became entangled with Rankin's syndicate, she was considerably better off than Diane McDermott had been, or so it seemed. For one thing, Laura had a profession—she was a licensed chiropractor in San Diego. For another, she had a business. Since the middle of 1933, Miner had been performing abortions out of her house. By early 1935, she had done as many as five hundred operations, maybe eight or ten a week. Like Ruth Barnett, Laura Miner had a deft touch, and so far, she had had no trouble with her clients or the law. The trickle of women in and out of her spare bedroom was light enough not to attract attention, but steady enough to bring in a sum that helped her to support herself, her husband, and her two kids. So far, the only people who wanted to know about Laura Miner were the ones she wanted to know about her—the unwed mothers, the exhausted young housewives like Diane McDermott, the middle-aged matrons caught by the change of life. These were her visitors, and she believed she served them well.

Given her straightforward setup, Laura had no reason to doubt the earnestness of Jane Toole, who came to her crying on January 25, 1935. Jane said she was an unmarried girl, and that she would rather die than have a child. Laura was not fondest of this type. Most of them had never had a pelvic exam before. But they were always grateful, and eager to get away when the job was done. This one was a little mousey girl, and her story had all the hallmarks of her type: first, love and promises; then, in rapid succession, passion, betrayal, shame. Last came the fear. Laura knew the story inside out, but she always sat quietly through all the chapters. She knew it was important to show the girls that she cared.

Laura did note one peculiar thing about Jane, but at the time she let it pass. Jane didn't want to climb on the table that day. She said she had come to find out how much it cost "to get rid of the thing," and to find out what the doctor would do to her. She had come, she said, to make an appointment. That was unusual but her tears were real, so Laura set her up for an appointment at the end of the week and turned her mind to other things.

There were three more callers that day and three abortions. By the end of the afternoon, Laura was worn out and glad to be finished, so she wasn't pleased when the door knocker sounded one more time.

Moving toward the door, Laura saw a man through the parlor curtains. He looked fortyish and dapper. Laura remembered later that she glanced at the man's face and thought to herself that he was the type who kept her business going. She was relieved that the caller was a man, and that she wasn't going to have to do another abortion just then.

The chiropractor let her visitor in. At first he said his name was Jim Meecham, and that he had come to make inquiries for a lady friend. He didn't look at Laura while he explained his business. He looked around at the furniture, the pictures on the wall, and he looked down the hall, toward the spare room. Laura had just invited Mr. Meecham to sit down and tell her the details of his lady friend's predicament when he began to speak to her in a low, threatening voice. He said that doctors in San Diego were mad at Laura Miner because she was underpricing them. He said, "You're too damn cheap!" Then, as Laura stood in the middle of her parlor, the man pulled out his card and opened his coat to flash a gold badge pinned inside the lapel. He said, "I am Bill Byrne, investigator for the State Medical Board, and I can make plenty of trouble for you. You know, don't you, that you could get six months just for making that appointment today to do Miss Toole. You are in a bad spot, lady, and you'd better listen hard."

William Byrne was a polished predator, and just in the way he was used to, his prey responded to attack. Laura looked down at the card Byrne put in her hand. It said: "Madison 1271. Station 563. William M. Byrne, Assistant Special Agent, Board of Medical Examiners, Department of Professional and Vocational Standards. State of California. 906 State Building, Civic Center, Los Angeles." She understood what was happening, and just now she shared Mr. Byrne's opinion that she was in a bad spot. Laura remembered, "I said, 'What is going to happen now? What do I have to do now?' And he answered, 'Well, consider today a warning, but I'm not going to want to come back here again. A word to the wise is for you to close up tonight and quit this work.'" Then Byrne turned and moved toward the front door. He stopped with his hand on the doorknob. He smiled and made Laura an offer. He said, "I'm going to Tijuana this evening and then I'll be back up in L.A. If you're ever up that way anytime, why don't you come in and see me." Laura said perhaps she would. And then Byrne was gone.

Over the next couple of weeks, Laura Miner cut her work down considerably, and those few abortion cases she took were done at night. But she did not feel secure. For the first time there were rumors, passed on by a druggist through a young woman who helped Laura out from time to time, that someone was defaming the chiropractor around town, saying she was a dirty abortionist who didn't know her business. The names George Watts and Jesse Ross dangled off the rumors, and Laura Miner was not too scared to find out what was going on. She had a hunch that Watts and Ross were associates of her visitor, Byrne. She believed that Watts and Ross intended to get rid of their competition in the abortion business, and she meant to protect herself.

Laura Miner began her effort to save her business the day after Byrne visited her house. First she checked the San Diego telephone directory and found a listing for George Watts. The chiropractor put on her hat and went downtown to the Commonwealth Building. She consulted the directory in the lobby, then took the elevator to the fifth floor. At suite 505, G.E. WATTS and J.C. ROSS were painted in black on the window glass set into the door. Laura did not hesitate. "I walked in and the nurse there in the waiting room said, 'What can I do for you?' I said, 'I'm not in trouble. I'm not here looking for an abortion. I came to see Dr. Ross personally because I have reason to believe that Dr. Ross has hired a solicitor to slander me in this town. And I want to find out why.'"

Laura was surprised that the woman did not stand in her way or ask her to leave. She acted as if the chiropractor's appearance in the office were an everyday kind of social occasion. She said, "Dr. Ross is not here very much. He is in L.A. most of the time, but he is here now. And he will be glad to talk it over with you." Then she took Laura in to meet the doctor.

Inside the surgery, Dr. Ross was standing at the sink. He was short and stout, shorter than Laura, a rather genial-looking Peter Lorre, she thought with relief. The chiropractor began to talk quickly and earnestly. As Laura recounted it later, she went straight to the point. "I told Dr. Ross my reason for hunting the office up was because there were numerous rumors circulating in San Diego that were damaging me. I said they were being circulated by a woman they'd hired as their solicitor." Laura said, "If you people want to open an office in San Diego, I have no objection to that. There is plenty of that sort of work for both of us. But why do you have to knife me in the back and slander me all over town to start a business for yourselves?"

Dr. Ross was genial and he was courtly, too. He said that if the solicitor, a woman he called Bea Hull, were doing anything damaging to Laura, it was without his knowledge and she would be stopped. But then Laura brought up the visit from Byrne, and the doctor grimaced in a way that made him look less genial than before. He said, "Yes, you have got to be careful of that fellow. He is liable to make it pretty hard on you." Then he went on. "Now, the man you want to see, that's Mr. Rankin. Our business manager. He's told me that he means to pay a call on you one of these days.

It would be an idea, in case he don't come, for you to go see him, up in L.A. I believe he has a proposition for you. He's been propositioning doctors down here, all over town. I wouldn't doubt he wants to talk to you about the same thing. He told me you could have some trouble doing work at your house now. That much I know." And then Dr. Ross seemed to run out of information.

But Laura had one more thing to say. She told the doctor that she would prefer to be left alone. She would prefer it if Mr. Byrne and Mr. Rankin and whoever else would give up bothering her. In return, she said, she would be pleased to mind her own business. Dr. Ross did not comment when Laura expressed her desire, and so she left.

Over the next couple of days, the evidence continued to mount that Laura's name was being dragged through the mud in San Diego. Another druggist told her that two women had come in, one at a time, asking for the name of a *man* who did abortions. They both told the druggist that they had heard about a woman on Thirtieth Street who did it in her home under bad conditions, and they wanted to steer clear of that. Both women had been referring to Laura. The druggist had hurried to let Laura know what was being said about her because he had sent many women her way and it had always worked out. The fact was, Laura was the sort of resource a druggist counted on, and he felt he owed her a warning.

Now Laura realized that her visit with Dr. Ross had changed nothing, so she decided to put on her hat and go up to Los Angeles. She would take up Mr. Byrne's invitation to pay a call on him. She needed to let Byrne know that she was a woman who had built a business during hard times, and she wasn't about to let a couple of thugs and somebody's Bea Hull ease her earnings out from under her. She thought she'd better let them see what she stood for.

First she sent Mr. Byrne a wire. She said she was going to be up in L.A. and that she would drop in to see him with reference to the subject that he had come to her house about. Byrne cabled back, "Phone me at office or at GLadstone 3961." He signed his message, "B."

A day later, Laura Miner was in Los Angeles. She described how first she looked for Byrne at his office. "I went to the State Building and some office girl there told me he was not there, but that he would be back in an hour or so. So I left the office and an hour later

I called on the phone and the girl said, 'Mr. Byrne is expecting you. He will be busy all afternoon, and he wants you to call on him at his home this evening.'"

Laura was exasperated, and she was leery about visiting this slick-looking man at his house. But most of all, she was determined to protect her name in San Diego, so she thought the danger was worth it. As it turned out, her visit with Byrne was strange and unsettling, and it was another encounter that pointed straight in the direction of Reg Rankin.

The first thing Byrne said when he let Laura into his house was that he hoped she had quit work. He said he guessed she knew what was good for her, and if she did, she knew that she'd better not press her luck. Then he got weird. He began to show Laura around his house, opening drawers and cabinets and pulling out opium pipes and boxes of opium, bottles of cognac and Armagnac, pornography and gynecological tools and dildoes that he said he had gotten from raids. Laura looked and she kept quiet. She said nothing when Byrne winked and offered her her pick, "from one crook to another." He opened a cupboard in the kitchen and Laura saw it was stuffed with pornographic photos. He lifted one picture delicately, between the tips of his thumb and forefinger, and waved it in front of the chiropractor. It was a picture of a naked Negro girl lying on a doctor's examining table. Her legs were spread apart and a white man's hand showed in the picture, resting on the girl's abdomen. Byrne waved the picture in front of Laura's face and he said, "I don't think you're planning to give up the business at all. So let me just tell you, if you're planning to do abortion work, you'd best go in with the doctors." Now he was using the same tone he had used in her parlor, and Laura was very eager to leave. By now she knew she was losing hold of her livelihood, and lingering here with Byrne—with his smut and his threats—was getting her nowhere.

But before she left, she made an attempt to salvage something from the visit. "I told him about my call at Dr. Watts's office. I said I had called there and saw Dr. Ross about some solicitor who was knocking me. I told Byrne that Ross urged me to see Mr. Rankin in L.A. about going to work for them." Byrne played coy that day, although nothing he said diminished his visitor's sense that her days as an independent abortionist were numbered. He said, "Well,

Dr. Ross has given you some advice there." He hesitated, then continued. "I think Mr. Rankin is a tax expert, and I think he has an office next door to Dr. Watts's office in the Signal Oil Building. I'm not sure," he said disingenuously, "what his connection is with those doctors, but I think it would be a fine idea for you to pay a call on Mr. Rankin and see what he wants."

Laura was certain now that whoever Rankin was, he was the man in charge. Twice she had been directed to him, and if she was to see this thing out, she had better go all the way to the top. Laura did not think of herself as a particularly brave woman, even though she knew that some people probably thought it took a certain kind of guts to break the law the way she did. But before Byrne's visit, she had been simply content. She felt suited to the work she did, and it was damn hard in 1935 for a woman—for anyone—to earn a living. If this man Rankin was going to break her back, she'd make him look her in the eye while he did it.

The night of her visit to Byrne, Laura stayed over with her sister in Saugus, and early the next day she drove to the Signal Oil Building. She didn't call ahead. As she put it later, "I just walked in." But Rankin was waiting for her nevertheless. His office girl took Laura's name at the door and told the chiropractor, "Step right in. Mr. Rankin is expecting you."

When Laura Miner went into Rankin's office, she found herself face to face with a man who did not doubt that he was in a position to shape her life. Reg Rankin did not bother with small talk now that the San Diego abortionist was in his office, or even with introductions. He barely said hello. He got right to the details concerning the place he had prepared for her. According to Laura, "Mr. Rankin asked me if I would like to go to work in Dr. Watts's office in the Commonwealth Building in San Diego. He wanted me to take over for Billie Nolan, the nurse down there who showed me in to Dr. Ross. He said that Billie was tired of San Diego, she didn't like the town. Then he said he'd pay me fifty dollars a week. I replied that fifty dollars a week was a joke for me. I pointed out that I could make more than that by myself, just doing a little work at home once in awhile."

At this point, Mr. Rankin began to speak to Laura more slowly and with more emphasis because he felt that she did not yet grasp his meaning. "Perhaps you don't understand," he said. "I am not exactly giving you a choice. I am—how can I put it—telling you the way things are." Then he said that Mrs. Miner would have trouble if she insisted on carrying on at home. Those days were over. It was too bad, but he couldn't say that she wouldn't be run out of town if she kept up her spare-room practice. Here he tried a benevolent smile and said she would be a whole lot safer if she took the fifty dollars a week and worked for him.

Laura asked for a few days to consider what Rankin had told her. The entrepreneur said he would be going down to San Diego in a day or two, and now that she understood what he had in mind, he didn't believe it would take her longer than that to respond to his offer. He said he would be by to see her when he was in town, and then he showed her out of his office.

Two days later, Rankin demonstrated his dependability. He called Laura and said he was staying at the Grant Hotel and would like her to come down that evening and talk to him. Laura demurred at first, She said she couldn't make it that night because she had to go to traffic school. She had gotten a ticket, she said, and she was required to go. But Rankin pressed her. "Come at nine. I'll still be here."

Laura had carried her effort to hold onto her business this far, and now she gritted her teeth and decided to take what felt like the final step. What other choice was there?, she asked herself many times as she drove down to the hotel just before nine.

Rankin met her in the lobby and showed her at once that he was more than dependable; he was vigilant. Again, he got right to the point. As Laura remembered it, "He said that evidently I didn't go to traffic school at all. He said evidently I had been doing a little work at my house that evening. I asked him how he knew that. And he said that one of the girls that had called at my house, around 7:30, was working for him. He had just wanted to check up on me. He wanted to know if I told him the truth, and he wanted a report on how much of a following I had. He said it would be useful for me to know that he was accustomed to checking up on people he was interested in. Then after he'd showed me how clever he was, he asked me if I'd given thought to his offer. I said, yes, I had thought it over, and it looked to me as if I couldn't fight him. He had more money than I had. And he knew what strings to pull. For a moment Rankin was quiet after I said that." So Laura repeated herself. "You have more money than I do. I can't fight you." Then she added, "I don't like your methods. You have hounded me, but what choice do I have? I will go to work and play ball with you because I am helpless." When she finished, Rankin looked satisfied, but he could not resist twisting the knife. He said, "That's a good girl. You know, if you'd said otherwise, I planned to have you run out of town. I'm glad I didn't have to do that."

Then Rankin got almost avuncular as he welcomed her into the syndicate. He put his arm around Laura and said this would be a much better arrangement and he knew she would be happier. He said they would both make plenty of money, her not so much at first, but things would pick up. He reminded Laura that she was not an M.D., so her position now was unreasonably risky. But with him, she would have the protection of the doctors, so things would be much better all around.

On March 4, 1935, Laura Miner became an employee of Reg Rankin's abortion racket, and Rankin himself began to teach the chiropractor how to become an office nurse according to his system. He instructed her in interviewing women and taking care of forms and payment, and in sending money to Mr. Shinn in Los Angeles. Soon Laura began to assist Dr. Ross, laying out instruments and helping with the curettement and the suction procedure at the end. For six months, Laura assisted Dr. Ross for fifty dollars a week, often taking care of patients or the friends and relatives of patients whom she had seen previously at her house. Then, in August, she and Rankin each saw a way to do better. For his part, Rankin decided to shift Jesse Ross to San Francisco. He needed a practitioner in the Elkan Gunst Building up there, and he expected that when Laura found out about the shift she would make him an offer.

Indeed, when Dr. Ross told his assistant he would be leaving, Laura wasted no time getting up to Los Angeles to make her proposition. She remembered the conversation. "I said to Mr. Rankin that I would like a chance to run the office by myself. I didn't want to be a nurse anymore. I wanted to be one of the operators. I told him I hoped I would—that I would conduct the office so that he would not be sorry that he allowed me to do the work." Laura added, "When I got the chance, I begged Mr. Rankin to let me do my work again."

Rankin was not particularly moved by Laura Miner's pleadings. But he did feel secure about the scene in San Diego, so he allowed Laura to demonstrate her abortion technique for Dr. Watts. When she passed muster, Rankin decided to break with policy and offer the woman a deal. He offered to pay her on the same basis as he paid his doctors. She would get a salary, Shinn would lay out for office expenses, and Rankin and she would split any balance left over. Laura was eager and she agreed to the terms.

But the terms did not hold for more than a month or two because the pressures were mounting on Rankin. All the arrangements he had made to hold his abortion racket together seemed to be fraying. In Seattle, Dr. Wilson and Paul De Gaston were giving him trouble. In L.A., Watts and Houston were telling him that Diane McDermott might not pull through. For Rankin, the money was still good, but the stress was sickening. Sometimes he thought his judgment was slipping as a consequence of the stress, and that was an unacceptable danger. And now he had taken on this woman, which was probably a bad idea.

So Rankin presented Laura with another deal. Once again he couched his offer in threatening terms: take it or get out of town. The conditions this time were rough: Miner would pay Rankin fifteen hundred dollars down and one thousand dollars a month, for thirty months, for full title to the business that had largely been hers at the beginning of the year. For $31,500, she could purchase back her abortion business and her independence.

By the middle of 1936, Laura Miner's life—like Diane McDermott's—bore little relation to its pre-Rankin shape. Laura's husband, who had lived contentedly for over a year off her earnings as a spare-room abortionist, was not content to see his wife controlled by Rankin. He was angry about the terms Rankin imposed. The loss of income was hard to take, but what was worse was the risk his wife incurred working for such an out-in-the-open operator whose greed ran before his judgment. By late summer, Marvin Miner couldn't stand the association and the risk, and on the day that Watts approved Laura's abortion technique up in Los Angeles, he took their two children and disappeared. As it turned out, his premonitions were keen: it wasn't long before his wife—the mother of his children—was under indictment in San Francisco, in L.A., and in San Diego as an accomplice in Rankin's abortion syndicate.

The independents, the small-time solo abortionists up and down the coast, were not bothered in 1936, but Rankin's boys and Laura Miner were all pulled in.

Laura Miner survived her encounter with Rankin in the mid-thirties and when the arrests came, she personally did not suffer very much. She had poise and skills and other resources to her credit. Some of Rankin's other victims were not so lucky. Indeed, one of the most resourceless of Rankin's victims was Shirley Packer, a young girl who had lived a checkered, sometimes vagabond, and always vulnerable Depression-era existence in the years before she got mixed up with the abortion syndicate. In the fall of 1935 when Reg Rankin found Shirley Packer, he hired her to work as a nursing attendant at a "convalescent house" in San Jose. Rankin intended that she would care for pregnant women brought to the house on Jackson Street after they had been "packed" in a downtown office building. These were women who had not gotten to an abortionist while a simple curettement could still be performed. Packing meant that an abortionist had inserted material up through the cervix that was meant to cause premature labor and miscarriage.

Shirley was hired to remove the packing at the right time and oversee the onset of labor. She was to manage the delivery of six-and-a-half-month fetuses, and maybe fetuses further along than that. And she was instructed to dispose of the evidence that an abortion had been performed.

Like Diane McDermott, Shirley's poverty during the Depression brought her into Rankin's orbit. Like Laura Miner, she had a skill Rankin could use. All three women were caught in the entrepreneur's web because the law against abortion created an opportunity for a man like Rankin who was willing to take it, and who was willing to squeeze it for everything it was worth. The law also created, of course, an arena of danger for many women, especially those who lacked basic resources such as money, employment, professional credentials, birth control, worldly contacts, and worldly know-how. Such women became deeply vulnerable when they felt compelled to transgress the law in order to take care of themselves. Once they stepped into the world of illegal abortion, these women became marked for men like Rankin as targets and as tools.

Shirley Packer was one of Rankin's tools in 1935. The story of how he used her and then cast her out is a real Depression era tale.

Shirley was one in the legions of forced wanderers of the thirties, in some ways not so different from the mostly male vagabonds and hobos who traversed the country in those years. Judging from her story, it was not an advantage to be a young woman on the road, especially a young woman travelling solo.

Shirley's journey into the dangerous arena of illegal abortion cannot be described as a straight line. It is a complicated story about what could happen to a young girl in times of economic dislocation. The circumstances of Shirley's life and her ultimate encounter with Reg Rankin point up the impossible and dangerous status of a rootless girl in the thirties.

Packer was young, about fifteen, when she began to make decisions for herself. In St. Louis, she left high school after ninth grade and spent the winter of 1928 caring for an old man her mother had sent her to because Shirley wanted to earn her own keep. When the old man died in the springtime, Shirley followed a family path and entered St. Mary's convent in the city. She was determined to become a nursing nun. For three years, she studied the nurse's course in the convent. By graduation she knew she had the stuff to be a nurse, but also that she had not become a nun. She was restless and had had enough of purity and prayers and quiet, clean-swept chambers.

A friend from the nursing class before hers had written to Shirley about California. She wrote from Los Angeles and said she could get Shirley a job. The girl said times were tough in California, like they were back home, but it was warm here and new people showed up every day. So nurses, she said, were always in demand. She sent a postcard to prove there were palm trees everywhere and sunshine, and that it was much more beautiful than grimy old St. Loo.

After three years in the convent, the letters and the postcard from Los Angeles were a thrill for Shirley, and all it took to get her on the road. She could take her skill with her, she figured, and like the young Paul De Gaston in Paris, she did not stop to sit for the professional examination. Hitting the road for southern California was a far more compelling idea, especially since the nuns had made it clear that most of the girls would not get work that year, even if they passed the test. In the fall of 1931, just weeks before the state licensing exam for nurses was held at Central High School, she went out on the highway going west, and waited for a ride.

Shirley Packer got rides all the way to California, and she was let off in Pasadena on October 2, 1931, by a truck driver who pinched her arm and told her that all roads out there led to Hollywood. "Don't get lost," he told her, and "don't get into no trouble." As Shirley later reflected ruefully, that was easier advice to give than to follow.

For seven days the girl tried unsuccessfully to find the nurse who had written to her. She took streetcars and walked the roads and went to the Pasadena library to read the city directories. She paid for a week at the YWCA, a place that reminded her of the convent, except that it was packed with wandering, ragtag girls all searching, like she was, for a friend. At the end of the week, Shirley had used up her funds, but she stayed on because she had no place else to sleep.

It was a problem, though, for Shirley to keep her bed at the Y. The rules were posted on the big front door, posted in the hallways and on the inside of the bathroom stalls. The rules were, you had to pay, and the matron, like St. Mary's Mother Superior, roamed the corridors looking for miscreants. On the third day that Shirley did not pay for her room and board, the matron called the police. As Shirley put it afterward, "The police came to arrest me for vagrancy, and I raised Cain. I was mad at the matron and mad at my friend for disappearing, and I made a scene right there on the steps of that Christian home. I hadn't done anything. The only reason they came after me was that I didn't have any money. If I had had any money, I never would have gotten into trouble. But it was during the Depression, and I came out here and couldn't find my friend and I couldn't find any work. What did they want?"

Partly because Shirley made such a fuss when they came to get her, and partly because the authorities in the Los Angeles area were empowered to use whatever means necessary in the mid-thirties to get rid of the wandering population, the police put her in the psychopathic ward of the county hospital to wait for her court hearing. On the second evening she was in the ward, a young doctor interviewed Shirley and afterward wrote *compos mentis*—faculties intact—on her chart. Then, for reasons Shirley could never fathom, he added "drug user" and "hold for observation" in the margin of the paper.

Shirley was kept under observation for two more days and then brought before Judge Newell in the Los Angeles County Court. The judge looked at the police report, at the doctor's comments, at the papers Shirley had been made to sign, and he looked at Shirley. He sentenced the girl to one hundred and eighty days in the county workhouse, for vagrancy. Then he said he would suspend the sentence and give her a ticket back home to St. Louis where she belonged. But she must promise, he said, to stay put. There was no place for her in Los Angeles County, and they didn't want to see her back again.

Shirley used that ticket to return home, but she did not plan to stay. There was no work for her in St. Louis, and her family could hardly feed themselves, much less put another plate on the table. So it was not long before she was back on the road to California, and as it turned out, on the road to joining up with Rankin's abortion syndicate. First, though, she would be arrested again in Pasadena, for vagrancy, by a vigilant policeman who'd been in court the day Judge Newell had warned Shirley out of L.A. County. Shirley described the encounter with the policeman in this way: "I didn't do a blessed thing. I was just walking along the street and he saw me. He knew Judge Newell had told me not to come back, but I wanted to come back. I wanted to find work. So there I was." According to Shirley, the charge against her the second time, in 1932, was "wandering from place to place without visible means of support."

The day after her second arrest in Pasadena, Shirley appeared in Judge Newell's courtroom. Years later, she remembered, "He was quite perturbed to think that I had come back. I suppose I didn't act very mannerly in his court, or answer him as I should have. Since then I have learned a lot better. But he sentenced me to the county jail this time. I had never been in jail, and when I got over there, I raised Cain, like I had at the YW. That was all there was to it, but they put me in for observation." Shirley was frustrated and mad that no one seemed to care that there was no place for a girl like herself to go.

For a long stretch after Shirley's outburst, things did not go well for her. Within a few hours, Judge Newell had been apprised that now the young girl from Missouri who had wandered loose on the street was further out of control. She was screaming like a banshee at the county jail. So he ordered her held in solitary until another hearing regarding her disposition could be held.

On November 15, 1932, Judge Thomas Gould of the Superior Court of Los Angeles County presided over this event. Shirley described Judge Gould's hearing that day: "They didn't give me a chance in court. The judge didn't say one word to me and the doctors said a few words, and that was all. I didn't say a word. The doctors whispered a few words to the judge, and he said, 'We will have to send her to Patton.'"

A document filed in the county clerk's office gives the legal version of Judge Gould's findings and demonstrates one desperate strategy the authorities felt pressed to use in those days in response to the wandering population that the Depression begat. "The witness, Shirley Packer, was found to be insane and she was then committed to and confined in the Patton State Hospital at Patton Hospital, California." The document also noted, "The Sheriff of Los Angeles County was to convey and deliver said insane person to the proper authorities of said hospital to be held and confined therein as an insane person."

This judgment and the confinement it mandated was to haunt Shirley Packer for some time. For one thing, Reg Rankin would dredge up these facts of Shirley's past to hold her in his thrall, or failing that, simply to debase her unmercifully, vengefully, in public, when he needed to.

Shirley was held at Patton for four months, until Zada Sullivan, a matron in the institution, convinced the court that the girl ought to be released. Shirley said about this woman, "I saw her all the time because she was very interested in me and thought I had been treated very unjustly." Mrs. Sullivan did not believe that Shirley was insane. She thought she was a normal girl and ready to work. Later Shirley described her first job in California, a position Zada Sullivan helped her find, after her two disastrous attempts to become self-supporting. She said, "I got the best thing I could do. I got a position in a motherless home taking care of two children."

For the next year and a half, Shirley Packer did well. After tending the children happily for several months, she felt restored and ready to look for work in her chosen profession, nursing. Finally, her timing was good. It took less than a week for her to find a position at Angelus Hospital on Trinity Street, where she was hired for nursing work despite her lack of a license. She was assigned to the obstetrics floor where she worked alternately in the delivery room and the nursery from February until June of 1935. Shirley felt good about the job she did at Angelus, and by June she was ready to advance herself. This time she found a job with the California Medical Association, taking on what were called "special cases." Shirley explained, "I worked for some of the best doctors in the city, doctors like C.W. Tice and Dr. Louis Gunther, Dr. Harlan Shoemaker. I took care of infectious cases and paralytics and heart cases and TB. I took care of practically everything."

Unfortunately for Shirley, now in her mid-twenties, in September 1935 there was a lull in special cases, and a girl who was night nurse on one of her jobs suggested she go down to the Signal Oil Building on Seventh Street and see Dr. Ross or Dr. Watts. "They're always looking for girls," she said. By this time Shirley was an experienced nurse with a specialty in obstetrics and more than five hundred hours in convalescent care, just the sort of girl that the doctors and Mr. Rankin were especially interested in.

Shirley met with Dr. Ross in mid-September, and the doctor passed her along to Rankin. Later Shirley remembered that Rankin seemed interested when she called on him, but said he had nothing at the moment. "But he said he would keep me in mind for the first thing that came along. I gave him my address at 1723 El Cerrito in Hollywood, and about two weeks later, I got a letter from Mr. Rankin. He told me to come up to San Francisco, to the Elkan Gunst Building there, and he would see me in Dr. Ross's office. He wrote that I was to come on October 6th." The Medical Association had not notified Shirley of any more special-duty positions, so she decided to go on up to San Francisco to see about Rankin's offer.

In San Francisco, Rankin told Shirley Packer that he wanted her to go to a "convalescent home" in San Jose and start working. He told her that Dr. Ross would take her down there, to 899 Jackson Street, and that her job would be to take care of the house and also of the patients convalescing there. That was all the information Rankin gave Shirley in San Francisco, and Dr. Ross offered no more when he drove the girl down to San Jose on October 19th. Shirley did not press her employers concerning the details of her new job.

As she put it, "At the time, I was just glad to be working."

Dr. Ross brought Shirley to the house on Jackson Street. It was a tall, white frame house, two stories. To the girl, it looked like a big farmhouse. Inside, it was almost barren of furnishings, particularly the three large downstairs rooms. The upstairs consisted of three bedrooms and a bath and what Shirley called "a sort of a delivery room." She described this room as having "a delivery table, quite a large sink with a drain board, and a sterilizer and that was about all." Dr. Ross walked Shirley through the house. In the kitchen, he introduced her to a woman whom he said was called Violette Pelligrini. He said Violette was Shirley's predecessor, and that now she was coming to work with him downtown in the Bank of America Building where they were opening a new office. Still no one described the convalescent patients, or what Shirley should expect. "They just told me I was to take care of them, feed them and nurse them."

For five days, Shirley stayed in the house on Jackson Street alone. There were no convalescent patients, and she did not see Ross or Pelligrini again after the first day. Then on the sixth day, about dinnertime, Violette telephoned Shirley and said she was bringing out a patient. She said she would tell Shirley what to do after they got there.

It wasn't long before Violette arrived with a young, blond woman who appeared to be in her mid-twenties. The woman looked slightly pregnant and very uncomfortable. She walked into the house in little, mincing steps, and Violette ushered her upstairs to the front bedroom. Then the older nurse came back downstairs and told Shirley that the woman—she called her Mrs. Brownell—had been "packed," and that the packing was to be removed in twenty-four hours. Violette said, simply, that Shirley was to give the woman care, and then she went away.

At this time, Mrs. Brownell had been pregnant for more than three months, and Dr. Ross had treated her in the routine way for such cases. He packed her dilated cervix with treated gauze in order to produce contractions that would expel the fetus. As an observer of Rankin's operation explained, "Any woman so packed would be sent away to any one of several lying-in hospitals or apartments maintained by the syndicate for cases of this kind, where the birth of a premature baby would occur."

Shirley looked in on Mrs. Brownell every hour or so that evening and the next day, and she tried to chat with her from time to time. But the patient did not want to talk. Most of the day she appeared to doze, and she kept the radio on. So a low murmur hung around the bed. At 6:00 in the evening, Shirley explained that it was time to remove the packing that Dr. Ross had put up inside her. Using a sharp tweezers, she pulled out the treated gauze. Mrs. Brownell grunted once or twice while Shirley worked on her, and forty-five minutes later, the labor pains began. Judging from the quality of the woman's grunts and moans, Shirley determined that Mrs. Brownell had moved quickly into hard labor.

At 9:00, Mrs. Brownell delivered what Shirley described as "a six-and-a-half-month living baby." Shirley was startled by the size of the fetus and how well developed it was. Instinctively, she tried to keep it alive. She tied the cord and she gave it artificial respiration. "It had quite a bit of mucus in its nose and mouth, and I used a catheter to get the mucus out. I put it in a tub of warm and cool water." But the baby was unmistakably blue. So Shirley tried harder. "I wrapped it up and put hot-water bottles around it and tried to keep it as warm as possible."

After an hour and a half of trying first one thing and then another, Shirley was frantic. She called down to the Bank of America Building, and as she put it, "I tried to get somebody to come out and see what could be done. I talked to Dr. Ross. I pleaded with him to come. I said, 'This baby is alive!' He said to leave it alone, that he couldn't have anything like that live around there." Stressing that the infant was in distress, she said again, "'This baby is *alive*.' I said it was cyanotic [blue] and I was doing everything I could for it. He said, 'You didn't tie the cord, did you?' And I said, 'Yes, I did.' So he said, 'Well, leave it alone. Let it die. We can't have anything like that living around there.' I begged him to come out. I said there were places to put babies that lived. But he didn't come out. He didn't come out until after the baby had died.

"When they did come—Dr. Ross and Violette came together— Violette said to me, 'Well, what have you done with it?' And I said, 'I have not done anything.' I said, 'It was a living baby when it came, and then when it died, I laid it in a pan and covered it.' She said, 'You should have gotten rid of it.' She says, 'You know the evidence has to be destroyed.' Dr. Ross was mad, too. He said I never should have tied the cord to begin with. Then Violette told me that it had to be flushed down the toilet. I told her I would not do it, so she put on a gown that they use when they do these abortions and took it into the bathroom and took a pair of scissors, and I saw her cut through the little left arm. I didn't see the leg dismembered, but I went back a few minutes later, and there was a mass in the toilet and she was cutting through the scalp, through the head."

Mrs. Brownell lay in the front room still, but could hear the voices of Dr. Ross and Violette and Shirley rise and fall through the bathroom wall. It is not known whether Mrs. Brownell was aware of what happened to the fetus. In fact, we can only surmise the barest facts about her history. It is likely that she was a woman who got pregnant at a time when she did not feel able to have a child, and Section 274 of the California Penal Code prevented her from acting legally on that feeling. It seems that it took her so long to find someone to help her that when she finally did find help, it came in this gruesome form.

We know more about Shirley Packer: she was a Catholic girl, for three years a novitiate, later incarcerated as an insane person by the State of California. The events at Jackson Street made Shirley think of both those past lives as she stared into the toilet. After a minute or two, she walked into the back room where she slept and packed her bag. Then, she remembered, "I just came downstairs and stood in front of those two with my things packed. I said, 'I am leaving.' But Dr. Ross stood in front of me and in front of the door and said, 'You are not.' I could not make much of a sound then. I whispered, 'I am a Catholic girl. I must go.' And Dr. Ross said, I don't care what you are. You will stay.'"

It was thirteen days before Shirley could escape from the house on Jackson Street. When she did escape, it was under the protection of a man whose wife had just undergone the same procedure as Mrs. Brownell, except that this woman, a school teacher desperate to keep her job, had been shown her baby before it was dismembered. The woman's husband took Shirley in his car and left her in San Mateo, where she began to make her way back to St. Louis, to the peace and safety of her mother's home. But like Diane McDermott and Laura Miner, Shirley found that her ordeal in the abortion racket was not to come to a neat conclusion. In the fall of 1936, exactly one year after Shirley had watched Violette Pelligrini dismember the fetuses, she was called back to Los Angeles to testify in court about those events.

Once again, the courtroom was not a congenial place for Shirley to be. This time Reg Rankin was responsible for her uneasiness, even though it was Rankin himself and the doctors in his syndicate who were on trial. Shirley never knew how Rankin found the records of her Pasadena arrests, of her banishment from Los Angeles County, of her incarceration in the insane asylum. She herself had never thought about the fact that following her release from Patton, no paper had ever been drawn up that gave her back her sanity. In Los Angeles, then, it could be argued that she was still insane.

Early in the fall, weeks before the court date, Rankin had found the nurse and told her that any subpoena she might be served was just a flimsy piece of paper, and he laid out for her a competing vision of her duty. Shirley remembered every detail of Rankin's presentation. "He said that he had plenty of money and I had none. He said that he was going to get out of this thing, but who knew if I would. Then he said that he was plenty smart, I must know that. I'd better not talk, he said. I'd better not have a word to say. And then he told me that he would stop at nothing. He could frame me in a second and give me the kind of publicity that makes people shrivel up and die. At the end he said he didn't think, once I had considered all the angles, that I would want to show my face in California, much less in a court of law."

Shirley Packer did appear in a court of law to testify in the matter of Reginald Rankin et al. But she—like Mrs. McDermott and Laura Miner and thousands of other women who came to court to testify in other abortion trials—came into the courtroom and left it with profound questions about the meaning and the purpose of the law.

In the courtroom where the activities of Rankin and the doctors were at issue, nobody asked about the past of Dr. Watts or Dr. Ross. Even Mr. Byrne was treated as a clean slate before his association with Rankin. But Shirley's past—her vagrancy, her insanity, her defiled femininity—became a centerpiece of the proceedings. Shirley begged the court to spare her from talking about the tawdry details of her life that had propelled her, finally, into Rankin's clutches. She looked at the judge and pleaded for protection. "Do

I have to tell all these things in front of everybody? Can't I say it just in front of the people who need to hear it?" Shirley was pitiful, asking again and again if she must review the details of her life, which sounded so sordid and seemed no explanation at all, no match for the team of lawyers who stood before the judge and intoned with authority when she finished trying to explain herself.

One of Rankin's lawyers said, "Your Honor. The record shows, by negative showing at least, that there has never been any proceeding under the provision of either Section 1470 or 1471 of the Probate Code—that being the provision for restoration of sanity under that Code. So inasmuch as there has never been any order of our courts restoring this lady to sanity, there is a continuing judgment on her sanity and that at the present time it is prima facie evidence of her insanity and therefore of her inability to testify in this proceeding under the provision of Subdivision 1 of Section 1880 of the Code of Civil Procedure."

Even as she listened to Rankin's lawyer assert and then repeat, "The lady is insane," Shirley Packer had known that something horrible, something like this, had been likely. She had been fearful about coming back to California to testify against Rankin. But the subpoena had said she must. What the law did not know was that Rankin had gotten to her first.

The women who got entangled with Reg Rankin and his abortion syndicate in the thirties had good reason to be confused about the law, even if they did not have the language or the political framework to help them articulate their concerns. In 1936 every state in the Union had a law forbidding abortion, even though countless women obtained abortions every year. In those days, hardly anybody bothered to talk about why the abortion laws were on the books, although from time to time a district attorney might have occasion to assert that the statutes existed to protect women.

But Diane and Laura and Shirley had reason to know that the law did not protect women. They had reason to believe, in fact, that the law's greatest accomplishment may have been its power to create opportunities for people like Rankin, and its power to channel opportunities for people like themselves. The stories of these women point the power of the law, as it worked in real life, to erect dangerous and demeaning filters for women unwillingly pregnant, unwillingly poor, but determined to define their own lives.

With abortion in the shadows, raw power replaced the civilized impulses that might have protected women in those days, and women were not equal players where raw power prevailed, even when it was their lives—their bodies—at stake. The fact is, no matter whom the D.A. claimed the law existed to protect, in the real lives of women, the law mandated danger, and it could never make up for the danger it caused, even if it tried.

Chapter Five

RENO

By the summer of 1936, Reg Rankin and his confederates had gone too far. Rankin's chain of abortion clinics, his chain of credit bureaus, his small army of doctors and nurses and shills—and the occasional mistakes they made—had all begun to draw the attention of law enforcement officials. It was not as if the district attorneys and the cops in San Francisco and Los Angeles, San Jose and San Diego didn't know about Reg Rankin's syndicate before June 1936. They knew. But they honored the agreement that had generally governed relations between abortionists and the law since the state of California criminalized abortion in 1849. It was the same agreement that protected Ruth Barnett in Portland: no death, no prosecution. But Reg Rankin's brash demeanor and his open operation of abortion offices up and down the coast had pushed the tolerance of the authorities beyond the breaking point, especially because the Internal Revenue Service had also gotten interested in Rankin's business.

That summer, the district attorneys in San Francisco, Los Angeles, and San Diego all cracked down. In L.A., police raided abortion offices in Hollywood, downtown, and Long Beach on June 5th and arrested Rankin, Watts, Shinn, and Byrne. They arrested three doctors, James Beggs, Jesse Ross, and Valentine St. John, and three nurses, including Violette Pelligrini. Also netted were a couple of individuals associated with the abortion ring's credit bureau, the Medical Assistance Corporation, including Rankin's brother-in-law, J.C. Perry. Three others were sought by the police but never apprehended: Dr. Houston, who had sold his Oregon drugstore to go in with Watts and Rankin; Beatrice Bole, Rankin's solicitor who had paid calls on Dr. Tatum, the drugless man; and the nurse at the Dryden Apartments who had watched silently over Diane McDermott. Others, potential witnesses, were subpoenaed in June, and some were offered immunity if they testified for the prosecution. Laura Miner, the San Diego abortionist and her assistant, Nedra Cordon, were offered this deal and accepted. Dr. Norman Powers, arrested with the others, agreed before the trial began to be a witness for the state. Paul De Gaston, so deeply involved in the complex life of Rankin's syndicate, was only too glad to turn state's evidence.

From October 5, 1936, through the 24th of that month, in Los Angeles Superior Court, prosecution witnesses provided gruesome tales and gory details in support of the charges contained in the nine-count indictment against the members of the abortion syndicate. The first count was the most inclusive, and ultimately eleven out of the thirteen defendants were found guilty on this count. It charged them with conspiracy and asserted that the defendants "knowingly, willfully, unlawfully and feloniously conspired, combined, confederated and agreed together and with each other to provide, supply and administer to divers pregnant women, citizens of this state and elsewhere, medicines, drugs and substances, and to use and employ instruments and other means upon such divers pregnant women with intent thereby to procure the miscarriage of such women and each of them, the same not being necessary to preserve the life of such women, or any of them." The other eight counts were more pointed, charging the defendants with "the commission of a criminal abortion" on specific, named women.

Testimony lasted for fifteen long days, but the courtroom remained a riveting place almost every minute of that time. Hard-boiled witnesses like Paul De Gaston alternated with soft, vulnerable women like Diane McDermott. Laura Miner described how her business worked on a day-to-day basis, and then the distinguished head of the State Board of Medical Examiners told how Rankin came to his office and brazenly threw his weight around. Unwitting participants and erstwhile collaborators took the stand and told stories about how and on whom the syndicate operated, and most of the time, one young woman or another was waiting in the wings or sitting in the witness box, compelled to describe how she got on a table and spread her legs.

In all, forty-three witnesses testified for the prosecution. Only a handful testified for the defense, and Reg Rankin, George Watts, and J.O. Shinn were not among them. Nor were the doctors Beggs,

Ross, and St. John. Bill Byrne did get up on the stand as the final defense witness, but only for a moment. After providing a shifty answer to one question put to him by his lawyer, Byrne was excused. The team of defense lawyers, supported by the judge, made it impossible for Byrne, under cross-examination, to shed any light on the question of his relation to the abortion syndicate. The judge ruled that questions about whether he knew Reg Rankin and whether he took a trip with Rankin to Seattle were incompetent, irrelevant, and immaterial, as the defense contended. The prosecution did not press hard. They had made their case and felt confident by the time Byrne was called that anything the man said the jury would disbelieve.

Indeed, the prosecution had made its case. After a short deliberation, the jury found all the defendants but two—Rankin's brother-in-law and a woman more or less arrested by mistake—guilty on various combinations of the counts. It is notable that in fifteen days of testimony, the issue of the unborn child, its potential life, its rights, was not a recurring theme or even a concern. The trial was about displaying the practices of a criminal syndicate, just as if it had been a bootlegging syndicate or a group of gamblers on trial. The difference, of course, was that in Rankin's operation, the client bought a chance to efface the wages of sex, and the clients were all women. So in addition to displaying the low-down tactics of a group of men willing to use the law to line their pockets, the trial provided a venue for displaying the sexuality and the vulnerability of women. Regarding the latter, the trial was an unqualified success.

But in the end, the jury's verdict was not the last word on the fates of some of the syndicate participants. Rankin himself made a few gestures toward appealing his conviction. He retained a lawyer and filed the necessary documents in the fall of 1936. In January 1937, though, he dropped his appeal and entered San Quentin. The three female defendants, Violette Pelligrini, Grace Moore, and Lillian Wilson, were permitted to file applications for probation, as was Mr. Shinn, Rankin's right-hand man.

Among the defendants who did not enter prison by the end of 1936 were William Byrne and the three doctors, Jesse Ross, James Beggs, and Valentine St. John, all of whom vigorously appealed their convictions to the State Supreme Court. The chief contention of all four men was that if the testimony of individuals who were accomplices to the syndicate's crimes—people like De Gaston and Laura Miner, and the women who had sought criminal abortions—were excluded, the evidence was insufficient to warrant conviction.

To be sure, the law was settled in California that a person could not be convicted of a crime upon the testimony of an accomplice *unless* that testimony were corroborated by other evidence that connected the defendant with the crime in question. What's more, Section 1108 of the California Penal Code specifically stated that the testimony of a woman who sought an abortion was tainted. It said, "Upon a trial for procuring or attempting to procure an abortion, or aiding or assisting therein, or for inveighing, enticing or taking away an unmarried female of previous chaste character, under the age of 18 years, for the purpose of prostitution, or aiding or assisting therein, the defendant cannot be convicted upon the testimony of the woman or with whom the offense was committed, unless she is corroborated by other evidence."

The identity established here between prostitutes and women seeking abortions was important not only in revealing the basis of the law's objection to abortion. The connection also shaped the outcome of the case because eventually this provision of the law did work to the benefit of the three doctors who appealed their convictions. On November 26, 1937, the Supreme Court of the state of California denied the strenuous efforts of the L.A. County D.A. to prove that the evidence against the medical trio was abundant and untainted. The Supreme Court found that the only substantial evidence amassed against the doctors had been offered, inadmissibly, by accomplices—the women who had received abortions and others involved with the syndicate. Consequently, the court decided, "Applying the foregoing rules to the instant case, we find with reference to the appellants Beggs, Ross, and St. John, that, after eliminating entirely the testimony of their accomplices, the record is completely devoid of any evidence even slight, which connects or tends to connect any of them with any of the crimes of which they were convicted [and] the judgments as to these appellants must be reversed for the foregoing reason."

Whether or not the State Supreme Court's decision in the Rankin case was an expression of solidarity between legal and medical professionals, the decision was consistent with the trial outcomes in abortion cases across the country during the illegal era: doctors were almost always exonerated on one grounds or another, especially if the charges did not include murder, and sometimes even if they did. In the Rankin case, community morals were outraged by the conspiratorial nature of the syndicate, but the court's decision suggests that professional ethics could absorb and tolerate abortion-performing doctors. After all, in 1936, perhaps as many as one thousand "therapeutic abortions" were performed by doctors at L.A. County Hospital, a number that would plummet to onetenth that many in less than twenty years.

William Byrne, however, was another story. The men and women who came to court and testified about his activities were mostly the same crew that testified against the doctors, that is, accomplices according to the law. But unlike the doctors, Byrne could not convince the state's highest court that his claim of tainted testimony was valid, and in the end, the court defined his situation entirely differently. Byrne was not a doctor. He could not claim medical expertise or draw on established collegial relations with other professionals to protect himself. In fact, his professional status was his undoing. As an investigator who consorted with his criminal targets, he had violated the public trust in the most fundamental way. There were no gray areas in his case, and the Supreme Court judges had no trouble dismissing his appeal.

Early in 1938, Byrne joined Reg Rankin and George Watts in San Quentin. Each man had been sentenced to a term in excess of ten years by an angry Superior Court judge, Arthur Crum. According to the *Los Angeles Times*, which followed the case closely, Crum "meted out the severest possible penalty by providing that the sentences on each of the five counts must run consecutively and not concurrently."

It is impossible to know much for certain about the activities of Watts and Byrne once they were incarcerated. Ruth Barnett wrote that her old mentor Watts died in San Quentin, but her account of this period is untrustworthy. What is known, however, is that Reginald Rankin, like most men convicted of the crime of abortion, did not stay behind bars for more than a fraction of the time Judge Crum intended.

By the summer of 1940, Rankin was out of jail, apparently unrepentant and unreformed. He was, in fact, busy trying to resurrect his former business, but on new terrain. Following an adage that advised, "If you can't do it at home, go to Nevada," Rankin had settled on Reno as a promising venue for an abortion clinic.

Rankin knew about Reno's reputation as a haven and an opportunity for all sorts of men who'd served time elsewhere. It was a small city in 1940, with no more than twenty-three thousand residents, but the word was that there was always room in Reno for a guy with shady ideas about how to turn a buck. The welcoming hand extended to Al Capone, for example, was legendary. When the gangster was scouting prospects in the Truckee River town, the mayor answered inquiries from his front men genially. "Al Capone is welcome in Reno as long as he behaves himself," he said. Later, Bugsy Seigel, too, made his headquarters there before moving across the state to Las Vegas. One person who observed Reno closely in those years explained why the city was so hospitable to such types. "The city police force increased in size, improved in equipment, and vanished from the scene of any important misdoings. The average citizen was living in a community of gangsters, bought politicians, thugs, and bootleggers, a community in which ancient bums had been pensioned into police uniforms."

Reg Rankin had reason to believe that Reno was a city that not only would tolerate a man in his business, but that needed him. After all, it was a town that built a big share of its economy on the trade in women's bodies, and where that was the case, abortionists had a ready-made clientele of some size. One Nevadan described Reno in those years as a "modern amalgamation of Sodom, Gomorrah, and Hell," where prostitution was a business "on a supermarket scale." The Stockade and The Bull Pen were the places to procure choice female flesh in 1940, and the two joints attracted locals and visitors alike. Common knowledge had it that The Stockade, particularly, catered to the tastes of travelling salesmen on the San Francisco-Salt Lake City route, and to businessmen from all over California. Years later, an historian recalled drily that the immense gross earnings both places produced proved unequivocally that "there were distinct possibilities in the area of unconventional approaches to attract visitors" to Reno.

Along with prostitution, gambling was entering its commercial heyday in Nevada. The year before Rankin showed up in town, William Hurrah opened his Tango Club on Douglas Alley, and a

number of entrepreneurs followed. Reno was jumping as it pulled
in a certain kind of man who associated money and short-term
pleasure. The fact that nine thousand divorces a year were
processed in Nevada during that era, the lion's share in Reno,
added to the transient flavor of the place and to the population of
women who might be carrying pregnancies they could not manage.
Rankin knew all this when he laid out his plans from San Quentin.

Between July and November 1940, Rankin put a great deal of
effort into setting up an abortion business in Reno. First, he assem-
bled a team of men to whom he could assign duties, just as he had
six years earlier in California. As for him, he took on the familiar
jobs of scout and strategic planner. He went to Reno in the first
part of July and met with a real estate man who showed him office
space appropriate for what Rankin called his "finance business."
Later in the month, Rankin dispatched Paul Cushing, a San
Francisco man, to sign a five-year lease for space in a downtown
office building. Rankin had approved the terms of the lease, which
called for a seven-room suite in exchange for a monthly rental fee
of two hundred dollars.

His brashness undiminished, Rankin instructed Paul Cushing to
take the real estate agent into his confidence and explain what the
offices were to be used for. Cushing complied. Before the lease was
signed, he explained to Norman Blitz, the real estate broker, that
the suite would be used by doctors for the treatment of women's
diseases, and that abortions would be done on the premises. He
hastened to explain further that the physician in charge, one
Valentine St. John, was retired but had controlled many such clinics and was used to having the best doctors refer their patients his
way. Cushing told Blitz that St. John had spent his lifetime developing his abortion method and the instruments used to perform
the operation, and that doctors particularly liked St. John's work
because it was painless and safe. He said that St. John had trained
many efficient young surgeons and, leaving out the mess that St.
John had recently escaped in L.A., he said that the doctor had never
had any trouble and had, in fact, been welcomed in any community he came to because doctors felt he was a "needed necessity."

Having laid the groundwork for opening the abortion clinic in
Reno, Cushing now asked Norman Blitz a question that reflected
the murky status of abortion in the pre-World War II era. He asked

if the real estate man thought that the medical community and the law in Reno would be receptive to an abortion clinic in their city. Blitz replied that if everything was as he described, he was sure Cushing, Rankin, and St. John would have no difficulty. Blitz remembered this part of the conversation. "I said the town and state were level-minded, and if the doctors approved of it, I didn't think they would make any trouble unless they made some mistakes."

Then Blitz gave Cushing a list of doctors in Reno who might be interested in sending patients to such a clinic. Maybe Norman Blitz was aware that the Nevada penal code stated that anyone who performed an abortion not necessary to preserve the woman's life could be imprisoned for up to five years, and that if the fetus had quickened before the operation, the sentence might be ten years. Maybe Blitz was not aware of the law. But his answer made it clear that the idea of an abortion clinic in a building he managed and shared ownership of with a physician did not raise a warning flag in his mind.

After obtaining this degree of assurance, Cushing and Rankin went ahead with their plans. They engaged a contractor to renovate the suite of offices and brought Valentine St. John to town to look over the premises. The chances that the trio would be able to open for business by September were looking good, but one outstanding detail remained: St. John was not licensed to practice in Nevada. This was a problem because Rankin was adamant, as usual, that they must have a proper doctor in charge. Blitz volunteered to arrange for St. John to pay a call on Vernon Cantlon, a longtime Reno physician and surgeon, and a member of the State Board of Medical Examiners. The plan was that Dr. Cantlon would expedite St. John's Nevada license.

Blitz, however, had sent the doctor to the wrong man. Vernon Cantlon did not think much of Valentine St. John that afternoon of July 20th, or of his foreign credentials. Sometime later, the Reno doctor remembered the details of the visit vividly. "We commented about news of local interest, and then Dr. St. John produced a container ordinarily used for diplomas and other credentials, and withdrew from the container several diplomas and other credentials; among them was a small credential which purported to show that Dr. St. John was a member of the Royal College of Surgeons,

London. I don't remember all of the papers he showed me. Among them were a list of the publications he had, with an appalling number of papers he had written. Also there was some sort of notice that he had been a professor of surgery in one of the Balkan states. I don't remember just which one it was, but I believe it was Budapest. Dr. St. John said, 'Obviously this will prove I am qualified to practice,' and he stated that he had performed over four thousand operations. I stopped him at that point and asked him if he had an American diploma from any American university of medicine, and he said no, that he did not. He intimated that it didn't matter very much because he was obviously well trained enough. I said that I was sorry, that we were rigidly enforcing the rule in the State Board of Medical Examiners that no one could be licensed to practice medicine in the state of Nevada without an American diploma. He was somewhat upset by my remark and left."

If Dr. St. John was somewhat upset by this turn of events, Rankin and Cushing were livid. Cushing blamed Norman Blitz for getting him to sign a lease by intimating that he would see to St. John's license. A week after the meeting between Cantlon and St. John, Cushing wrote to Blitz about "the mutually misleading information you received and relayed concerning licensing of a foreign doctor." He went on, "The difficulty lies in our absolute necessity of having a regularly licensed physician to act as titular head of the Reno offices. You will understand that the disappointment regarding St. John's license was a considerable setback in our plans." Feeling that Blitz owed him one at this point, Cushing made a request. "Efforts are now being made here to find a man eligible to receive a Nevada license for this purpose. In the interim, can you suggest any man in your locality who would, for a consideration, be interested in lending his name to the office? Naturally, such an individual would have no responsibilities other than those implied in the use of his license and name."

Norman Blitz had nothing to offer Cushing and Rankin in this line. He simply continued to collect rent payments through the summer of 1940, though the offices in the Lyons Building sat idle. In the last part of August, Reg Rankin found himself still committed to opening an abortion clinic in Reno, but without the key ingredient—an abortionist. So at this point, he turned to an acquaintance. He turned to Ruth Barnett.

When Rankin made his proposal to Ruth late in the summer of 1940, she accepted. First she agreed to join him in San Francisco to consider the details of his plans for a Reno clinic, and then she agreed to go to Reno for the purpose of performing abortions. It is difficult to know today what had changed since 1934. Back then she had been adamant that Rankin leave her out of his schemes. She was happy where she was, she had said, in the Broadway Building in Portland, the new owner of Dr. Van Alstyne's practice, the beneficiary of Dr. Watts's training and his loyal clientele. It is difficult to know for sure why Ruth accepted Rankin's proposition, mainly because she took some trouble to efface the episode from the story of her life. She did not want her daughter to know what happened in Reno, nor anybody else. The fact is, from 1952 until the end of her life, Ruth Barnett wrote and rewrote versions of her life as an abortionist, and always she omitted the events of 1940 in Reno.

It is possible, however, more than fifty years later, to piece together some speculations about why the Portland abortionist took up with Rankin when she did, and also to imagine why she altered her life story to erase the episode. To do so reveals the kinds of calculations an abortionist was compelled to make in the illegal era and the kinds of pressures that shaped her professional life. It also reveals the kind of danger that conditioned Ruth's private life in those days. It was not the same danger that stalked and nearly killed Diane McDermott or that threatened Laura Miner. But the act of altering one's life story suggests anxiety and fear. The extent to which Ruth could not tell the truth about her life, even though the point of the autobiography she wrote was to expose the abortionist as a good woman, tells us something of the forces that broke her control over her life in those days and beyond. To paraphrase Carolyn Heilbrun, in the fall of 1940, Ruth Barnett was trapped in a script that she didn't write and could never write about, and that begins to describe her danger.

In the early 1930s the abortionist had plied her trade in the context of the Depression. The traffic flowing through Ruth Barnett's office reflected the length of the unemployment line, the lines at the soup kitchen, the crowd at the Salvation Army. But by 1940, things were changing. Portland was creeping out of the Depression as the country began to prepare for war. Within a few years, over two hundred thousand youthful migrants would arrive to take jobs in the war industry there, a demographic event that would boost Ruth's practice enormously in years to come. In 1940, the locals themselves, still disporportionately middle-aged, were feeling the economy warm up. The Commercial Iron Company got the city's first federal contract for shipbuilding that year, and Alcoa opened a reduction plant to produce aluminum ingots in Vancouver, just across the Columbia River from Portland. Every week things looked better, and more growth was expected. In a hopeful climate—even with the clouds of war forming on the horizon—many women who found themselves unexpectedly pregnant were not as beset by fear and desperation as they would have been a few years earlier when money was so scarce. The men were going back to work, and women had not yet become the welders and riveters they would become soon. For the moment, Portland felt almost flush, as if the best of the prosperous 1920s were coming back home. But by 1940 the conditions of home life had changed in one way, at least, that had direct implications for Ruth's business.

In the late 1930s, conjugal life in Portland (and elsewhere) began to feel the influence of Margaret Sanger's national birth control campaign. It had been twenty-four years since the crusader for contraception had come to Portland, and now few people remembered how she had been locked up for distributing birth control literature. Linda Gordon has described the changes of the late 1930s in this way: "Judges, doctors, government administrators, and pharmaceutical houses entering the contraceptive business were all persuaded by an enormous change not only in public opinion but in public demand for birth control." A poll commissioned by the *Ladies' Home Journal* at this time reported that seventy-nine percent of its readers approved of birth control, and over the course of the thirties, the National Committee for Federal Legislation for Birth Control claimed that it had grown from one thousand backers in 1931 to twelve million in 1937. Under this kind of pressure, the American Medical Association at last endorsed "artificial contraception" in the late thirties, and a landmark federal court decision poked holes in the old Comstock Law of 1873 that had defined contraceptive information and materials as obscene. Like many new converts to the birth control cause in the waning years of the Depression, the court expressed its interest in contraception as a "healthy alternative to the national epidemic of illegal abortions" that had been performed during the decade of economic dislocation. It can be argued that these years marked, in fact, the first surge of both mass and elite support for contraception.

This is not to say, of course, that any woman in Portland or anywhere else who wanted to use birth control in the late thirties or early forties could get her hands on the information or materials she sought. Even the women who could afford to pay private physicians in those years had a hard time finding doctors willing to provide them with contraception, yet many did. For the first time, hundreds of married women in Portland, some of them the patients of Dr. Jessie Laird Brodie, a tireless advocate for the cause, now had a choice beyond the old alternatives of an unplanned, problematic pregnancy or a trip to the Broadway Building downtown.

A Portland labor organizer active in the Federation of Woodworkers in the late thirties knew that working women in that city were ready to think about contraception and to do what was necessary to get it for themselves. Julia Ruuttila remembered that during a lockout, the women's auxiliary of the Federation tried to raise money for layettes because, as she put it, "the people that were locked out had no money to buy clothes for babies." But the women rapidly moved beyond that strategy. "We got the idea," she said, "that we should have someone come and speak to our auxiliary meetings on birth control because it was no time to be bringing any more children into the world when we couldn't even feed the ones that we had. I had heard that Dr. Lena Kenin was interested in birth control. So I went to see her and she agreed to come and speak at a meeting on different methods of birth control, something that most of our members knew absolutely nothing about. It was the largest meeting that we ever had. We advertised it in all areas where the workers lived. It was just absolutely jammed.

"Well, she advocated the use of diaphragms to be used with some kind of antiseptic cream; however, they had to be fitted. So she volunteered her services. I think she agreed to fit diaphragms to a large number of women, maybe twenty. But we realized to get all of our people covered and to get those diaphragms bought, we were going to have to get other doctors interested. So we sent a committee up to the medical school. What a fight that was! The head of the medical school was a Catholic. Well, we had a sit down up there. That's right! So they finally agreed to fit the diaphragms. We had a tussle with the welfare to make them buy the diaphragms, but we won that one too."

Julia Ruuttila's report is strong evidence that women in Portland were prepared to fight for alternatives to unhappy pregnancy and abortion at the end of the thirties, and that, to an unprecedented extent, it was possible to succeed. At least to some degree, the diminished traffic in Ruth Barnett's office reflected these events and also the demographic and economic shifts in Portland. On the one hand, by 1938 the birthrate there and elsewhere had bounced back to its pre-Depression level, suggesting that women were feeling a new willingness and ability to augment their families. On the other hand, the new birth control option was affecting the number of abortion clients. The abortion business in 1940 was not what it had been just a few years earlier during the Depression, or what it would soon become under wartime conditions. Moreover, while the number of respectable illegal practitioners in Portland was smaller just before the war than it had been, and despite the retirement of Dr. Van Alstyne and the departure of Dr. Watts, Ruth still had a formidable senior colleague in the Broadway Building with whom she shared the trade.

Ever since Ruth came to work for Dr. Watts in 1929, she'd known Ed Stewart as a fellow practitioner, and she held him in awe. In her opinion, Stewart's reputation was flawless and his office was "the most famous clinic of its kind in the Pacific Northwest, if not anywhere." According to Ruth, Stewart brought distinction to the profession they shared. At the end of her life, she saved some of her highest praise for this man, whom she considered a very classy gentleman. She said, "He came from one of Oregon's pioneer families and for years remained a brilliant surgeon. He was a cultured man without pretensions. A connoisseur of art, he kept his impressive collections of paintings both in his clinic and his home. He spent a great deal of money on worthy causes, including sizable grants he made on an anonymous basis to colleges and medical schools. Like the hero in "Magnificent Obsession," he made these gifts under pledge of absolute secrecy. He was a very generous man."

What Ruth did not reveal about Dr. Stewart then or ever was that, since 1934 at least, Ed Stewart had a close relationship with

Reg Rankin and was more than once in on the entrepreneur's deals as a silent partner. Stewart was not a man whom Rankin could hector or move around like a pawn on a chessboard, as he did the other abortion doctors he collected in the thirties. Stewart was more dignified and more successful than the others, but not too refined, it turned out, to make deals with Rankin. Unlike most of Rankin's associates, Stewart knew how to stay in the background, to keep his name off the contracts Rankin was fond of drawing up, and he usually knew how to stay out of the way when things got hot. Yet the evidence shows that he was deeply involved in 1934 and 1935 in a number of aspects of the syndicate.

Early on, Rankin believed he could count on Stewart to participate in underwriting the capitalization of the Medical Acceptance Corporation, the credit business that Rankin hoped would replace the traditional practice of accepting engagement rings and fraternity pins from desperate women as collateral payment for abortions. In the summer of 1935, Rankin told Paul De Gaston that it was time to start such an operation, and he began to plot his strategy. First, he said, "I am going to call Dr. Stewart to see how much cash he can invest in it, and if I can get five or ten thousand dollars from each doctor, I will have something to start with." Then, De Gaston remembered, Rankin picked up the phone and called Ed Stewart in Portland, and the two men worked out the details.

That same summer and into the fall, Rankin sent De Gaston to Portland to Stewart's office a number of times. According to De Gaston, he was sent there to "show Dr. Stewart our method of abortion, this local anesthetic and also this sucker, how to use that." Of course, by this time Ruth was a master of the method herself and occupied an office in the same building as Stewart. If Stewart merely had wanted to learn the aspiration method devised by his old colleague Watts, it is likely that Ruth would have been honored to teach him. But Stewart was, by this time, in business with Rankin, and Rankin generally insisted on using doctors, even when that meant an unlicensed doctor recently involved in a murder trial, as in the case of De Gaston.

In addition, Rankin and Stewart travelled together several times to Seattle and California in those years, and extended their partnership beyond the abortion business by investing together in a ranch in eastern Oregon. De Gaston had a role in this part of the relationship, as well. He said, "I would have, from time to time, to go to Portland and relieve Dr. Stewart while Mr. Rankin and he were away together on trips."

When Rankin's clinics were raided in 1936, the authorities in California were well aware that the syndicate had offices all the way up the coast in Portland and Seattle. They were well aware of the nature of Dr. Stewart's practice, the location of his office, and his connection to Rankin. Yet they and the Portland police left him alone. At that time and for the next fifteen years, the authorities in Portland cracked down on many kinds of criminal activities, but displayed a willingness to recognize abortion practitioners as "needed necessities," particularly if they appeared content to pursue their specialty quietly and with care.

However Rankin's arrest and imprisonment may have personally affected Ed Stewart, it did not turn the doctor against the entrepreneur, or make him wary of participating in future schemes with the man. In fact, as soon as Rankin was released from jail and engaged in the task of assembling his old cohorts for the purpose of setting up a clinic in Reno, Dr. Stewart was right there with him. The Rankin-Stewart partnership was the key factor in Ruth Barnett's removal from Portland to Reno.

The two men made the calculation that Ruth would be a more valuable asset in Reno, and so they sent her there. Business was off in the Broadway Building, and Rankin was desperate for an abortionist in Nevada. Stewart, holding an investment in both locations, could see that Ruth in Reno would be a solution to both problems.

Rankin had plenty of experience putting the screws on people, getting them to move when he said so, and where. He had reason to question whether he could strong-arm Ruth Barnett, but with Stewart's help, Rankin thought the odds were better than even that she could be moved. Maggie, Ruth's daughter, has a recollection that Ruth and Rankin became lovers that year. She also remembers that when Ruth left for Reno, she sent ahead her beautiful things—the oriental carpets from her office and the settees, oil paintings, and Chinese urns. She meant to stay for some time.

On the 14th of October, 1940, Ruth Barnett and Reg Rankin arrived together in Reno. Along with her finery, Ruth brought her medical instruments and the books of her trade, volumes she'd acquired during her studies for the naturopathy license in the early thirties and that she always kept nearby. One was a tome entitled *Minor Surgery* and another was the third edition of *Preventative Medicine*.

Warren Campbell, a contractor Rankin hired to refurbish the premises, was waiting for the couple in the Lyons Building. As soon as Ruth and Rankin arrived, Campbell pointed out some large boxes stacked in the corner of the suite's front room. The boxes had arrived over the past couple of days from Bishoff's of Oakland, California, a surgical supply company. They held a full set of equipment to outfit the sort of abortion clinic that Dr. Watts had taught Rankin to invest in: a Van Burdick aspirator, some rubber tubing, an irrigator and a pail, some operating tables, cabinets, and a sterilizer, all shipped from Oakland to Reno via the Oregon-Nevada-California Fast Freight Company. As Rankin opened the cartons, Ruth ticked off their contents. She was familiar with every item, not only because the pieces duplicated the contents of her office back home, but also because she herself had purchased this set in Oakland the month before.

Ever since he and Ruth had met with Cushing and St. John at the St. Francis Hotel in San Francisco on August 19th, Rankin had been clear about what he wanted from her. He wanted her to take charge of everything—medical equipment, decor, recruitment, and abortions. There was, however, one gray area. Despite the fact that, by this time, Rankin knew that St. John's licensing situation in Nevada was hopeless, he let Ruth come to Reno under the impression that Valentine St. John was still in the picture. So when she arrived in Reno, she believed that it was only a matter of time before the doctor received his license in that state. Her understanding was that when St. John was properly credentialed in Nevada, he would be nominally in charge of the clinic, and Rankin had assured Ruth that there would be plenty of work for both practitioners. Ruth was used to working under these conditions. And she was satisfied that, under the circumstances, it was in everyone's interest to have a medical man on the scene.

The rest of October was taken up with getting the clinic ready for business. J.C. Perry, Rankin's former brother-in-law, the man who had had a part in running the Medical Assistance Corporation in L.A. back in 1935 and 1936, lived near Reno now, and Rankin gave him the job of taking Ruth around to buy the accoutrements still required to complete the office. By the first of November, Ruth was itchy to open for business. Everything was ready, but still St. John did not have a license. Ruth was not pleased that in this strange city where she knew no one but Rankin, there was no titular doctor to lend his protection to her work. At this point, Ruth complained to Rankin. She threatened to pack up her carpets and go back to Portland if things didn't get moving soon.

Rankin was loathe to lose the only abortionist he had at the time, so the next day, he, his son (a young man in his twenties), and Dr. St. John took a trip to Las Vegas to find a doctor. They were looking for a certain old man who drank too much and didn't have many patients anymore, but had, at one time, worked as a surgeon in the same hospital as St. John in Los Angeles. What made this man, Z.A. D'Amours, worth a trip to Las Vegas was that he possessed a Nevada medical license. St. John promised Rankin that D'Amours was just the man they needed.

When Rankin, his son, and St. John arrived in Las Vegas, they had some trouble at first locating D'Amours. Fortunately for them, before too long they chose the right stranger to ask, an attorney named Fred Alward who was standing in front of the Clark Building downtown. They asked him if he knew old Dr. D'Amours, and indeed, Mr. Alward had known the doctor well for ten years, and knew where his office was. The lawyer told the trio he would arrange a meeting at the Boulder Drugstore that evening. When Alward went to the doctor's office to tell him he had visitors in town, however, he found the old man sleeping off a heavy evening of drinking. So at the appointed time, Alward met the men at the drugstore and told them, as he remembered later, that he "didn't think that the doctor could very well see them that evening, that he was having a little drinking celebration, but that they could see him the next morning when he was sober."

When Dr. D'Amours sobered up, he was glad to meet the visitors in the drugstore. He was fond of Dr. Valentine St. John, and he was in the kind of straits where unexpected callers bearing a business proposition were welcome. As Dr. St. John well knew, Dr. D'Amours was a guileless old man. It never occurred to D'Amours that there was anything untoward about the proposition that his friend from California and the other two gentlemen made him. No one mentioned the word abortion, and as far as D'Amours knew, Dr. St. John was a good man. Sometime later he described their common history with affection: "I was resident surgeon in the French Hospital in Los Angeles. He was a surgeon there, too, a very fine surgeon. I really did appreciate him, especially after he operated so well on my little daughter's foot. Then I really learned to like him. In fact, I never knew anything bad about this man."

The fact was, Dr. D'Amours had been waiting for something good to come along for some time. He was not disposed to scrutinize what the men told him about their intention to open a reputable "medico-surgical clinic" in Reno. St. John was one of many old friends and colleagues D'Amours had written to that fall, hoping one of them could give him a hand. As he put it, "I wrote that I wasn't doing well in Las Vegas, and now St. John came along and said he could get me a collaboration. I told him I had no money to make a change, but Dr. St. John said not to worry, that they would help me if I could go right and be myself."

Rankin and St. John left D'Amours that day with the notion that at last his life had turned the golden corner. They said he should wait and as soon as the clinic was ready, they would send for him. In the meantime, they said, they would leave him provided for. Indeed, before the trip back to Reno, Rankin stopped in at the Boulder Drugstore and made arrangements for the old man. Frank Crookston, the pharmacist in charge, remembered the transaction. "I seen Mr. Rankin on that Monday morning, I think it was. He came in the store and said he was about to leave town, and they wanted to leave some money with me for Dr. D'Amours, and I said, 'Well, allright.' Mr. Rankin told the young gentleman that he was with to write a check for fifty dollars and then he asked me if I would give it to Dr. D'Amours in small payments. He didn't think it would be advisable that he get the whole fifty dollars at one time. I wrote a receipt for the check to the gentleman and that was the last I knew."

That same day, while Rankin and St. John were recruiting old Dr. D'Amours, Ruth Barnett engaged the superintendent of the Lyons Building in Reno to paint "Nevada Clinical Group/ Z.A. D'Amours, M.D." on the door of Room 307, the main entrance to the abortion clinic. She put in the work order that morning because St. John had assured her that the trip to Las Vegas would yield them the "titular head" they needed. He said there was no need to wait. For the next several weeks over in Las Vegas, and then down in Los Angeles, D'Amours waited to hear from his old friend St. John about when he was to come to Reno and take up his new duties.

Rankin and the others came back from Las Vegas on November 3rd and assured Ruth again that everything was set. Consequently, Ruth began to take abortion patients. Since the clinic was new in town and neither she nor Rankin had ties to doctors who could refer patients their way, the traffic was slow. Day by day, however, word was getting around, from matron to matron, from shopgirl to shopgirl, to the prostitutes and to the women in town waiting out their divorces, that an abortion clinic had opened for business.

One woman who heard about the clinic was Claudia MacDonald, a nurse at the Washoe General Hospital in Reno. Claudia was deeply relieved when another nurse at the hospital told her about the office in the Lyons Building. The other nurse said her sister had gotten rid of a pregnancy there just after the first of November, and everything had been fine. The place had been clean and quite professional, she said. Claudia was relieved because on October 5th, the day her period was due, she had not bled.

When her period did not come on the fifth, or then on the sixth or seventh of October, the nurse was thoroughly distressed because, she said later, the facts of her life could not accommodate a pregnancy. To begin with, she was nearly forty, and she had a daughter in high school. Also, she had a second husband, a disabled man who earned almost nothing. All three of them—her daughter, her husband, and herself—depended on Claudia's nursing work to keep a roof over their heads. Claudia put it very simply, "I couldn't afford to have a baby, no way."

On October 10th, Claudia went to see Dr. Henry James Valenta, a physician attached to the general hospital where she worked. She hoped the doctor would be able to tell her some reason why her period hadn't come, a reason other than pregnancy, although she was doubtful. By this time, Claudia had been working as a nurse for seventeen or eighteen years, and she knew full well that usually when a woman missed her period, that's all there was to it, she was pregnant.

The appointment on the tenth, though, did soothe her somewhat. Dr. Valenta was a kind man and he understood her concern.

The way he remembered this visit was that Claudia came into his office near tears, and she had a very bad cold. "I decided," he said, "most likely a physical examination at that time would not determine a pregnancy, being too early. I told her not to worry. Most likely, I told her, due to her bad cold she would be delayed."

Claudia went home repeating the doctor's words in her mind, but she said nothing to her husband or her daughter. For the rest of October, as her cold dried up, and then into November, as she began to feel nauseous, she kept her misery to herself. On November 10th, she went back to Dr. Valenta. This time the doctor did a bi-manual exam. He determined that Claudia was pregnant, eight to ten weeks along.

Dr. Valenta was uneasy as he watched the nurse put her clothes back on and leave his office. He saw that she did not try to hide the fact that she thought the pregnancy was tragic. The doctor had seen that look on the face of many a woman, and he figured that this one, being a nurse, would not shrink from doing what she felt needed to be done. He noted that she hadn't said a word, she hadn't begged him for a name, but the doctor could tell from experience what she would do.

Indeed, Dr. Valenta could read the face of a determined woman. Two days after her pregnancy was confirmed, Claudia went to the Lyons Building on her lunch hour. She said, "I went over there on the twelfth, to try to contact a Dr. St. John, and the elevator girl went to the door and told me it was locked. But she said there was a note tacked up on the door to call Ruth Barnett at the Riverside Hotel for an appointment." Claudia tried to reach Ruth that afternoon from the hospital, but the switchboard operator at the Riverside said she was out for the day. The next day, November 13th, Claudia again took her lunch hour to go to the Lyons Building. The note was still on the door, and again, Claudia called the hotel when she got back to work. This time she left a message. She said that Mrs. Barnett could return her call when she came back, and Claudia gave the operator her extension at the hospital.

The night of the thirteenth was not a restful one for Claudia. Mostly she calculated, over and over, how many weeks pregnant she could be. She spent the night trying to squeeze the weeks down and compress the size of the fetus inside her, to make it smaller and smaller. When she was closest to sleep, she could see it vanish. But when she was most alert, she worried about who the woman was who had left the note on the door, about where the more comforting-sounding Dr. St. John had gone, and about whether this Ruth Barnett at the Riverside Hotel knew when he was coming back. If she were ten weeks along, and Dr. Valenta had said she might be that far, then she did not have much more time to hunt these people down.

On November 14th, Claudia went to work in a daze. She had not been there long when a call for her came in to the nurse's station. Ruth Barnett was on the line. Their brief exchange stayed with Claudia. "I told her I would like to see her. She made an appointment for me to come over to the Lyons Building 307 at quarter after twelve that day. I told her that would be convenient because it was when I took my lunch hour."

Claudia went for the third time to the Lyons Building that day, and Ruth Barnett let her into the clinic. The nurse was still hoping for Dr. St. John, but inside the office there was no suggestion that anyone but the woman was available to help her. At least, Claudia thought, she seemed like a solid sort. To her medically trained senses, the furnishings and equipment looked professional and the scent of the place was fresh. So Claudia relaxed the slightest bit, and as she put it in her professional parlance, she "began to find out the terms under which an operation would be performed."

First she asked how much the operation would cost. Ruth, who had been through this negotiation countless times before, was easy with her client, and straightforward. Claudia remembered, "She told me it would be fifty dollars for two months and seventy-five for three, and seeing I was a nurse, she would do it for fifty dollars. I told her I would have to go out and get the money, and she said she would wait until I returned." The reader must imagine where a nurse with no cash reserves and a dependent family who did not share her secret might find the sum of fifty dollars in the middle of a Friday afternoon. But a determined woman could do such a thing. At 2:00, Claudia came back to the Lyons Building with the fifty dollars in her pocketbook.

Ruth took the money from her, and Claudia watched as the abortionist made a note in a small black book with gold letters spelling out National Date Book on its spine. Then, according to the nurse, "Mrs. Barnett took me into another room and told me she wanted me to undress and put on a gown and lie down for fifteen or twenty minutes. Then she brought me a Nembutal capsule. After I got into the bed there, she brought me a movie magazine to look at, and I did look at it. After about twenty minutes, Mrs. Barnett told me to come into the surgery and get on the table. Then she proceeded to give me the local anesthetic and do the curetting."

So far, Claudia was comfortable with the abortionist because Ruth seemed comfortable with her work. Claudia could tell, because Ruth chatted with her about the abortion business as she completed the procedure. "She said she preferred to give locals so that her patients could be aware, and then we discussed the office, how nicely it was furnished, and she said they had offices like this one in Seattle and Portland and San Francisco, too. At the finish of the operation, Mrs. Barnett said that should I have any trouble at all to come back to her and that she would take care of that with no additional charge."

The remainder of Claudia's stay in Room 307 seemed routine at the time. She climbed down off the operating table and went back to the bed she had occupied before. Now she rested for fifteen minutes or so, with a heating pad on her abdomen. She flipped through the movie magazine some more. Then, as she put it, "I got up and dressed and called a cab and went to work."

After that, things did not seem routine to Claudia again for some time. "On Friday night I couldn't sleep. I was having chills and fever. Saturday I went to work as usual, but I had to go off duty and I laid down there for a time and the supervisor called Dr. Valenta to take me home. I stayed in bed all day Sunday. Sunday night I was sick and I became scared and called Dr. Valenta." On Saturday, Claudia had told the doctor when he drove her home about her trip to the Lyons Building. He had looked at her sadly but had not chastised her, so now she felt it was safe to turn to him again. Besides, she had no choice. She knew that she was very ill.

Dr. Valenta did not hesitate when he heard Caludia's voice on the phone. She sounded weak and scared. He hurried to her home on Wells Street and found that Claudia MacDonald was very sick indeed. "She had a temperature of 104.6, a rapid pulse. She was quite acutely ill. I did an external manual examination on her since I knew what had happened, and found her quite tender over the lower abdomen. I told Mrs. MacDonald she had better come to the hospital. She tried to refuse, saying that the gossip around the hospital would fire her from her position, but I told her it was a case of either going to the hospital or possible death staying home."

The doctor further recalled, "I took her to the hospital and got in touch with Dr. Rodney Wyman, chief of staff at the Washoe General Hospital. It is imperative that to do a curettement on any type of abortion, criminal or accidental or natural, I had to call the chief of staff to okay my procedure." Rodney Wyman sanctioned the curettement. He told Dr. Valenta, "Go ahead, it's the safest thing to clear her out." He also cautioned the doctor to be extremely gentle and to pack Mrs. MacDonald lightly afterwards.

With permission granted, Dr. Valenta began the procedure. He saw to it that Claudia MacDonald was prepped and sedated. Then, as he described it, "I caught the upper portion of the cervix to pull it out. With a sound which passed freely to approximately four to four-and-one-half inches, I tested the distance between the superior pole of the uterus and the terminal part of the cervix. A Hagar dilator dipped in Merthiolate to dilate the cervix—the usual procedure—wasn't necessary in this case because it was quite well dilated already. After that, I proceeded with my curettement."

There was no question in Dr. Valenta's mind that Claudia was suffering from a septic, infected abortion. If he had had doubts before, the condition of the woman's cervix would have been definitive proof. By this time, too, he had the name and location of the abortionist whose services had gotten his patient into this fix.

Claudia MacDonald recovered from the raging infection she'd contracted, though her condition was touch-and-go for awhile. On the face of it, Claudia's ordeal seems to bear out the truth of the popular idea that lay practitioners like Ruth were dangerous back-alley butchers, women who were not doctors but who plied their trade cravenly and inexpertly for money. But the preserved remains of a criminal life are almost always evidence of failure. The underground abortionist could not keep and so did not leave, a record of the thousands of clean procedures she completed. Ruth Barnett, like the scores of illegal practitioners who were her unacknowledged colleagues in those years, was sometimes defined by the rare errors that sent her patients to the hospital.

Nowadays, it is even more tempting to equate a woman like Ruth with the dark ages of coat hanger-wielding charlatans. The equation serves the cause, of course, of legalized abortion, and at the same time demonstrates that a person without a medical degree had no business doing an abortion. Yet, between 1918 when Ruth Barnett began in the abortion business and 1940, twenty-two years and thousands of abortions later, there were no recorded errors. And again after 1940, there were none for many years.

In the 1940s a botched abortion was, in a sense, not so much a problem of the back alley as it was typical of the risk run by all practitioners, legitimate and illegitimate, who performed surgery before the advent of antibiotics. The history of medicine, after all, is littered with cases of post-operative septicemia. Halbert Dunn, an expert on this issue at the time, estimated that the number of deaths in the United States from abortion—illegal and "therapeutic"—in 1940 was between three and four thousand. Some years later, a study of abortion-related deaths in New York City showed that after the year 1940, the annual number of such deaths declined dramatically because of the introduction of antibiotics. For example, in 1931, a hundred and forty women died as the result of abortions; by 1941, the number had declined to forty-eight, and ten years later, to fifteen.

Where the back alley did play a role was in preventing the practitioner from routinely providing an antiseptic environment for abortions. By 1940, hospitals were performing surgery under good antiseptic conditions, but the professional outlaw abortionist, no matter how skilled, did not have the resources to match the typical municipal general hospital. An article in the *Saturday Evening Post* pointed out that "even a competent surgeon [operating outside of a hospital] without sterilizing equipment, oxygen, plasma, nurses or anesthetist can easily lose a patient." It is noteworthy in this regard that Ruth herself was frustrated over her inability to stock her new office in Reno with the all the supplies that she was used to having in Portland. Early in November, she wrote home asking friends to purchase and send her some basic antiseptic preparations that she simply could not get her hands on in Reno.

The fact that Claudia MacDonald landed in the hospital meant that Ruth Barnett would probably be arrested. Indeed, it was not long after Claudia's fever dropped back down to normal that she had law enforcement visitors in her room at Washoe General Hospital. By this time, of course, the nurse's cover had been blown;

her colleagues had informed each other up and down the hospital corridors, as she had known they would, what was the matter with Claudia.

The policemen who visited Claudia on the morning of November 19th at 11:30 also paid a call on Dr. Valenta, and by the time they left the hospital, their investigation was virtually complete. They had the name of the perpetrator and her address, and a posse was formed to bring in the abortionist. It included John Parks, the chief criminal deputy sheriff of Washoe County, a man named Driscoll who was also a deputy sheriff, and Ernest Brown, the district attorney. The men proceeded to the Lyons Building, third floor, arriving there before noon. It was a classic encounter between an illegal abortionist and the law: Ruth tried to hide the evidence, but she didn't have a chance.

John Parks remembered Ruth coming into the reception area of Suite 307 to greet her callers. She was wearing what he called a nurse's smock or apron. He said, "She was dressed in the fashion of a nurse, I would say." Judging from what Ruth said to the gentlemen, this was her intention—to look like a nurse, like somebody's helper, not like the person in charge. Parks recalled the encounter. "We asked Mrs. Barnett who ran the place. She said she was taking care of it for some doctor. We asked her who, and she said Dr. D'Amours. She said that her part was to stay there and mind the place while the other offices were being fixed up. We asked her where Dr. D'Amours was, and she said she didn't know. She said she'd never met the doctor, in fact. So she said at the time. We asked if she'd mind if we looked around the premises. She said no, so we looked into all the different rooms, noticed what was going on, what it looked like." Specifically, they noted the beds and the operating tables fitted with stirrups, the sinks fitted with suction hoses.

Parks went on, "She wanted to know what we were there for and we told her the truth: we were making an investigation of an abortion that had been reported to the law, and she denied everything. They always do. Then we immediately asked her if she would go with us to the hospital so that the young lady in question could confront her. Mrs. Barnett said okay, and she asked if she could be excused for a minute to put on her coat. Well, we excused her, and she locked the door leading to her main office. I gather she locked the rest of the doors, too. It took her considerable time, longer than it would for a person to put on their coat. Then she did go with us to the hospital. In Mrs. MacDonald's room, the young lady took one look at Mrs. Barnett and said, 'That's her.'"

After that, the D.A. took Ruth Barnett down to the police station and booked her while the other men went back to the Lyons Building and conducted a search. They found the abortionist's medical books, a carton labelled "Dr. Valentine St. John, 307 Lyons Building, Reno, Nevada," with the return address "C.A. Bishoff Co., 1618 Franklin St., Oakland, California," and a bill of sale for medical equipment. They found some bottles containing what the deputy sheriff referred to as "poison pills" and some bottles containing hydrochloride, also several prescription pads and Ruth's appointment book in which Claudia MacDonald's name was neatly inscribed. In addition, they found an incriminating letter Ruth had written to her associates in Portland several weeks before but had never mailed.

The letter had been hidden inside a nurse's smock and folded among a stack of freshly laundered linens. It made reference to the many patients Ruth expected to see at the Lyons Building, to "'R' who called last night from Las Vegas," and indicated that "he has finally got stuff moving." It referred to Ruth's daughter Maggie in San Francisco, who was at the time employed as an abortion recruiter based in the office of Dr. Stuck, the Oakland practitioner long associated with Reg Rankin. The letter ended wistfully. "Sure is going to feel funny," Ruth wrote home, "on my birthday and Thanksgiving, to be so far away, but it can't be helped. Hope business there is better."

Most damning, the police found Ruth's surgical bag. It had been tucked under a blanket and a pillow on the very bed where Claudia MacDonald had rested with a movie magazine five days before. The deputy sheriff observed laconically about the bag, "I'd say it was hidden."

At this point, with the case against the abortionist all but sewn up, the sheriff of Washoe County, Mr. Ray Root, got involved. He called a formidable group of five law enforcement officials to the D.A.'s office and brought Ruth Barnett in to face the men and provide them with a confession. Later Root referred to the meeting as "quite a conversation." Ruth admitted everything, and under the prodding of the authorities she went further than that. As Root put it, "She mentioned a lot of individuals who went in this thing with her. Mr. Rankin and Mr. Cushing. She named Dr. St. John. She mentioned Dr. Stewart. She mentioned Dr. Stuck in Oakland. In other words, she involved more or less all of them."

Ruth sat with the district attorney and his colleagues on November 20, 1940, and spilled the beans. It was true, she said, she had performed the abortion on Claudia MacDonald that nearly killed the woman. There was no percentage in trying to deny it now, because they had the goods on her. But privately, Ruth was scared and angry. Rankin and Dr. Stewart had put the screws on her to come to Reno, and when she did, nothing was ready. Rankin had promised a doctor, but there was none. There was barely a clientele, and the clinic was still under construction. Clearly, no one had bothered to make friends with the law. It was obvious that the D.A. was taking a serious attitude toward the MacDonald abortion. She could tell that he was about to see to it that she went to jail.

But Ruth was determined not to go down alone, or at all, if she could manage it. So she named names, and in the end, seven members of Rankin's new Nevada syndicate, including Ruth, were charged with conspiracy to commit what the newspapers in Reno, L.A., and nearly everywhere else mysteriously referred to in those days as "an illegal operation."

Over the next couple of weeks, the defendants were pulled in. Rankin and Cushing had scattered to points in northern California; hapless old Dr. D'Amours, still waiting for the medico-surgical clinic to open, had gone to L.A., where he was apprehended. Dr. Stewart was brought down from Portland. Valentine St. John had simply vanished. Clearly he'd had his fill of abortion trials back in 1936.

When the Reno trial began late in 1940, Ruth sat in the courtroom with her co-defendants, took the stand, and then, in the middle of her testimony, she turned state's evidence. Ernest Brown, the district attorney, made a motion to dismiss all charges against her, and at the end of the trial, only Rankin and his assistant, Paul Cushing, were convicted of conspiracy, largely on the evidence Ruth provided. Dr. Stewart, Dr. D'Amours, and Mr. Perry were exonerated; Dr. St. John was never apprehended.

For Ruth the matter boiled down to this: she had to tell the truth to save herself, even though it meant violating her personal

creed, a creed that demanded silent loyalty to colleagues. To name
the names of the men who had gotten her into this fix was low but
understandable in her book, but to turn state's evidence was a complicated and shameful matter for the abortionist.

After the trial was over, Ruth did not hang around in Reno. As
Maggie put it many years later, "She got back to Oregon as fast as
her little woofies could take her." But it turned out that the trip
back wasn't as easy as all that. Ruth brought her shame home with
her, and for many years, as she wrote and rewrote the story of her
life—which was always constructed as the perfect expression of her
principles—she had to lie about her dealings with Rankin in 1940.
In a reversal of her behavior in Reno, she was ever after compelled
to deny the truth.

Ruth's sense of integrity was built on more than a commitment
to loyalty, although that was always important. Beyond loyalty, in
fact, were a number of other convictions, all of them compromised
by Reno. Ruth's story of her life, the story she wrote and told to her
family and to strangers, and that she carried in her heart, was first
of all about the abortionist as a good, moral, independent woman.
It was even about a woman who grew more moral because of her
work, and as she grew in this direction, she never wavered. Maggie
once observed in this regard, "Let me tell you what influences you
in the abortion business. When you listen to the stories, when you
listen day after day to the stories these women have to tell, and you
become so involved and so sympathetic to their situations, it makes
a person out of you. In a funny, offbeat sort of way, it gives a person
tremendous strength to be able to do something about all that
trouble."

The way Ruth told the story, being an abortionist was *about*
being good and moral, and about figuring out what was right in her
own terms, and on her own. It was about having the personal
resources to be truly independent. It was decidedly not about the
life of a woman moved around at the will of men who used her,
making her do their bidding, employing her.

Ruth once said, "I have heard a number of physicians say that
no one can perform as many abortions as I have done without losing a patient. They talk about the dangers of rupturing or perforat-
ing a womb and the ever-present danger of hemorrhage. These doctors," she went on, "whose knowledge of abortion techniques is

minuscule at best, are talking through their hats. In all the abortions I have done—maybe 40,000—I never lost a single patient." These facts were central, really crucial, to Ruth's identity. It was only okay to be an abortionist if one were crackerjack, up-to-date, virtually infallible. She defined the other sort, the "alcoholic doctor and the untutored butcher," as her opposite. Yet there she was in Reno, botching the works as an untutored butcher might do. *That* was shameful and had to be hidden. *That* had to be written out of her life.

In the story that she wrote of her life, moreover, this paragon of women and of abortion surgeons was protected by forces stronger even than her own integrity and skill. She was protected by the community that needed her and by the police who recognized that her worth outweighed her criminality. But in Reno, no one had come to her defense or recognized her worth. There she was no better than a back-alley woman with no right to her *métier*. They said she was dangerous and dirty and unskilled, and no one in town but her co-defendants knew otherwise. This was a public degradation too hard to live through once, and so Ruth determined she would never live through it again.

Instead, Ruth's version of her life would be filled only with evidence that the abortionist was above all and always a woman of principle. To admit to an old association with a man like Rankin would cast the shadows of opportunism, greed, and criminality across her life, and that was something Ruth would not have. Rankin and the law together had forced her into an arena where those motivations prevailed, but she spent the rest of her life denying that she had ever had anything to do with low motives or scum. In the official life story, any arrest reflected opportunism on the other side. Ruth's arrests in the 1950s and 60s were the work, she said, of "the young, politically ambitious district attorneys who hound the abortionist" when it suits their political needs. A criminal of conscience could argue no less.

More than fifty years later, Maggie, who knew the complexities of her mother's life better than anyone else, remembered the Reno episode with clarity. Nearly eighty when she summoned up the details of those weeks Ruth spent in Nevada, Maggie acknowledged that her mother had not told the truth about what happened there. The lie was one of many examples, Maggie felt, of Ruth's compulsion to sugarcoat her life story, to deny the lowdown, raunchy parts. But the irony is that the version of Reno that Maggie knew was sanitized at its core, just as her mother wished it to be. In Maggie's version, *Ruth's* role in Reno was innocent; only the law was corrupt. Ruth told her daughter the only version of Reno she ever told anyone. It had the narrative elements the abortionist loved, and it was a lie. The fact was, Ruth was determined that not even Maggie should know the worst part of being an abortionist, and that meant no one could know.

This was the version Maggie knew: "Mother went to Reno to open an office for Rankin. She went to Reno and took all her gorgeous oriental carpets. But I don't think she ever had a chance to operate on anyone there. The funny thing was that a girlfriend and I solicited business for their office. I was working out of Dr. Stuck's office in Oakland, and my friend May and I would travel the road between Reno and Oakland and stop at all the druggists' and leave our card for them to send their patients who were in trouble to Stuck or to the place in Reno. I don't know if it worked. But I was in the office when they arrested everybody in the place, and they arrested me, too. It was the first time in my life that I was arrested for soliciting.

"Everything happened so fast, with the roundups, the arrests, the circle being closed. I went to jail. I gave them the name of Cohen [Maggie's father's name], not Barnett. I took my I.D. that said Margaret Barnett, and I was very busy quietly tearing it up and flushing it down the toilet, so I didn't have any identification when they searched my purse. I never said I was her daughter.

"Ruth was in Reno getting arrested at the same time I was getting arrested. Mother just got out of that by the skin of her teeth. She got news of the big bust coming up there in Reno—she made friends with some of the high commissioners or something. They came and told her what was happening with Reg Rankin and the rest of them. They told her that the best thing she could do would be to get her butt out of there, and leave what she had. They said the only way they would let her go back to Portland scot-free was for her to turn over all her oriental carpets and leave all her beautiful things, five or six thousand dollars worth, and that much in cash payoffs, too. They let her back out of it that way. She just scooted back to Portland.

"But she always felt she shouldn't have been there. She had bad vibes on it. The thing was, Rankin was a good talker, and they were flirtatous together. He was just a smart business con man. The whole experience did have an effect on her life to the day she died because any talk, any talk at all of a syndicate made mother gag."

Chapter Six

PORTLAND

As soon as Ruth was released by the authorities in Reno, she rushed back to Portland, to safety. The irony of the situation did not escape her: a few weeks' sojourn and a couple of abortions in the sin capital of the West—where anything and everything could be had for a price, including police protection—had very nearly landed her in jail. Portland, on the other hand, was never in the Sodom and Gomorrah league with Reno, but it had always tolerated the abortionist. At the time Ruth left for Reno in the fall of 1940, she had been plying her trade in various respectable downtown locations for twenty-two years, with no trouble from the law.

Now it was good to be home, and back at work in a town where everyone who counted knew she was a quality practitioner. But the experience in Reno had raised some questions in Ruth's mind about abortion and the law, about why the cops in some towns winked at illegal operations in one season but not in another, while their brethren elsewhere, charged with enforcing substantially the same statutes, kept a different schedule entirely. But as World War II began, just months after the Reno caper collapsed, and Ruth's offices were swamped with unwillingly pregnant defense workers and the girlfriends and wives of men who were shipping out, she did not have a great deal of time to ponder these questions. But the questions that occurred to Ruth in 1940 point to the heart of the law and how it works. They point, as well, at the subjective meaning of "crime" and "criminal." In fact, Ruth's questions are just the place to start to understand what the world was like when abortion was illegal yet commonplace, when the laws ostensibly written to stamp out the practice were rarely but selectively enforced, and when they were enforced, it was more often than not a sensational media event. Ruth's experience in Portland is a far from unique case study of these matters.

Ruth Barnett returned to Portland in early 1941, just as the city was beginning to need her services more urgently than ever. Maggie says that in the early 1940s, "the fat years began to roll. The shipyard workers were swarming to Mama and the war brides and sweethearts. Ruth kept a nurse and a receptionist in each of her two offices in the Broadway Building, Dr. Van Alstyne's old place and Dr. Watts's chambers, both of which were now hers. Portland so openly acknowledged her competency, she just worked two or three hours in each office and carried her instruments wrapped in a towel with her up and down in the elevators. She was a busy woman." During the war years, business was always good. The abortionist was not bothered by politicians or police; nor was she harrassed by individuals like Rankin, seeking to shake her down or control her business.

Even if Ruth had attempted to hide her practice in those years, chances are her efforts would have been to no avail. One law enforcement official in the 1940s explained why. "The abortionist cannot for long keep his business secret from vigilant policemen. The patrolman on the beat or in the radio car will inevitably mark the telltale signs. The abortionist is rarely visited by a man unaccompanied by a woman, and most women come singly or in pairs. They usually leave assisted or showing physical weakness and are commonly borne off in taxicabs whose drivers know the character of the place and wait there for fares. All these are red flags."

The law in Portland did not single Ruth out for special favors, far from it. Many others in the Rose City who made their livings in ways that violated municipal ordinances and state statutes were similarly allowed to flourish. Portland was no sin city, but the slide from Prohibition through depression and wartime sustained the right conditions in the Northwest and across the nation for gamblers, bootleggers, and pimps, as well as abortionists, to make out handsomely. And no one tried to break up their operations.

In the early 1940s, the mind of the typical Portlander was on the war. The common goal was to give your all to the war effort, and have a good time on your day off. In general, the Multnomah County D.A. and the city police supported this wartime way of life. The cops might be quick to break up a barroom brawl or see to it that a troublemaker at one of the shipyards was removed. But they didn't push themselves much further than that. They stayed clear of the gambling syndicates, the after-hours bars, and the whore-houses, except, it was said, for the routine first-of-the-month rounds, when everybody concerned expected the visit and the envelope was waiting. Just after the war, a law enforcement agent described the scope of outlaw activity in Portland in the early forties in this way: "The city during the war years was nearly overrun with a vicious criminal element. Federal investigators became aware of the fact that Portland had become the clearinghouse for dope, bootlegging, whiskey, prostitutes, and other contraband for the entire area from north of California and west of Colorado." The same lawman declared that the activities he cited went on with what he termed "the knowledge and acquiescence of the Portland police," under a system of police protection that cost the vice-mongers sixty thousand dollars a month. The point is, whether these criminal activities were as widespread or as remunerative for both the purveyors and the police as accounts of the time would have it, the locals thought they were both. One scholar of the era noted that Portlanders "strongly believed" that the town was saturated with vice of every kind, and everyone, from the mayor on down, either tolerated the situation or milked it.

After the war was over, vice-mongering, especially gambling and prostitution, continued unabated in town. But by 1946 or '47, the climate had changed somewhat as the country entered an era characterized by what Robert Lacey has recently termed a "nationwide hysteria" about crime that was almost as high-pitched as the hysteria about communists. "Cracking down on crime," or at least appearing to, became the municipal analogue to stamping out foreign agents on American soil, and its moral equivalent. The federal government made cracking down a high priority, too, and lent heroic status to the D.A.'s and the cops in San Francisco, Cincinnati, Wichita, and across the nation who brought in successful indictments. No law enforcement team from coast to coast was untouched by the purge mentality abroad in the land. None wanted to be left out, and the chief of police in Portland was no exception.

In the late forties, Chief Leon Jenkins went to see Portland's mayor, Earl Riley, about his concerns. He told the mayor that he was alarmed about the crime wave that was sweeping the United States and had assumed serious proportions in Portland. According to one account, the police chief told Riley that his apprehension was based on data sent out by FBI director J. Edgar Hoover citing the fact that twenty-two hundred U.S. cities reported a record-breaking number of crimes in 1946. The chief told the mayor that Hoover had urged cities everywhere to "substantially increase their vigilance." Chief Jenkins recommended "dramatic steps" to curb crime in Portland. He wanted to increase the law enforcement budget by ten thousand dollars, put all policemen on twelve-hour shifts, and discontinue all vacations and time off for members of the force.

Mayor Riley was never terribly keen on crime-busting himself, no matter the jeremiads from Hoover; his style was government by cronyism, and that was that. But the times were such that a politician could sidestep the subject only at his own peril. By 1947, the *Oregon Journal* declared that *something* had to be done about local crime, and pointed out that responsibility was broad-based. The paper editorialized, "Reports that Portland is again an 'open town' put a group of public officials on the spot, and particularly the mayor, the district attorney, and the chief of police. But public opinion is also on the spot." Indeed, a number of city fathers took heed. The City Club of Portland launched a vice investigation that year and the Portland Ministerial Association weighed in with an expression of its concerns.

It was the sense of both groups that Portland had a serious vice problem. The city's religious leaders were clear that gambling and police negligence were at the heart of the "scandalous conditions" infecting the city. The ministers pointed out that in 1945, the IRS collected something like a quarter of a million dollars in tax revenues from Portland operators of slot machines and similar devices prohibited by state law and city ordinances, and more in 1946. The ministers went on to complain to the authorities, "If the clerks in the revenue bureau of the government have no difficulty in locating these gaming devices to collect a tax, why should you be unable also to locate them? Or is it to be assumed that the operation and location of these gambling machines are known to the police but they are winking at the crime being committed?" The president of the Portland Ministerial Association, the Unitarian reverend Dick D. Morgan, was frustrated enough by the persistence of sin to raise the threat of employing a popular postwar strategy. "We will name names," he said, unless the mayor shows that he is serious about breaking the gambling rings for good.

The prominent citizens who conducted the City Club's vice investigation suggested that vice was everywhere in town, in two hundred forty-eight locations to be exact, including one place that had sustained fifty-nine repeated, but obviously ineffectual, arrests for gambling and another that had been hit sixty-seven times for prostitution. The City Club investigators were willing, in their thoroughness, to take crime into their own hands. A chronicler of their activities explained how staid burghers fanned out, incognito, in search of the bawdy, the lewd, and the low. "City Club members combed the various nightclubs, after-hours joints, bootlegging operations, and places frequented by prostitutes. They found the crooked operations: high dice tables, crap games, lottery pools, horse booking, and slot machines in full operation. They played the games themselves and made mental notes. The joints were sure-fire rendezvous centers for stickup men, burglars, dope peddlers, whores, pimps, and other underworld characters. Behind peephole doorways there were Chinese gambling and poker parties." The City Club's final report was a fascinating, detailed document that shook Portland. It exhorted politicians and the police to do their jobs. It urged a crackdown.

About the same time that City Club members were snooping around whorehouses and gambling dens and letting the word out that their report would be "tough" and "stinging," Mayor Riley made a concession to reality. He hired August Vollmer, a retired police chief from Berkeley, California, to study the Portland police department and let the mayor know what needed to be done. Vollmer's report was of a piece with the City Club's findings, and it was harsh. He declared that "the responsible police authorities have no established policy and no definite program for the control or suppression of gambling, prostitution, and other forms of vice." The only established program Vollmer could find within the department was one involving extortion for protection. He found that ununiformed officers made regular collections at vice establishments and some patrolmen brought in "additional exactions" on their beats. In exchange, police adhered to the traditional practice of tipping off a joint before it was raided.

Month after month, the citizenry of Portland sustained these body blows to their city's reputation and to their own sense of propriety and safety. There was no doubt left that vice was rife or that it was sustained by the large and frequent payments that gamblers, pimps, and dope dealers made to the police. Many even believed that Mayor Riley was the chief beneficiary. One observer claimed that Riley had a special vault-sized room built in City Hall, right next to his own office, for holding the City Hall percentage of the vice protection payments. Riley, it was said, "got the loaf," others the crumbs. The mayor responded to these and other rumors about his close association with Portland's underworld by using another popular postwar strategy. He simply accused his accusers of being in league with the vice lords and left them to deny it.

Still, throughout the flaps over the City Club and Vollmer reports, Riley managed to retain the support of the principal men of the city, some of whom owned the real estate where gamblers and pimps paid good rents. As long as Portland had a mayor who could play along with the real estate interests and the vice elements, both businesses could proceed as usual.

If business as usual was the order of the day for the mayor and the vice lords and the real estate interests in the years just after the war ended, it was boom time for Dr. Ruth, who now, with the retirement of Ed Stewart, was the sole remaining abortionist in the Broadway Building. The fact is, the years most commonly associated with the postwar baby boom produced an unprecedented number of other pregnancies that could not be counted by the census takers. Already by the mid-1940s, hundreds of thousands of women—married and unmarried—were exhibiting two striking forms of behavior that could be called protofeminist: a willingness to break the law to protect themselves, and a determination to control their own fertility, even in an era when women's role as baby maker was more glorified than ever. As striking as these secret, illegal forms of behavior were, it is at least as striking that neither the ministers of Portland, nor the city fathers, nor the visiting former police chief from Berkeley chose to call public attention to the incredible number of abortions that Ruth Barnett and her colleagues were performing. The men who checked out dope peddlers and who were, if we take their word for it, entirely committed to scoping out the full, dark contours of Portland's underworld, never mentioned, much less explored, the downtown office buildings where the city's most female, and arguably most frequent and lucrative, crime flourished.

The ministers were most upset about the quarter-million-dollar total the IRS was able to collect from dozens of operators of slot machines in Portland in 1945. Yet neither they nor the secular authorities raised the issue of the IRS's interest in Ruth Barnett in those years. All by herself, between 1945 and 1947, the abortionist amassed a tax bill of over 1.1 million dollars, according to the revenue service. Her unpaid tax bill was somewhere in the neighborhood of two hundred thousand dollars for each of the three years; the remainder was for penalties and interest. Bea Cook, the receptionist Ruth had inherited from Maude Van Alstyne, herself owed over four hundred thousand dollars for those three years.

Abortion was every bit as illegal as gambling and prostitution, and yet thousands of women were getting illegal operations every year. It was a crime that produced millions in unreported income for practitioners. But nobody lifted a finger against a competent practitioner like Ruth Barnett. There were no deaths, there were no prosecutions.

Today, when the opposition to abortion is so bitter, so political, and in some quarters, so religiously zealous, it is well to look back only fifty years to a time when abortion was illegal but prevalent. It was a time when most ordinary citizens were not particularly bothered by that fact. Even religious leaders who decried public debauchery in the form of gambling had not a word to say in public against abortionists.

What, then, was the status of abortion in the 1940s? Ruth Barnett's experience in Portland makes a strong case that abortion was not really considered a crime at all, at least not in that time and place. A medical commentator of the era who assessed the way ordinary citizens felt about abortion may have put his finger on the sentiments of Portlanders when he wrote, "Since the number of individuals who make use of abortion is large, since induced abortion is an everyday occurrence, it is not possible that the prohibition of abortion expresses the true opinion of the masses; in this case, we must assume that there is a gulf that separates so-called 'public opinion' and the 'secret' but real convictions of the people."

Indeed, studies conducted in the postwar decades, before the legalization of abortion, claimed that vast numbers of women secretly obtained what they required. Studies showed that as many as two out of every nine pregnancies ended in illegal abortion, and nine out of ten illegal abortions were said to be performed in those days on married women. If these estimates of clandestine behavior bear any relation to the truth, it is possible that nearly every adult in Portland had had an abortion, or knew someone who had, or at least knew someone who had a friend or relation or co-worker who had had one. In this way, abortion indeed became a "daily occurrence."

It became an unfortunate and secret, but commonplace, event in the lives of all sorts of women, rich, poor, and middling, few of whom typically participated in criminal activity. A woman who went down to Ruth's office with her husband or her best friend or her aunt for an abortion was probably most often treated afterwards like a woman who'd had a miscarriage, not like a criminal. The combination of the matter-of-factness of abortion, then, and the cross-sectional character of the abortionist's clientele—my mother, your wife, me, you, and the girl next door—made it difficult to associate abortion with the sleazy scent of vice, no matter how the law read.

It is a fact, too, that the mayor, Chief Jenkins, and the men on his force knew about the frequency of abortion in town, not only as officials charged with upholding the law, but also as private citizens. Ruth frequently raised the fact that she served their wives and sweethearts just as she did other women. A contemporary observer identified the typical relationship between abortionists and law enforcement in this way: "Informal police protection was the quid pro quo for taking care of their women who needed some 'local treatment' on a reduced or no-fee basis." The need for an abortionist could strike any woman, and the men of Portland, from cops to businessmen to doctors and lawyers, were not motivated to get in the way of Ruth Barnett. The leading newspaperman in the city was certain about the scope of Ruth's practice. He said, "I'm sure Barnett gave abortions to political people and to their mistresses and wives."

And besides, Ruth Barnett was a quality practitioner, a fact that made her a public health asset in town. Anyone who bothered to keep track knew that Portland did not have the death rate for botched abortions, or even the incidence of septic abortions, that were said to afflict other cities, even into the forties, when it was not uncommon for a whole ward in the municipal hospital to be given over to victims of self-induced operations or shoddy abortionists. Ruth's record (the error in Reno aside) was a powerful factor in her favor. It was a blessing, too, for the women of Portland, and the men in charge knew it.

What Ruth Barnett could not know in the late 1940s was that things would not stay the same for her in Portland much longer. At the end of the decade, her practice was enormous, and so was her income. She married Earl Bush, a businessman and nightclub owner from Coos Bay, in 1948. They lived the gay life she loved so dearly: parties in her Portland mansion and at their ranch in eastern Oregon. They raised race horses and white-faced Herefords. She still bankrolled Maggie, who by this time was on husband number four or five and never dreamed of a life without Ruth's resources. But the "crime hysteria" in Portland did not abate. It kept pace with the anti-communist fervor and a strong national self-righteousness. It was just a matter of time before Ruth became a target.

She never would have guessed it at the time, but 1948 was a pivotal year in determining Ruth's fate. In that year, the citizens of Portland rose up and threw their mayor out of office. They did so despite the fact that, according to most experts on Portland politics, all the city fathers supported Riley. The big men were not disenchanted with Mayor Riley's alleged cozy relations with the purveyors of vice or with his business-as-usual style. But here they parted company with the vast majority of their neighbors.

In the spring of 1948, Dorothy McCullough Lee, a founding partner with Gladys Everett of the first female law firm in Portland, was drafted by what a *New York Times* reporter called "Portland's women" to run for mayor. The *Times* reported that the city's women presented their reluctant choice "with innumerable petitions and pleas [but] once in the contest, Mrs. Lee put her male adversaries to rout." In Portland, as in many communities across the country, women who had left their domestic roles to contribute to the war effort were making themselves heard politically in the late 1940s.

Mrs. Lee was appealing because she was plainspoken about her mayoral intentions. "I will enforce the law" was her campaign slogan, and it was a promise that resonated with the voters. She was given to utterances that cut through the usual garble of politicians and got straight to the point. For example, she declared on the stump, "The difficulty is that you can't be a little bit illegal, anymore than you can be a little bit dead. You are either law-abid-ing, or you aren't." Some newspaper men in town made fun of Lee, tagging her Do-Good Dottie and then, when she vowed to sweep the Chinese gambling dens out of town, No-Sin Lee. But others cast her as a Carrie Nation radical, a public housekeeper, a woman of superb housecleaning talents. In the end, it appeared that the citizens of Portland did not hold her gender against her, and may even have honored her for it. They expressed their desire to clean up the town by giving Lee seventy percent of the vote and sending Riley to the showers.

The day before Dorothy Lee took office on January 1, 1949, the *Oregon Journal* gave the mayor-elect a guest column in which to remind Portlanders what they voted for. Lee did not mince words. "I have," she wrote, "as one of my major objectives, making Portland free from organized crime and vice as humanly possible. I do not feel that the best method of attaining this objective is by spectacular or sporadic operations but rather through the constant and unremitting efforts of a police department with high standards of efficiency and effectiveness." In other words, Mayor Lee promised to be the reliable sort of housekeeper who practiced tidi-ness day in and day out.

Dorothy Lee began to enforce the law, as promised, as soon as she took office. Within the first week, the headlines began flashing news of police raids on after-hours nightclubs and Chinese gam-bling dens. The *Oregon Journal*, known for its raw, blood-and-guts style of journalism, ran lurid front-page photos of axe-wielding cops hacking and slashing their way into vice venues all over town. Lee had the citizens of Portland behind her and the national press, too. Public opinion was high on the crusading mayor who could act like a lady and clean up a city at the same time. The *Ladies Home Journal* featured Dorothy Lee's crime-busting administration in an article entitled, "When a Woman Runs the Town." The magazine praised her for the anti-vice agenda she championed. Like the men who had catalogued crime in Portland before she took office, Lee referred to her dedication to the cause of eliminating bribes, boot-legging, slot machines, pandering bellhops, punchboards, football pools, horse parlors, brothels, and dice games from the face of Portland. And like her predecessors, the word, "abortion" never crossed her lips. It was not on the agenda, despite the fact that from time to time, crime spotters around the country sent out alarms in the pages of the *Saturday Evening Post* or *Ebony* that warned Americans of the connection between abortion and other vices. One such alert announced that "wide open towns where gambling and prostitution flourish are often abortion centers."

From the beginning of her term, Mayor Lee found it necessary to conduct sensational raids and spectacular operations on a regular basis. She was aware that her constituents got satisfaction out of big, splashy headlines and pictures showing that the law was being enforced. By spring of 1950, however, Portlanders were beginning to wonder if Lee's crime campaign was actually having the desired effect. One analyst reported that "the people felt that the mayor was harassing minor officials while serious gamblers and out of town racketeers went unscathed." Many had come to believe that all the mayor's hoopla about crime-busting had become a circus that was focussing far too much effort and attention on penny-ante crime while leaving the worst offenders alone.

It was true that Do-Good Dottie was having a hard time getting things right. The big businessmen in town had never supported her or her crusade, and she couldn't seem to find a police chief who would work effectively with her. Early on, she had fired Riley's man and hired Charles Pray, the popular retired supervisor of the Oregon State Police. He lasted less than a year, then resigned and complained, "Everyone at the police station seemed to know where gambling was conducted but the chief, and nobody would tell him things that were otherwise common knowledge." Pray was replaced by a police department insider, Donald McNamara, who promised to control the department and work closely with the mayor at the same time.

McNamara and Lee concentrated on prostitution and slot machines and seemed to be making inroads, but their public relations were lousy. Everyone knew the police department was hopelessly fractured into several warring factions. The *Journal* began to denigrate the mayor's cleanup efforts, claiming that the drive against hookers had only affected the most visible prostitutes, the streetwalkers. The brothels and the call girls were as active as ever, according to the paper.

It was common knowledge around town that the gambling joints were rarely padlocked, but even when the police went that far (most often with prior warning), the big operators like Swede Ferguson and James Elkins just opened again in the same location or at a new address. *USA Confidential,* a smutty publication that purported to expose the particular smutty flavor of every major city in the country, made it clear that under the lady mayor, Portland remained a fine place to look for a certain kind of good time. The authors classified Portland as "every kind of dirty town with a spotless record," and explained, "Portland always was rich pickings for smart guys. It's the leading logging port of the world, and lumberjackers, flush with money, are sports, suckers for a broad or a hot deck of cards."

In the summer of 1951, Mayor Lee and her anti-vice allies turned up the volume. As the election of 1952 came closer, her desire for action and for media support intensified. At first she didn't take on new targets, but instead went after the hearts and minds of her constituents with a new fervor. After all, Lee had been elected on an anti-vice platform. That was what the citizens wanted, and what they were going to get.

During the first weeks of July, the City Council discussed, and endlessly refined, a proposed ordinance that would "prohibit the ownership, maintenance, and play of any coin-in-the-slot devices." City Council Commissioner J. E. Bennett, Lee's staunchest ally in the crusade, explicated the nature of the emergency surrounding slot machines in terms that the whole city could understand. Bennett's remarks mesmerized his listeners. They are equally fascinating today because the commissioner made so clear the *stakes* of the anti-vice crusade, and its larger context.

Bennett said, in part, "One of the things, in my mind, that is doing this country more harm and is more dangerous than Joe Stalin, is these underworld characters that would use the provision of the Constitution that guarantees freedom for the purpose of destroying the freedom of all the nation. Poison will kill poison, and freedom will kill freedom! Punchboards are just one of the dangers facing us from the people who would use the provision of freedom in the Constitution to destroy the freedom of the rest of the people." In other words, the purveyors of vice (including the distributors of punchboards, a vehicle for petty gambling) were more corrosive of American democracy than communists. The commissioner justified the mayor's fervor in the most apt terms he knew, and exhorted Portland to stand by the mayor as an act of patriotism on embattled and imperilled terrain.

The very same week that the City Council was debating its response to the punchboard emergency, Ruth Barnett's whole world fell apart. After at least sixty-five years of official avoidance and passive acceptance of abortion activities in Portland, the silence ended with a coordinated investigation of the abortion scene. The *Oregon Journal* dropped its bomb on July 6, 1951, and Ruth Barnett was at ground zero.

On the day the police marked for raiding the Stewart Clinic, Ruth and her husband Earl Bush were up at their ranch in the eastern part of the state for a long holiday weekend, and Maggie called up there to let Ruth know what had happened. Maggie remembers, "I called the ranch, and I said, 'Trouble downtown,' and 'Git to gittin!' I didn't know whether the ranch phone had been tapped and so I said, 'Take the long way and stop where a friend has a nightclub.' She knew I meant go through Washington State and stop at the Evergreen Hotel where Leo Jeroff had a club. The 'git to gittin' was a signal from childhood. If Mama said that to me when I was staying too long somewhere, it meant 'get home now!'"

Years later, Ruth remembered Maggie's call. It came while she and Earl and their guests were out, cowboy-style, "riding the range, hunting strays in the canyons and draws of the sagebrush country." Ruth drove to the tiny hamlet of Riley to return Mag's call from the only phone for miles that wasn't hooked up to a party line. Ruth recalled, "Maggie said, 'There's a warrant out for your arrest,' and she told me about the raiding party of sixteen who stormed into the office like they were players in a big, Hollywood-type production. 'Brave lads in blue,' Maggie said, 'stomping up and down, flashbulbs poppin'.' They even had a hospital alerted, and an ambulance standing by, in case they found a patient on the table."

The news was stunning. Ruth drove back to the ranch in a daze, but her memories of that afternoon remained sharp for the rest of her life. "Earl and our guests were waiting on the patio. I told them what had happened. They were as stunned as I, blankly silent for a moment, then we all began talking at once. 'I've got to get back to Portland,' I said. 'Please, Earl, we're going the long way. I don't care how much extra driving it means—five hundred, even a thousand miles. I'm going to walk into that courthouse and give myself up.

They'd like to catch me at a roadblock, with a lot of fanfare and pictures and newspaper headlines saying I was arrested while trying to get away. I'm not going to be trapped like that. I've never run away from anything and I'm not going to start now.'" Ruth and Earl started out for Portland immediately. Ruth knew the days of tolerating abortion in Portland were over for now. Suddenly, after decades of looking the other way, the authorities had decided to redefine Ruth's practice as a crime and bring her in.

She and Earl drove half the night, taking the long way around. "About one a.m.," Ruth remembered, "we reached Pendleton, the round-up city, where we stopped long enough to buy the late-edition Portland newspapers. Then we continued homeward. I turned on the map light and saw my name in big black headlines for the first time in my life. 'How bad is it?' Earl asked. It was a few moments before I could answer him. 'Worse than I ever imagined,' I said.

"Here was my life's work vilified and smeared. I had long believed that every woman has the right of abortion if she believes it is necessary. How could I believe otherwise after talking to thousands of women—sick, lame, frightened, and hungry—in need of help. I had worked hard to make my establishment a beautiful and friendly place, where every possible safeguard was taken against infection and accident. And where—most important of all—none need fear that today's secret would become tomorrow's idle gossip. I was proud of the clinic and justly so. And now the newspapers made it appear something between a plush-lined house of ill fame and an abattoir catering especially to the young. All my years of work for hapless women had been drowned in a torrent of newspaper sensationalism.

"We were a few blocks from the Columbia River ferry that would take us into the state of Washington when Earl stopped in front of a small all-night cafe. The parking lot was quiet and dark. Through the lighted window I could see the clock on the wall. It was three a.m. We went in, sat down at one end of the horseshoe counter. We were the only customers, but not for long.

"Headlights flashed through the windows as a state police car drove up and parked beside ours. Two officers emerged. One went to the rear of Earl's car, took a slip of paper from his pocket and beamed his flashlight on the license plate as I watched through the window. It seemed an eternity before he shook his head. They were looking for my license number, not Earl's. The officers came into the cafe and sat down at the other end of the counter, opposite us. They looked us over casually. Earl finished his coffee, paid the check and we walked out as slowly and nonchalantly as we could.

"In a few minutes we were on the ferry, heading for the Washington shore. By six a.m. we reached the Evergreen Hotel in Vancouver, Washington. Fourteen hours of high-speed driving was exhausting. Earl took a hot bath and went to sleep. I lay awake, restless and fearful of what the next day would bring.

"Vancouver, Washington, lies just across the Columbia River from Portland. After a few hours rest we drove across the Interstate Bridge and directly to the Multnomah County Jail, stopping only once to telephone my attorney.

"While an officer at the courthouse took my name and address, the room began filling up with people. Although Saturday is usually a quiet day, word of my arrival to turn myself in got around quickly. Reporters and photographers appeared as out of nowhere and were soon buzzing around us. A uniformed officer stopped by the desk and said apologetically, 'Dr. Barnett, I'd rather have been anywhere else in the world than in your office yesterday.' Then the flashbulbs started popping and the reporters began their questions. My attorney said, 'No comment.'"

No comment was issued from another prominent quarter in the city that day, and in the days following Ruth Barnett's arrest: the lady mayor had nothing whatever to say on the subject of the abortion bust. She kept mum despite the fact that the raids carried out on July 6th amounted to the most spectacular operation of her tenure. That week, Mayor Lee continued to preside over a City Council glued to the subject of punchboards. In retrospect, her obsession throughout the month of July with the manly vices of gambling and liquor offenses renders her silence on the subject of what the newspapers were calling the "abortion nests" very curious indeed. A law enforcement operation of the magnitude of the abortion bust must have required the sanction of the mayor's office. But the bust seems to have been made with the understanding that the mayor could keep her distance from this most female of vices. Dorothy Lee could handle gangsters and slot machines and even prostitutes without flinching or mincing words, but the subject of abortion revealed the limits of her mettle. This time she would only enjoy the reflected glory; her law enforcement team had scored, and Portland would be a cleaner town for it.

However squeamish the mayor was, she knew—and the D.A., the police, and certain newspapermen knew—that abortion was a crime whose time had come. All over the country, as women were being exhorted in the postwar years to return to the domestic sphere and focus on raising children, it was inevitable that abortion would come under fire. The news was coming in from southern California, from Cincinnati, from New Jersey, and points south, that long-practicing abortionists, and particularly female practitioners, were being arrested. As for Mayor Lee, her administration needed a boost, a big boost, in order to remind its constituents that effectively eradicating vice was the number-one priority. It is possible that someone clever figured that a summer abortion bust would mean a highly publicized trial the next spring, just what Lee needed to kick off her 1952 reelection campaign, which some of her advisors in the summer of 1951 believed to be on shaky ground.

Whatever arrangements had been made behind the scenes, by the middle of 1951 it was clear that the authorities were ready to go after Portland's abortionists in a big way. It was not, apparently, an altogether easy decision, despite the favorable climate. After all, having abortion on the front pages for days and weeks could have its downside for politicians and law enforcement. Splashy arrests of people like Ruth Barnett, who everyone knew had been operating unmolested for years, would surely underscore the fact that the authorities had neglected abortion for as long as anyone could remember. In addition, the favorable climate notwithstanding, the mayor and her minions were taking the chance that Portlanders receiving the news would simply shrug, expressing the belief that abortion was an essential fact of life that did little to corrupt the city and its officials.

In many cities, the powers that be knew the same thing that Myer Tulkoff, a law professor, knew about the risks of abortion raids and prosecution in the early fifties. Tulkoff argued that "many citizens and public officials look upon criminal abortions with toleration, the citizens because they don't care, and some officials because it is easier for them to convince themselves there is nothing morally reprehensible in accepting bribes or protection from abortionists." And, he added, "it is very difficult to obtain evidence to secure convictions."

Paul Keve, a probation officer in the early fifties who'd made himself an expert in these matters, pointed out at the time that "abortion is an art so much in demand and so well-paid that it attracts practitioners [who are] intelligent and aggressive and skilled at hiding their activities." Plus, he said, "the skillful abortionist who performs his work with care is extremely difficult to catch," because he is "solidly protected by clients who protect him because their own need of protection is just as great."

One engine pushing hard on the politicians and police to make their move in Portland despite the difficulties was a newspaperman named Rolla Crick, a young, crackerjack reporter who specialized in covering the vice busts after World War II. Many years later, Crick remembered that he did not have a personal agenda at the time. It was a simple matter for him: he saw a news story that wasn't being covered. As Crick put it in 1992, "Abortion was an unpopular subject and no one really cared. So they didn't want to waste their time on it. It was a law on the books no one prosecuted and I wanted to know why, and that's the way I went into it."

According to Maggie, Crick's agenda was a little more personal than he let on. "*The Oregonian* and their star reporter, Wallace Turner had been working on busting the gambling and pinball and slot machine rackets that were run by Lonnie Logsdon and coining gold like mad. After several secret grand jury meetings, the D.A., police, and *Oregonian* reporters conducted a mass raid on about a dozen spots simultaneously and scooped the hell out of the *Oregon Journal* and their white-haired boy, Rolla Crick. So nothing would do but dear little Rolla—and I've no doubt he had plenty of help— conceived the idea of a secret indictment and similar raid on all the abortionists' offices."

Whether or not his project was meant to even the score, Crick was a seasoned journalist, and he knew he would need cooperation to build a good story. So he shopped around. The medical community, a natural ally and a possible source of good information, was not enthusiastic about Crick's plan. As he put it, "The medical people and medical examiners at the time, I mean if you looked at the board, they had split opinions on whether or not anything should be done. After all, these were M.D.'s who wouldn't do abortions themselves but it was nice to have somebody to refer a patient to. Not all were that way, but some were. So the board wasn't all that eager for the big crusade."

Crick also went to the Multnomah County D.A., John McCourt, and laid out his idea. At first McCourt expressed only guarded interest. "He wasn't certain what the public mood was. He didn't know what the people would do if he moved against the abortionists." The more the D.A. walked around the idea, however, the more attractive it began to look. As Crick put it, "After a while, McCourt liked the idea of looking and getting lots of publicity because he was running for office again." By this time, the D.A. may also have gotten the okay from Dorothy Lee.

Later, after the raids had taken place and the public appeared to support them, Crick and McCourt vied with each other for the credit, but it appears certain that early on, the newspaperman was the catalyst. Once McCourt signed up, though, he spared Crick nothing. If Crick would do the legwork, he said, and share everything, he'd see to it that the reporter got whatever he needed to do a good job. First, McCourt arranged for Crick to get access to the files of the State Board of Medical Examiners, in which there were a couple of relevant names. As Crick remembered, "We got some names to start with and then I talked to those women and when they became assured that we were not going to parade their names through the press, then they would talk." Crick found early on that not everyone went to Ruth Barnett, although the ones who did gave her very high marks for her work. Other women had had very unpleasant experiences and didn't mind telling what they knew if it would help. "Dr. George Buck, for example, was a brutal man, he really was. Some of Dr. Buck's cases went bad, really bad. The women would talk about how brutal it was. He was medically qualified, but his bedside manner was awful." Buck's patients were willing to talk, as long as they were sure their identities would be protected. "One woman would tell us about other abortion patients, because she had become aware of the abortion business from other patients or some friend of a patient or somebody. Like that, that whole thing spread out."

McCourt also assigned personnel to the newspaperman, in the form of a rookie policewoman who played the part of Crick's girlfriend. Together, the ersatz lovers did the legwork over a period of weeks during the summer of 1951. "We went from place to place," according to Crick, "and gave them a story about her need for an abortion, and gradually we established they were in the abortion business, and by one excuse or the other, we would get out of there and go on." (Maggie always said Crick should be "hung by the balls" for entrapment because of this strategy.)

Crick went methodically about the business of building his case. It took some time, but the effort was paying off. Day by day he was amassing more than enough evidence to support the most spectacular raid Portland had ever seen, as well as a major spread in the newspapers and, it would turn out, Portland's highest journalism award for the year 1951. Two things were clear from the beginning of the investigation, and Rolla Crick took careful note of both. The first was the prominence of Ruth Barnett. As Crick recalled, "I first realized how large the abortion operation was when we zeroed in on Ruth Barnett. She was the largest operator, and to give her credit, she was a very good operator. We soon found out that if you wanted an abortion, the place to go was Barnett's. Lots of doctors were referring patients to her. They didn't want their names used or anything, but that's what they were doing."

The second point that Crick picked up quite early on was the fact that getting an abortion in Portland was not a dangerous affair, even though it was a crime. Years later he said, "I know some of the pro-abortion people would hope that you could prove how dangerous it really was in those days. In Portland, anyway, I couldn't say that it was as life-threatening as they claim." The reporter was aware, even as he pushed for a full-scale investigation and a major crackdown, that women's lives were not put at risk by Portland's abortionists.

On a daily basis, Crick reported back to his editor at the *Oregon Journal* and also to John McCourt, the Multnomah County D.A. He passed on the material that was pointing toward a major exposé. What would become most evident by the first week in July was that both Crick's editor and the D.A. were willing to capitalize on the starring role of Ruth Barnett. But both men would choose to ignore Crick's point that abortion in Portland was not a dangerous proposition.

It was nearly nine years since Ruth Barnett had returned to Portland from Reno to practice her trade in safety, undisturbed by the law. But by 1951, there were no safe havens anymore, as politicians and law enforcement officers undertook the job of persuading Americans in cities across the country that abortion was a serious crime and its practitioners were dangerous criminals.

Chapter Seven

PRIME-TIME CRIME

*P*ortland, Oregon, wasn't the only town in the fifties where a determined newspaperman focussed the minds of local authorities on abortion. It would not be too much to say that in those years, as newspapers flourished and competed heatedly with each other and with the emerging medium of television for customers, a reporter following his nose for news would likely find an abortion exposé to be good for circulation.

Ernie Warden was Rolla Crick's counterpart in Wichita. He worked his beats in the same postwar climate, capitalizing on his ability to fill the prime news holes with "purge" stories of all kinds. In Wichita in the early fifties, federal and local investigators swarmed across the city exposing gambling rings, grain price-gouging rackets, and liquor scandals. Just as in Portland, no one breathed a word about abortion, even though it wasn't much of a secret that Wichita was a major abortion center in the Midwest. But once Ernie Warden determined to expose the abortion trade in the early 1950s, Warden's editor, the D.A., and the police all piggybacked on the reporter's zeal, now that the time was right. Then, day after day, the cops staked out the "abortion mill," peering through windows, taking secret pictures. When the story broke, the *Wichita Beacon* ran screaming headlines across page one, such as the one that declared, "ABORTION RING SMASHED HERE: LOCAL POLICE SWEEP DOWN ON VICE HOME, ELEVEN WOMEN TAKEN IN RAID UPON WICHITA ABORTION MILL." In Wichita, Warden pursued Grace Schauner, the proprietor of the "mill," all the way to jail.

The scenario in Portland was strikingly the same. When police staked out Ruth Barnett's offices in the Broadway Building in preparation for the raid, they were conforming to a tactic that abortion squads used in Wichita and all over the country. The favored strategy was for police to man observation posts for days, even months, and watch girls and women entering and leaving the alleged abortionist's office. The cops behaved, in fact, a lot more like insatiable voyeurs than like crime-busters, sometimes taking moving pictures of the female traffic, sometimes pointing their cameras at windows of what they took to be the surgeries inside. The police in San Diego lingered in a boarding house across the street from an abortionist's office for one hundred and six days, taking moving pictures for hours at a time with a Bell and Howell Model 70 fitted out with a three-inch telephoto lens, and recording license-plate numbers. In Baltimore, between May 1, 1950, and August 11th of that year, police reported scores of different women going in and out of an abortion doctor's office. Police observed and photographed women for weeks getting on and off a yacht where abortions were performed in San Francisco Bay. In 1949, two police inspectors characterized their observation of a building where Alta Anderson, an abortionist, worked as a "vigil." Day after day, abortionists in San Francisco Bay and Baltimore, just like Ruth Barnett in Portland, performed dozens of abortions under covert police scrutiny. Who knows now, so many years later, why the police typically waited so long before they moved in to make arrests. Surely in each of these cases, the police had sufficient evidence to make arrests after a day or two of surveillance. Perhaps they were waiting for a woman to be injured before they moved in, although that was a condition of no state law, and if it was what they were waiting for, they were rarely satisfied. Perhaps they were waiting for the most politically expedient moment to make an arrest, a moment timed to underscore a mayor's or a D.A.'s vigilance. Whatever accounted for these extended stakeouts, it is clear that the abortions proceeded while the cameras rolled.

So it was in Portland during the summer of 1951, until the first week of July, when Crick, along with the man assigned from the D.A.'s office and the rookie policewoman, indicated that they had wrapped up the investigation and suggested it was time for the raid. The team had been thorough. It uncovered seven practitioners in addition to Ruth, and Crick said there were no more. Everyone on the abortion detail knew the raids would be a break with tradition: there had been no death. There wasn't even a lady in the hospital, suffering from high fever and a tender abdomen, ready to talk. Without any experience staking out abortion offices, the D.A. and the chief of police would have to make this one up as they went along, although improvising would not prove difficult. After all, law enforcement officers in Portland had gotten a lot of practice over the last eighteen months in methods of explosive exposure as they carried out Mayor Lee's crackdown program against vice offenders. The application was new, but it was a seasoned force.

At about 11:00 on the morning of July 6th, a total of thirty-one officers of the law split up into raiding parties in preparation for moving in on eight abortionists all over town. Over half of the team was assigned to the Broadway Building. A few minutes after 11:00, a young patrolman appeared on the corner of Broadway and Morrison. He walked idly up and down the block checking parking meters, keeping track of the time. At the appointed moment, while fifteen of his colleagues seized the building's two elevators, he sprinted around to the the back of the building to cover the fire escapes. Inside, the elevator operators were warned to keep their hands on the controls and go straight to the eighth floor.

According to officials on the scene, Edith Weigar, Ruth's receptionist at the time and the wife of a medical colleague at the Stewart Clinic, was interviewing a prospective patient when the police burst in. She shrieked as the cops broke through the door to Suite 801. Mrs. Weigar had to be forcibly restrained, but she continued to scream invectives at the cops and the press who were piling into the office. A detective held her arms to keep her hands off the telephone and away from "a button concealed in her ornate desk," he said later. But she kept on shouting, mostly at a persistent photographer. She yelled again and again, "One more flash and I'll break your camera all to hell."

Rolla Crick was there to document the fruits of his efforts. He noted that the men crowding in were astonished by what they found inside the Stewart Clinic. "Police officers," he wrote, "were completely unprepared for the lavishness they saw in Dr. Barnett's suite of offices." He also noted the police moving "uneasily" down the corridors of the clinic, past a series of curtained cubicles. Behind each curtain, Crick and the others said later, there was a woman in some state of undress. Behind one curtain they could see a young woman struggling desperately "to put her clothes on." Dr.

Weigar was caught in the act, working over a woman prone on a surgery table. Although these women were relatively safe from harm at the hands of abortionists, they were suddenly subjected to harsh treatment from the police and the press. Maggie, who had been nearby, although out of the way of the police, years later described the flavor of the raid. "You'd have thought the martians landed," she said. "Photographers, police cars, sirens screaming all afternoon."

Ruth, who was up at the ranch at the time, could only describe what the raiders left in their wake. "They ransacked the offices without a proper search warrant, yanked drawers out of desks and cabinets and spilled their contents on the floor. They confiscated my unopened mail, a file of paid bills and current bills. They took several hundred dollars in cash that was kept on hand for operating expenses and salaries. One deputy, who must have been a fan of Fu Manchu stories, was certain that the hand-carved Chinese desk contained secret drawers and panels. He wanted to smash it. They scooped up every instrument they could find, no matter what the design or purpose." The raiders' "thirst for melodrama" was insatiable, she said. In time, Circuit Judge Martin Hawkins would call the work the police did that morning at the Stewart Clinic a "promiscuous search of the premises."

All over town that day police broke down the doors of abortionists' offices and exposed the full range of practices to reporters and photographers, and through them, to the city of Portland. It was notable that on this random morning in July, abortions were in progress in at least five different offices. On Southeast Hawthorne Boulevard, Dr. George Buck had two patients "under treatment" when the police burst into his office. The doctor told his visitors that he would be tied up till 2:00, and the cops, who had been instructed not to bother patients, settled down to wait. In the reception area, a man who said he was a Sacramento businessman told police he had just paid Dr. Buck three hundred and fifty dollars. According to a reporter on the scene, the man had come to Portland on the train with a woman "who he said was not his wife."

When the force arrived at Dr. Kenneth Dewey's office, a place of business he shared with his uncle, also an abortionist, they found that the premises were situated under a blue neon sign that flashed the doctors' names. Inside they found a teenage couple cowering in the corner of the waiting room, and a nurse whom one of the photographers captured on film throwing a screwdriver, hard, at the chest of an arresting officer. A deputy D.A. on the scene at Dewey's scampered around trying to maintain order while one of his colleagues whisked the teenagers off for "a good talking to" by John McCourt, the D.A.

At Dr. Ed Brandt's place of work in the Times Building downtown, the police and reporters pushed through a door with a sign on it reading, "Dr. E.V. Brandt Clinic, Chiropractic Physician, Physiological Therapist, Sinus Infection, Colon Therapy, Female Disorders." Despite Brandt's numerous specialties, the raiders found his setup disappointingly shabby. The furnishings consisted of "three old wicker chairs, a gray plush davenport surrounded by an old wicker table piled high with magazines." There were three rooms in the suite, including a "book and paper-cluttered office with an old rolltop desk and two examining rooms with examining tables covered with sheets which were not very clean. A stack of towels had fallen over on the floor of one, and there were boxes, their bottoms dusty and ragged, shoved under both examining tables. All the equipment was old, including a chair with stirrups." One reporter reached for a detail that sharply distinguished this office from the luxury and elegance of Dr. Barnett's when he noted that Brandt's coat and hat hung on a nail in the wall.

Dr. Ross Elliott's office was also in the Times Building, one floor below Dr. Brandt's. The intruders noted immediately that Elliott's setup was several cuts above his neighbor's. They called his place "pleasant," and "clean and well-cared for." In an unusual show of respect, one observer remarked that Elliott was "immaculately dressed all in white." Operations were in progress in this office, too, and the cops were willing to wait until the doctor was through before putting him under arrest. In the meantime, they took the measure of a young man in the waiting room who was "particularly mad" to find himself in the presence of the law while "his pretty, blond wife" was lying on a table in the other room. They also noted the contents of the suite, including a large wall chart that showed the stages of fetal development. Just before noon, as the deputies, a newspaper reporter, and photographer waited for Elliott to finish with his patients, a young woman came through the clinic door "to see about an appointment," she said. She was plump and blond and had curlers in her hair. The young woman sat down on a settee in the waiting room nervously and one of the deputies "casually" asked for her name. At this, Dr. Elliott's would-be client must have realized what she had walked into. As a reporter present put it, "Suddenly her eyes big, her face unhappy, she clutched her purse to her and lit out for the elevator at great speed."

Years later, Ruth Barnett said that the raiding parties on July 6th behaved as if they were straight out of a grade B movie. By all accounts, the grade B movie was, indeed, the governing genre. Cops, reporters, photographers popping flashbulbs, all piling into the doctors' offices, were clearly willing to frighten almost everyone they found inside the clinics, including the clients, technically guilty of no offense. In the style of the day, the crackdown on these abortion clinics that everyone had known about for years was staged as heroic if tawdry theater. And more important, the way newspapermen captured and conveyed the news of the raids was enormously exciting and perfectly simple at once. The point was the moral starkness of it all: the cops were the forces of good, the abortionists evil predators, the clients their prey. It was no more complex than that. At least at first glance.

In fact, the public face of the abortion raids expressed a great deal more about life in an American city after World War II, about law enforcement and authority, about women and their bodies and sexuality, and about the public's appetite for these subjects. In the twenty-four hours after the raids on Friday morning, the two Portland dailies together published fifteen articles and a full thirty photos of the events, beginning with heated, 120-point headlines proclaiming, "MASS ABORTION RACKET RAID SNARES TWELVE," and "CITY, COUNTY COPS STAGE RAIDS ON ABORTION NESTS." The tone was set. The headlines were the first course of a media feast for Portlanders, rapt as the genteel veneer of ordinary life was peeled back to reveal its dangerous, wormy underside.

The headlines, the pictures, and the tenor of the stories on July 7, 1951, and the days that followed reveal that the editors of the *Oregon Journal* and *The Oregonian* shared a sense of what the citizens of Portland would find a shocking revelation in 1951. The editors knew that when the ordinary citizens of Portland picked up their newspapers on the day after the raids, they would find that a tolerated practice had been transformed over night into a crime. Cops and editors took a chance that even if the sudden public transformation of abortion into a prosecuted crime was in part ridiculous, it could be rendered entertainingly. They took a chance that Portland would thrill to the images: the face of the criminal, the valor of the cop, the venue of crime, and the suggestion of its pervasiveness. And they provided fodder for a more full-bodied thrill when the newspapers drenched the whole business in sexual innuendo and titillation. The raids became highly satisfying news because they could so readily be shaped into a story that resonated with the daily concerns of being an American in that era, and for this reason, the news sold papers. The story was stretched across weeks of front pages and appeared again and again throughout the decade, in Portland and across the country.

The abortion raids story was as good as its mix of ambiguities, surprises, and secrets. In Portland, from the start, nothing was absolutely clear about the crackdown except its status as a sensational front-page event. For example, there was the first order of business: casting the perpetrators as criminals. It was not too much to expect that the perpetrators in a crackdown of this magnitude would look like criminals, say the kinds of things that criminals say, and otherwise give the impression of criminal behavior. But in this case, some of the practitioners looked like criminals in their mug shots, others did not. A reader could get confused.

Consequently, the papers did not handle the abortionists in a unified way in their effort to portray the perpetrators. On the one hand there were Dr. Elliott, Dr. Brandt, Dr. Buck, the Drs. Dewey (uncle and nephew), and Dr. Weigar—all but Dr. Buck, who was an M.D., were chiropractors. The papers called them "doctors," letting their readers know, through the use of quotation marks, that these men were impostors or quacks. There were other pointers, as well. Some worked in settings a real doctor would avoid. There were hints that the abortionists were "businessmen," not healers at all. Some looked like old men in the front-page mug shots, and some of the shots made the men look rather like perverts caught in the act. Dr. Weigar, in his picture, looks up, vulnerable and stunned, into the faces of two fedora-hatted deputies from the D.A.'s office. He still wears his rubber gloves, he is that close to his victim's vagina. Dr. Buck looks like a criminal as he tries to escape the news photographer's camera. As a group, the abortionists look like criminals because they are losers: they are abortionists, not proper medical specialists like cardiologists or obstetricians, and they got caught.

On the other hand, there were also hints that the male abortionists were quite ordinary. The young, attractive Dr. Dewey sports a crisp-looking suit and tie and an up-to-date chapeau in his photo, making him virtually indistinguishable in type from a fashion drawing on the paper's front page advertising men's wear from M.&H.H. Sichel, "importer of lightweight suits, borsalino hats and haberdasheries." He looks *normal*. Dr. Brandt looks at the reader out of a long, sagging, middle-aged face almost the same as that of Sid Woodbury, a leading businessman in the news because Governor McKay had just appointed him chairman of the Oregon defense mobilization committee. Brandt looks normal, too. The same abortionist who looks like a pervert in one picture looks like an ordinary professional man—anybody's doctor—in another. So who were these "doctors"? Criminals? Abortionists? Commonplace middle-aged men?

Someone in charge at the *Oregon Journal* must have sensed the potential for confusion about the "doctors" identity. Someone recognized that the readers needed to be certain that, with all the public hoopla over the abortion crackdown, the perpetrators deserved punishment. So the *Journal* went beyond even its own rather loose definition of reportage, and beyond even the scores of photographs it used to illuminate the events of the day, to drive home the message that these men were criminals to the core. The *Journal* provided its readers with the most trenchant sort of commentary in the form of "cartoons," or interpretative line drawings, of the abortionists that incorporated what one could call the full range of anti-abortion iconography of the era. In one drawing, the abortionist is depicted as a prosperous, heavy-lidded dandy. His accoutrements—a boutonniere, a walking stick, a broad silk tie, fedora, cufflinks—mark him as not-a-doctor. He stands erect, gazing shrewdly to his left, against a background of multiple dollar signs overlaid by a scalpel-like tool. The companion cartoon has the abortionist in medical garb. The man looks straight out of the picture, a sinister cast to his eye. Rising from his head is a great, fat, black question mark, like a thought balloon. It puffs out above the "doctor's" head and wraps around the his torso. The question mark is filled with ghostly lines, a woman's face, and graves. In trying to make sense of this unprecedented event in Portland, the artist portrays the male abortionist as alternately a lubricious gent and a death-dealing impostor, a criminal.

If the male practitioners were offered up as a colorless bunch that required invented, graphic interpretations to bring them to life, Ruth Barnett was another story entirely. In fact, she *was* the story; the male abortionists were a mere side dish. No D.A., no cop enjoined to bust an abortion joint could have wished for a target more ideally suited to stimulate public discomfort. Ruth Barnett's style and her practice, together, were a public relations godsend guaranteed to push the citizens of Portland—who presumably couldn't have cared less, yesterday, about abortion as a crime—to reconsider the subject. Ruth gave the story a personality with visual heft and glamour. For the story to fly, she was indispensable.

In some ways, Ruth was an even more complicated package to unwrap than her male colleagues, and her complexities—as a woman, an abortionist, an entrepreneur—seep out of every attempt to capture the woman for Portland's riveted readership. The papers worked their hardest to cast her as an unmistakable criminal, a perfectly recognizable breed of female transgressor, hard-bitten, avaricious, and unwomanly, but at the same time they revealed the ambiguities that leavened her criminality, gave her story depth, and made it a fabulous read.

The most important qualities of Ruth's story as it was shaped for the public was her stunning success and her personal style. They said she ran "the most elaborate abortion parlor" in town, in the Pacific Northwest, maybe anywhere. When the police swooped down on the Stewart Clinic, they found not merely one or two pathetic, cowering women, but at least eight or ten "unclad girls in cubicles," some shrieking, some trying to escape, and staff all over the premises. This was an enterprise of an altogether different magnitude and tone than the others: up-to-date, antiseptic, and luxurious at the same time, an utterly successful concern. There is no question but that the Stewart Clinic, as it appeared in the newspapers, severely challenged the popular back-alley demonology that cast the woman abortionist as an old witch, a harridan who relied on toxic brews or a steel hatpin. Whatever she used, the common wisdom had it that the female abortionist worked over the woman, as one demonologist put in, "in wanton disregard of the health of the victim."

In a touch that heightened the drama and appeal Ruth lent to the crackdown, the premier abortionist managed to be absent at the crucial moment. All the other abortionists were *in situ* when the raids came, but Ruth had special resources in this as in every other regard that it was hard not to admire. The fact is, the accounts of the scene the cops and reporters found at the Stewart Clinic *are* admiring. Ruth's clinic was a fantasy achieved, her post-war American Dream. Medically, financially, aesthetically, personally, it was a triumph, and that came across. Wally Turner, Rolla Crick's counterpart on the morning paper, gushed, "Both the clinic premises downtown and the 'hospital' at the Ramona Motel were lavishly furnished with thick rugs and fancily-carved massive furniture. The clinic has a one-room apartment with a tiny kitchen, furnished in deep pile rugs and expensive draperies and furniture." Turner and the others would have agreed with Maggie that the little girl from Hood River was indeed living high on the hog. Ruth's surgery, pictured on day one in the paper, was spotless and professional, her surgery table notably distinct from the old midwife's kitchen table.

Many decades later, Rolla Crick wondered how the cops and the press would have behaved if Dr. Ed Stewart had still been the proprietor on the eighth floor of the Broadway Building when abortion became a crime in Portland. It was a good question because, along with their admiration for Ruth Barnett, reporters transmitted other messages about the woman abortionist, and those messages were about her sex. As the stories appeared day after day in the aftermath of the raids, Ruth's elegance slid into a vain sensuality, her medical prowess was recast as a perverse willingness to prey on women's bodies. Her lucrative practice became a vehicle for transforming the wages of women's sex into a cash crop. In the transition, Ruth's power became the venal power of the Seductress, the bloody power of the Lady Vampire, the lewd power of the Madam. In this way, the female abortionist lent levels of new meaning to the crime, exactly what was called for to keep the story hot.

It also helped that, to a surprising degree, the "victims" themselves—the unwillingly pregnant girls and women—could be ambiguously rendered for public consumption. In deference to ideas about the sexual shame attached to abortion, and about the victimized status of women who went into the back alley, some of the reports sidestepped evoking the clients in any vivid, flesh-and-blood way. In Dr. Buck's office, for example, the patients on tables remained hidden to cops and reporters who knew they were there but accepted the fact that Dr. Buck stood between their desire to see them and the women's need to be protected. In fact, almost all the male abortionists managed to shield the women under treatment in their offices. Even the "pretty blond wife" on a table at Dr. Elliott's office was a device; none of the observers on the scene actually laid eyes on her. It was as if the simple fact that these abortionists were male was sufficient to give both their business and their clients a veneer of legitimacy.

At the Stewart Clinic, of course, it was another story. Nobody was a "wife." Nobody had a husband or boyfriend along for protection or support. The females at the Stewart Clinic on July 6th were on their own. They were "unclad," shrieking, "waiting in cubicles" like prostitutes, then resisting, escaping, sexual. There was no hint anywhere that these naked, eroticized women were potential mothers. Instead, the coverage hints that although Ruth Barnett's power (even in absentia) was in part predatory, these females were not real victims. Rather, they were offering themselves up as snacks.

One Portland chiropractor suggested in print during the first week of July that he and his colleagues were really upset about the abortion mills and felt their profession had gotten the "blackest eye" when blame should have been assigned to the women involved. The president of the Oregon Chiropractic Association issued a statement the day after the raids claiming the entire association believed that "women who submit to and pay for abortions are equally guilty with the doctors." It was they, he said, whom the law should punish.

In line with this view that associated guilt with the women who sought out abortions, many doctors claimed that any woman who wanted to end a pregnancy was an aggressor against her mate. She was using abortion, according to a psychiatrist, to castrate her husband, "usually emotionally, but occasionally even in actuality."

Knowing that the public was naturally curious about what sort of woman would get herself into a fix like that (and maybe also curious about how far the papers would go in supplying that sort of information), both dailies featured a set of what they called "nurse's notes." *The Oregonian*, the morning paper, was coy: "The exact meaning of the notes is obscure, but it appears they are the nurse's descriptions of patients." The nurse's notes constituted, in fact, a most illuminating typology of an abortionist's clients, and deepened the moral ambiguity surrounding these women. The nurse described visitors to the abortion clinic, one by one:

> Gullible woman has two children by ex-husband. Became pregnant by boyfriend who committed suicide and now she puts her faith in another man who says he'll marry her. Living in trailer park.

> Very dramatic mother of young, husky patient from California. Pleading for her daughter whose boyfriend ran out on her on their wedding day.

> Doped patient 49 years old. Has daughter and son in college.

> Very young patient. Only 14. Self-assured and very outspoken. Cute, hair done on top of head. Who fought and swore.

> Patient with three children whose husband came back periodically for her forgiveness and got her pregnant again. On relief. Would beat her up. Cried all the time.

> Patient thumbing ride to California for money and will thumb her way back.

> Man brings in 14 different girls and thinks nothing of it.

> Stubborn youngster only 14 who wanted her baby and was badly spoiled by parents.

Arguably, the nurse's set of thumbnail sketches taken together created an association between abortion and disorganized lives— women seeking to end pregnancies in this particular clinic were victims of abandonment, violence, the suicide of a lover. But weren't there a great many readers, glued to the news of the raid, who could recognize some aspect of their own ordinary lives in this litany of poor, resourceless women? Weren't there many who read the nurse's notes and knew that their own lives were also touched by irresponsible or violent men, by some version of these desperate situations? Just how many readers pictured the traffic through all those abortion clinics, exposed for the first time to public consideration, and thought, "There but for the grace of God . . ."?

Amidst all the bizarre sensationalism of the raids, no reporter dared to name the most obvious and shocking news of all. No one mentioned that the events of July 6th made the abortion business in Portland *visible*, with all its multiple offices, its multiple practitioners (almost all of whom were doing abortions on a random morning), and its multiple patients from all walks of life.

Now that everyone knew, indubitably, that abortion was occurring all over town, it would be hard to deny the corollary, that ordinary women all over town had secrets, that anybody's wife or daughter might harbor the dangerous secret that she had been unwillingly pregnant and had resisted. The big secret now revealed, though still unstated, was that these women had taken their reproductive lives into their own hands, the law be damned. As one commentator who'd seen those screaming headlines put it at the time, "Criminal abortion has swept over the entire country! It happens all around you, down your street, across from your place of business, and it may even be happening right in the building where you live or work." In other words, it might be happening to your own wife. That message, too, leaked through the headlines in Portland, and gave a ludicrous cast to the whole business because it multiplied the layers of hypocrisy Portlanders had to penetrate in order to reach the moral indignation that the headlines demanded.

If neither the "doctors," the "victims," nor the "crime" itself was quite as it seemed at first glance, neither, finally, were the cops, who in the purge climate of the cold war did not have a straightforward job. Besides fulfilling their traditional "protective" function, law enforcers in the 1950s were called upon to serve functions that were politically profitable, explicitly titillating, and morally bracing all at once. When the police broke through the doors to abortionists' chambers, they were not only enforcing the law, they were also creating an opportunity for heroics and for making political capital.

Yet sometimes the problem was a surfeit of opportunity, and the abortion situation in Portland was apparently one of those times. The cops and the deputies who appeared heroically in the newspapers in early July, staging the raids, looked somewhat different the next day when one of the abortionists told the press a story about cops who had offered to protect him for the sum of ten thousand dollars. The abortionist told the *Journal* that he had gone to the D.A. and to the chief of police with his evidence in hand. At this point, he said, "he was at a loss to know why the detectives are still on the police force." Now the headlines screamed, "ABORTION RAIDS LAID TO SHAKEDOWN TRY," and the moral terrain looked murkier than ever.

The two cops in question recognized the contagious properties of guilt when they promised to "exonerate [themselves] and law enforcement in general." *The Oregonian* had no trouble whatever believing that the cops could have an interest in responding to abortionists on the basis of something other than professionalism and heroism. After all, just a few years earlier, when one of San Francisco's most prominent abortionists, Inez Burns, was arrested, the news got around that this practitioner had regularly paid off the cops to the tune of three hundred thousand dollars a year in exchange for protection. When Burns's clinic was closed down after World War II, it was a sign that arresting an abortionist could win the authorities political capital that was more valuable even than the money they collected for protection.

The Oregonian editorialized in July 1951, that extortion in cases like these was to be expected: "This sort of thing is the logical byproduct of illegal business which is immensely profitable when operated in mass production, as was the far-famed and notorious Stewart Clinic over a period of many years." The editorial concluded on a harsh note that unexpectedly shifted the public's gaze and its opprobrium onto the police. "The practice of abortion on a large scale almost inevitably leads to corruption of law enforcement . . . and perversion of justice and government. There is less excuse for those who fill their pockets with graft from such a racket than there is for the abortionists." Thus the men who shaped the news and packaged it continued to underscore the difficulty of defining the crime, the criminals, and even the victims with certainty.

By the time Ruth Barnett and her husband, Earl Bush, arrived at the sheriff's office on Saturday afternoon, it was not yet clear how the press would cast the proprietor of what everyone had begun calling Portland's "swankiest abortion parlor." The headlines of the *Sunday Journal* trumpeted the news of Ruth's surrender over a portrait of the abortionist, who had a knack under any circumstances for striking marvelous, elegant poses. Now that the authorities finally had their most important suspect in custody—an event for which they could take no credit—they treated her like a glamorous movie star, albeit one touched by a scandal that only served to make her all the more fascinating to the reading public. "The fashionably dressed Dr. Barnett," Rolla Crick wrote (using no quotation marks to sully the honorific), "who had been the object of a police search since 11 a.m. Friday, greeted reporters affably, but refused to discuss the abortion business. She said she wanted to be identified as Ruth Barnett, but that she was 'happily married' three years ago to Earl M. Bush." If she wouldn't talk about abortion, Ruth quite comfortably entertained questions regarding her racehorses ("bragging," said Crick, "that her horses had won six times recently at Portland Meadows"), her cattle ranch, her dude ranch, her breeding farm for racehorses and white-faced Herefords. Allowing Dr. Barnett yet another touch of careless glamour, Crick reported that Ruth did not say where she had been during all the time the police were hunting her. She said she left the Suntex ranch Friday afternoon, but "had some errands to run and shopping to do" before she surrendered. And then Crick conveyed his final take on the essence of the stylish abortionist, that is, on her wry poise and defiance. "At one point," wrote Crick, "while newsmen were photographing her, [Deputy D.A. Charles] Raymond asked, 'Why have you been doing this?' She smiled and said, 'Are you kidding?'"

In an accompanying column, Crick himself acknowledged that many people in town besides Ruth found the dumb earnestness of the authorities a bit incredible, even in the midst of all the high melodrama. The whole investigation has been "highlighted with cloak-and-dagger-type experiences," he wrote, "but many persons contacted wondered why all the fuss about abortionists. Many believe the only crime in the abortion business is getting caught."

The strange thing—and Crick knew this, too—was that as the details piled up about the abortion business, about the abortionists themselves, and about Ruth Barnett in particular, the moral ambiguity gave way to moral condemnation. The ambiguity faded because at its heart, the story of the abortion raids contained elements that resonated deeply with the story of being an American, a Portlander, and a woman in 1951. The fact was, no matter how difficult it may have been for the police, the press, and even the citizenry to define the principals and the crime, the larger narrative was familiar.

One-half of the big story, after all, was the shocking part that revealed the instability and vulnerability of the community. It was the part that told about how yesterday's secure hometown was today under threat from an enemy within. It was an immoral and clandestine enemy. In 1951, Americans knew about the very thin and often broken line between subversion and its twin infiltrator, perversion. These were the insidious strains that flourished in secret cells and "nests" and seeped out aggressively, infectiously, attacking all that was good and strong and true. The underground abortionist, not unlike the Red it turned out, could be anywhere and everywhere, unmarked and apparently normal, like you and me.

It required real heroism to ferret out this criminal, because no ordinary citizen was equipped to recognize the danger. Only the experts—the cops and the press, and the authorities behind them—could expose the hidden places where evil forces did their dirty work. These were the places where the purveyors of perversion undermined community morality and safety in order to satisfy their own gross appetites, particularly their appetite for the alchemy of changing the living wages of sex into cash. The headlines, the mug shots, the photos of plush interiors and dusty surgeries exposed this hidden danger. It was lurid, familiar, and exotic at the same time, and it was good to be able to see what it looked like.

Any American could appreciate this morality tale. But perhaps you had to be a Portlander to appreciate the local angle. Perhaps you had to have lived through the Riley era, when a cop was only good for a wink and a nod, and through the humiliation of the Vollmer Report, which called the police force a sham, and then suffer through the recent ineffectuality of Dottie Do-Good to really appreciate the hometown pride that surged when the cops caught a whole industry red-handed in one morning. There was something very satisfying about splashy front-page evidence that the Portland police department could still perform and, in the process, make the community a safer place to live.

The other half of the big story was, of course, about sex. It was about criminal practitioners who positioned themselves between the legs of prone women to insert god knows what up into those

women, for cash. It was about presumptively lewd women who
wanted sex but not babies. And it was about semi-secret places
where many women at a time took their clothes off in cubicles, in
defiance of femininity and maternity. And the raiders said NO! But
not without making abortion and the naked women visible at last.

That is what the raids accomplished first and foremost. A few
people, Ruth included, eventually did go off for brief jail terms
after the raids, only to get out and start up their businesses again.
A far more important outcome was that abortion was made visible,
and women's sex lives were put on the table, so to speak. Of course
it didn't always look that way at the time. Ruth and her colleagues
were the ones in handcuffs. Their pictures were in the paper. They
were the ones on trial. The letter of the law, together with the jour-
nalistic ethics of the day, protected the faces of the girls and women
in the abortionists' offices on July 6th. But this was a case where the
most arresting function of the spotlight was its ability to draw
attention to the shadows beyond the circle of its glare. After July
6th, an observer did not have to peer too deeply into the darkness
to see that it was thick with female forms.

What the fertile girls and women of Portland must have recognized in the midst of the raids, and certainly afterwards, was that
the terms of their fertility had changed, virtually overnight. It was-
n't only Ruth and Maggie who remembered the halcyon days
between the wars and the constant wartime traffic through the
clinic. Thousands of women in town, who at one time or another
had been unwillingly pregnant, remembered too. In spite of the law,
thousands of women had made the choice to either continue with
a problematic pregnancy or make the trip downtown to the Stewart
Clinic or the Times Building. They had chosen, unimpeded by the
cops or the likes of Rolla Crick, for as long as anyone could remember. And apparently those days were over.

If abortion had been secret but accessible before, in 1951 the
signs were increasingly clear that the authorities were stepping in to
manage what had for so long been women's personal business. And
they were not alone in carving out a public stake in the terrain of
pregnancy. In fact, the spectacular abortion raids in Portland and in
most cities in the country in these years were only the most public
aspect of what had become a whole new set of postwar constraints
on pregnant women.

By the late 1940s, new, oppressively supervisory structures in the fields of medicine, law, and criminal justice had emerged to govern the meaning and the course of the pregnancies of millions of women. The existence of those structures often made the decision to end a pregnancy much more dangerous than it had ever been before. The rise of police raids on abortion offices was only one element in a new cultural, medical, and legal commitment to the proposition that pregnant women must stay pregnant, no matter what. This meant ensuring that the abortion decision would be taken out of the hands of women and placed in the hands of experts.

In medicine, a great many doctors began to take an aggressive position against abortion after several generations of doing fairly large numbers of abortions themselves, looking the other way, or even facilitating, through referrals, countless illegal abortions. It was a fact that before the war, many women found cooperative doctors because the list of approved medical indications for abortion, which kept expanding through the thirties, justified thousands of "therapeutic abortions." And even women who didn't have a medical problem had little trouble finding one of the thousands of illegal practitioners across the country who practiced undisturbed, in the shadow of the law. One way or another, women who wanted to end their pregnancies found a way. But after the war things changed. Many doctors said abortion wasn't necessary any more.

For one thing, the list of illnesses that doctors had defined as incompatible with pregnancy began to shrink year by year with the advent of new therapies and technologies. By the early fifties, influential physicians began to stand up and make the claim that there were almost no medical contraindications to pregnancy left. Even a woman with breast cancer or cardiovascular disease, who could have gotten a routine hospital abortion in the thirties, was told after the war to go home and not worry about the baby.

The doctors' turnabout, however, did not stop the ever larger number of women who had grown accustomed to a certain degree of abortion availability from coming to their offices, begging for abortions or referrals to abortionists. It was a terribly awkward situation all around, and most doctors were simply not willing to break the law, no matter what their private thoughts might be about abortion. But they still had to find a way to deal with all these women in their offices.

Doctors dealt with these women by explaining to them and to each other that pregnancy no longer represented an added burden or an increased strain on a woman, even one with a preexisting illness. In many cases, of course, this rationale had the effect of diminishing the relevance of a pregnant woman's condition *and* her own assessment of it. Doctors implied now that pregnancy was an event that transcended a woman's body and had, in an odd way, ceased to be a medical issue.

In these postwar years, pregnancy became fundamentally a moral issue. As new imaging technology allowed doctors to construct the fetus as a little person, they tended more and more to describe pregnancy *first* as a process of fulfillment and realization for the fetus, and to refer to the pregnant woman's body in terms that suggested a safe reproductive container. Now the pregnant woman, along with her physician, had the moral duty to keep the container fit. One obstetrician explained the suitability of women for this role: "Woman is a uterus surrounded by a supporting mechanism and a directing personality." Completely effaced, the woman-as-uterus simply housed the child.

As doctors adopted these ideas, the number and the rate of therapeutic abortions performed in hospitals plummeted all over the country. But women did not necessarily accede to the new medical definition of pregnancy. They did not stop seeking abortions. Ruth Barnett and her underground colleagues in Portland and elsewhere knew that. And so did hospital-affiliated obstetricians and gynecologists whose dilemma was graver than ever. In some ways, the situation was paradoxical. On the one hand, many people believed that doctors were scientific and humanitarian heroes for subduing the dangers of pregnancy and for developing methods to conquer diseases threatening to pregnancy and the pregnant female. On the other hand, state laws still required that a pregnant woman's life be endangered in order for her to get an abortion. This meant that legal demands could not be squared with medical advances that claimed to have virtually removed the basis for medical judgments recommending abortion. Nor, of course, could legal demands be squared with the determination of many women to get abortions, the law and their doctors' proscriptions notwithstanding.

There is no question that doctors were feeling the squeeze from all sides and from within their own ranks, as well, since any two doctors would be likely to disagree about which woman should be given permission for an abortion under which conditions. Nevertheless, doctors still had a legal responsibility to make the decision. And they were still interested in holding on to their medical authority to do so. So many physicans struggled to find new grounds for making medical decisions about abortions. To a significant extent, psychiatrists helped out in the crisis, providing myriad esoteric ways of selecting who should and who shouldn't be permitted an abortion.

Even with help from psychiatrists, though, physicians felt a need for something more to strengthen their position as abortion decision makers. In the late 1940s and early fifties, they began to assemble themselves into hospital-based abortion committees. These were official groups from which professional, expert diagnoses and decisions regarding individual women could be issued in one voice. The abortion committees gave doctors legal protection and ensured that the "right" ratio of births to abortions was maintained in the hospital. The ratio varied from hospital to hospital, but doctors everywhere believed that a high ratio of births to abortions would protect the reputation of their hospital.

By associating abortion decisions with a scientifically objective group of doctors, and with the probity of the profession, committee members could disassociate themselves personally from widespread concerns that an unreasonable number of abortions—legal and illegal—were being performed. Through the committee, doctors could diminish their individual vulnerability and perhaps their crises of conscience. And they could promote an aura of medical solidarity and legal compliance. For all these reasons, many doctors were satisfied that hospital abortion committees were a good solution.

As might be expected, unhappily pregnant women were not so thrilled with them. Imagine the physically exhausted mother of three little ones, determined to have no more children, being told by her doctor that abortion was unnecessary and immoral. Imagine that the woman was determined enough to persist and make an application to the abortion committee (a humiliating and coercive innovation, from her point of view, that no one had even heard of last year). Dr. Alan Guttmacher, a great champion of these committees, wrote a description at the time of how his committee worked at Mt. Sinai Hospital in New York. "The director of the obstetrical and gynecological service is chairman of the permanent abortion committee. The other members are the chief, or a senior attending, from the departments of medicine, surgery, neuropsychiatry, and pediatrics. The board has a scheduled weekly meeting-hour, and convenes routinely whenever a case is pending. No case is considered unless the staff ob-gyn desiring to carry out the procedure presents affirmative letters from two consultants in the medical field involved. Five copies of each letter must be filed at least forty-eight hours in advance of the meeting. The ob-gyn whose case it is, and one of the two consultants who made the recommendation must make themselves available at the meeting for further information when desired. In addition, if the chairman feels that an expert from some other department would be helpful in arriving at a proper decision, this specialist is requested to attend as a non-voting member. The case is then carefully discussed and if any member of the five on the committee opposes therapeutic interruption, the procedure is disallowed."

Women who went through this ordeal in the fifties and sixties remember their experience with the abortion committee as among the most awful of their lives. Many could not bring themselves to submit to such a process and went off on their own, in search of an abortionist. Many women did submit and were denied, but emerged with their determination undiminished. These women, too, often went into the so-called back alley.

It is a shocking fact that many women who were "successful" with the committee found out, to their horror, that they had been granted permission to have an abortion only if they agreed to be sterilized at the same time. One doctor explained, "A serious effort is made to control the need for dealing with the same problem in the same patient twice." One doctor who objected to this practice drew the most pointed analogy he could to explain why. "For some while now, I have called attention to this irrational policy of insisting that a patient be sterilized at the time of the therapeutic abortion as a guarantee that the patient will not return again pregnant seeking another therapeutic abortion. Such an argument possesses hardly less logic to recommend it than one which advocates amputation of the penis along with routine leutic therapy because, unless this is done, the patient may return with another chancre sore." Another doctor, equally angry at his colleagues for their hostility to women seeking abortions declared, "The fairly common practice of insisting on sterilization if an abortion is permitted may have arisen from dealing with epileptics or feeble-minded women. It carries on as a punishment or a threat—as if the physician is saying: 'All right, if you do not want this baby, you are not capable of having any.'"

Studies conducted at the time showed that sterilization had indeed become a fairly common practice in the early fifties. Over fifty-three percent of teaching hospitals made simultaneous sterilization a condition of approval for abortion, and in all U.S. hospitals, the rate was 40 percent. One doctor, unhappy about the fact that unwillingly pregnant women were being forced to accept sterilization, observed that the practice had the effect of driving women to illegal abortionists to escape the likelihood that dealing with law-abiding physicians would entail the permanent loss of their fertility. He added, "I would like to point out because the package [therapeutic abortion/sterilization] is so frequent, I therefore consider them fortunate to have been illegally rather than therapeutically aborted and thus spared sterilization."

The doctor had a good point. It was, however, a point rarely made at the time, but many of this man's colleagues knew it was true, even as they proceeded, week after week, to gather in their abortion tribunals and warn each other that, as one put it, "the physician must have a high index of suspicion for the patient who tries to pull a fast one." Another doctor spoke for many committee members when he raised the spectre of the "clever, scheming women, simply trying to hoodwink the psychiatrist and obstetrician" when they appealed for permission to abort.

Despite what they could plainly see in their own offices and at the weekly committee meetings about the determination of ordinary women to make their own decisions, doctors bolstered their personal righteousness about intervention by referring to the hefty and growing body of literature affirming that women's role on earth was to have children, and that a woman's healthy sex life was predicated on her desire to have children. Two leading postwar experts in the psychology of women argued that women who insisted on separating sex and procreation, by deciding to abort, for example, were consigned to the hell of "sexual limbo." A day after the raids, a Portland doctor expressed his pleasure at the police action. He believed in stamping out abortion because the operation caused guilt complexes, frigidity, and divorce. Stamp out abortion, he believed, and these neurotic symptoms would die off naturally. Many doctors told each other about women like "Laura," whose case exemplified the problem. After her abortion, Laura "lost her sexual desire and moved to a separate bedroom. So seriously was her marriage affected that Laura was sent to a psychiatrist for treatment. She was on the brink of divorce. And all this was caused by interrupting the most vital biologically sacred function of womanhood—conception." In line with this 1950s orthodoxy, the committee doctors forced a woman who did not want to carry any given pregnancy to term to declare herself insane. That was what the structure demanded.

Doctors also justified their committee work by referring to the force of women's will to have children. They basically accepted the adage that nobody gets pregnant who doesn't want to be. In this way, any and every pregnancy became a choice. It may well have been an unconscious choice (a favorite Freudian explanation in the fifties), but it was a choice nonetheless, despite what the woman herself might think she wanted. (A doctor said at the time, "If we have learned anything in psychiatry, we have learned to respect the unconscious far more than the conscious and we have learned not to take abortion requests at face value.") In a cruel twist on the meaning of choice today, a woman who said she wanted an abortion could be understood to be proposing to violate her own choice to be pregnant.

As they made their way through this nightmare maze of newly conceived psychological and cultural ideas about pregnancy and abortion, many pregnant women declined the opportunity to become supplicants before the abortion panels. They did not accept the new definition of pregnancy that granted primacy to the fetus, nor did they give up the idea that a particular pregnancy could be dangerous or damaging to them. So while abortion boards were sitting in hospitals around the country, hundreds of thousands of women each year did the only thing they could. They sought out abortionists elsewhere.

And this is where the politicians and the police came in from time to time, when the political climate dictated that a raid would pay off. Law enforcement did not typically raise the issue of the meaning of pregnancy or motherhood, or of the sanity of women who sought abortions. But they did raise the public health issue of "dangerous operations." Like the *Oregon Journal*, they raised the spectre of the abortionists' torture-type instruments and the deaths of victimized young women. But Rolla Crick, the newspaperman, knew better than this. He knew that women in Portland were not dying from the operation, despite the fact that hundreds upon hundreds of abortions were being performed there each year. He was aware that reliable experts estimated that at the time of the big bust in Portland, about three deaths occurred for every ten thousand illegal abortions performed in the United States annually, and that number included self-induced operations.

Crick also knew that when things *had* been dangerous—in the thirties, for example, when the abortion rate in Portland was so high during the Depression, and there were no antibiotics—women *had* died: eleven women in 1934, nine women in 1935, fifteen women in 1936. But there had been no sensational raids then. As Crick put it, "The traffic flourished unchecked for many years." The reporter and the other men who broke open Portland's abortion business on July 6, 1951, were not insensible to the fact that the raids came at a time when the women on the tables were relatively safe in medical terms. But the irony was that the raids themselves (both the threat that they could occur at any time and the actual busts) were what put so many women in danger by exposing them, and what kept all women on edge.

But exposure was the name of the game in the fifties, and there were plenty of reasons why exposing abortionists and their clients was a fruitful pursuit. Some of the reasons were not so subtle, such as demonstrating that the D.A. and the cops were doing their job. Nor was it hard to see the raids as a bald statement of the determination of the city government and its agents to stop women from ending their pregnancies. It may have been a little harder for some citizens to read what might be called a municipal pro-natalist policy into the abortion raids, but many women in town knew that's what the situation amounted to. With doctors closing ranks against abortion and the city cracking down on abortionists, every pregnancy meant a baby. There would be no way around it.

Reading a bit below the surface, the raids became a way to clarify what passed as "violation" in the new postwar world, and to clarify who was a "violator." Conversely, it became a way of asserting which authorities and institutions were in charge. For example, transforming abortionists overnight into front-page criminals unmistakably affirmed the authority of doctors and of the law in this area. The law might have languished sadly in the past, but now, the raids suggested, things would be different. Similarly, exposing all those women in the clinics as transgressors made a double-barreled point, first that people shouldn't be going around acting as if sex and babies could be separated from marriage, and second, that women were put on this earth to have babies, first and foremost. Moving against abortion and abortionists in 1951 shored up a lot of traditional notions about women and family that were indeed in need of repair.

Finally, the raids made for good newspaper sales. The Portland newspapers virtually stormed the public with abortion news, day after day. The abortion nests, the plush parlors, and the unclad girls steamed up the front page, and they titillated the readership no end. In some ways, the raids *belonged* to the newspapers because the newspapers packaged them up, dished them out, left them on front stoops all over town, and sold them by the hundreds from corner newsstands. The abortion raids were hot entertainment flavored with news, and Portland bought the product. As Maggie said years later in her own especially clear-sighted way, "We were headliners in those days, and it was an everyday thing. We'd be driving home and find ourselves behind a big *Journal* truck or an *Oregonian* truck, and we might have to stop while the newsboys threw the big bundles of papers out on the curb. There was always a crowd waiting for the paper and those big headlines. Everyone knew Ma was always good for selling the papers."

Chapter Eight

WOMEN ON TRIAL

No one who knew Ruth Barnett in her glory days ever doubted that the abortionist was a clever woman. Yet she had not anticipated the troubles that came to her in 1951. She had not read the handwriting on the wall, perhaps because the decade following the Reno caper was professionally tranquil and remunerative for her. Ruth had become so accustomed to feeling secure in the Broadway Building that when she began to hear about the arrests of her counterparts in other cities after the war, she was likely to cluck over a colleague's misfortunes and, at the same time, feel certain that the excellence of her own practice and connections shielded her absolutely and made her different from less well-situated practitioners. In this, Ruth miscalculated.

Had she been more of a political animal at this time, the abortionist might have paid closer attention to the news that travelled the underground circuit, the stories about old midwives who'd been performing abortions for years, middle-aged chiropractors and nurses and naturopaths like herself who had never botched a case but had nevertheless lately been subjected to the hell of arrests and front-page mug shots, trials, and incarceration. It wasn't only in Portland that the old deal with the cops was off by 1951; all up and down the West Coast and across the country the police were moving in on abortionists who'd never lost a patient. And more often than not, the cops moved against women abortionists on the theory that it was a darn sight easier to score a conviction when the defendant was a presumptively untrained, unskilled, and unprotected female.

Ruth was aware, for example, of the recent troubles of Laura Miner, the San Diego chiropractor Rankin had strong-armed in the thirties. Back then, Miner had been netted in the California raids, but the authorities had given her immunity in exchange for

testimony against Reg Rankin, and afterwards, she had been more
or less allowed to resume her own abortion practice once the furor
died down. For eleven years following Rankin's trial, Laura Miner
pursued her work undisturbed by the law, but in the late 1940s she
was targeted early in the postwar crackdown. Through her contacts
in L.A. and Oakland, Ruth Barnett heard how, in mid-September
1948, Miner and her associates, Josephine Page and Nedra Cordon
(who had been with her since the Rankin days), became suspicious
that their office was being watched and might be wired. The
women were correct. Investigators from the San Diego D.A.'s office
had been observing the office for months, using binoculars and
movie cameras. They had been filing regular tallies of women coming in and out of the place. Later the police revealed, showing films
in court of Miner's clients, that they had recorded fourteen women
on June 9, 1948, twenty-two on June 11th, twenty-one on June
16th, and so on. The D.A. was able to mount a successful case
against Laura Miner and her associates despite the fact that no
client's death or injury was at issue, and no matter that all those
present at Miner's trial could hear for themselves the testimony of
the witnesses for the prosecution—the women who'd sought abortions from Miner—that they had been brutally coerced to testify
against the abortionist and her associates. In the late forties, none
of this mattered, and the three women were sent to jail.

Ruth Barnett's contacts around the country also told her in
these early postwar years about the fate of women like Florence
Stallworth, a fifty-two-year-old black public health nurse who had
trained in the thirties at the Freeman's Hospital in Washington,
D.C. For years, Stallworth held a series of very responsible positions
in hospitals in North and South Carolina, until she allegedly agreed
to perform an abortion on a young black woman who didn't have
enough money to meet the fee of a doctor she'd consulted first.
Doctors and other colleagues, her neighbors and minister, all of
whom had known Florence Stallworth for years, lined up to testify
at her trial. They spoke of her excellent character and her high level
of professional competence. Her medical colleagues took pains to
cast considerable doubt on the charge of abortion. But Florence
Stallworth was convicted anyway and sent to prison, leaving her
near thirty-year career as an effective and respected health-care
provider in shambles.

The fact was, the climate in Portland that sanctioned Ruth Barnett's arrest in 1951 prevailed around the country. In cities everywhere, politicians and police exploited the power of the exposé, the fear of a corrosive enemy within, and the widespread desire to enforce maternity in order to fuel the postwar crackdown on abortionists and on women who persisted in seeking abortions. It seemed that abortion was acceptable, albeit illegal, when people were standing on breadlines or when husbands were being shipped out to man the infantry lines and might never return. But abortion was quite another thing when the United States was glowing triumphant, the land of plenty. Under these conditions, abortions were unnecessary. They were unbecoming and unacceptable.

Looking back across the postwar landscape, one notices a marked elevation in the number of abortion trials in the decades just before *Roe v. Wade*. But a second look reveals that, relative to the vast number of illegal abortions performed in that era (estimates range from two hundred thousand to over one million a year), the number of practitioners prosecuted and the number of women forced to appear as witnesses against their abortionists in court was still tiny. No doubt the fact that women likely to seek abortions (or likely to be exposed in a raid) were from every socioeconomic group, were from every racial group, were pubescent to menopausal meant that, unlike participants in other criminal activities (but rather like some Prohibition era imbibers), they were not always so easily cast as the malefactors one loved to hate. In other words, many D.A.'s and police departments continued to leave abortionists alone out of a distaste for embroiling their otherwise respectable and ordinary female clients in public scandal. Moreover, many men, including powerful ones, continued to have a stake in the termination of many pregnancies and did not want to see all the abortionists run out of town, either before or during the crackdown time.

It was mostly in places like Portland (and Los Angeles, over and over again) that the authorities, needing to bolster their public image, perceived abortion busts and abortion trials as a valid ticket to that end. But what does stand out, alongside the elevated, if still modest, rate of arrests and the sensationalism in which anti-abortion activity was couched, was the special vulnerability of lay female practitioners, no matter that the violations committed by other abortionists, including male doctors, were exactly the same.

Carlson Wade, a chronicler of abortion activities in the postwar era, cited a situation in Iowa to make the same point. Two cases were brought before a court in that state. "In one abortion the defendant was a physician, offering proof that it was necessary. The court agreed with the physician and the case was dropped. In the second abortion case the [female] defendant was not a physician. While the conditions in favor of abortion were almost identical in both cases, the court filed suit against the second person and offered this reason: The defendant was not a member of the medical profession and has no right to practice medicine and no presumption is indulged under such circumstances that the act was performed in good faith and for a legitimate purpose.'" Wade remarked, "From the above it is clear that in many prosecutions, the court is primarily interested in *who* performed the operation, rather than *why* it was done."

Ruth Barnett's experiences in 1951 and throughout the decade of the fifties were exemplary in this regard. The manner of her arrest and the way she was portrayed by the press set her apart from the other—male—practitioners arrested with her in Portland. Her trial, and the trials of other female abortionists elsewhere, would be heavily spiced with the sexual flavor of gender, as well. In fact, gender differences continued through every phase of the punitive process. After the 1951 raids in Portland Ruth Barnett was the first of the abortionists to be imprisoned, and many of the men never served time at all. Dr. Harmey Dewey, for one, the elder of the two Dewey chiropractors raided on July 6, 1951, was acquitted of the abortion charge on December 7, 1951. His case, in which a woman client was brought to court to testify about the injuries she sustained at Dewey's hands demonstrates one crucial way, in particular, that the trials of male abortionists were distinguished from those of women like Ruth.

In Dewey's trial, a pathologist from the University of Oregon Medical School, Warren Hunter, appeared for the prosecution and testified that the woman in question (who was, by the way, named in the newspapers) had sustained injuries to her uterus that were, as he put it, "too severe for her to have done them herself." Despite this expert opinion, Dr. Dewey was able to convince the jury that the woman had, indeed, aborted herself. His success was apparently related to the fact that he was able to produce two colleagues, Dr. James Silvas and Dr. Thomas Burke, to corroborate his claim. The woman with the torn uterus also testified. She said that Dr. Dewey had done the job and that she had never even laid eyes on Silvas or Burke so they couldn't possibly know the facts of her case. But the jury did not buy her account. They believed the trio of practicing doctors. (Several years later, Dr. Silvas committed suicide after multiple charges of performing illegal abortions had been leveled against him.)

Things never went so well for Ruth Barnett in the courtroom as they had for Dr. Dewey, not in her first trial in the spring of 1952, nor in subsequent trials that stretched across the 1950s and deep into the 1960s. The fact was, the courtroom was no better place for an accused woman to be than the front page of the morning paper. The front page carried prosecutorial weight and conviction, although these thrusts were occasionally and temporarily muddied by the ambiguities necessarily embedded in an abortion bust. In the courtroom, on the other hand, the narratives were starkly unambiguous. The story that the prosecutor typically told about a female practitioner's greed and lack of skill and perversity was so unambiguous that the woman abortionist rarely fought her way out from under them. Ruth never did.

Ruth Barnett's abortion trials reveal the courtroom pattern that emerged and held steady whenever and wherever these women were on trial. The elements of the pattern were bold and fixed, and produced an effect that was both ordinary and bizarre. To begin with, the abortion cases became first-rate occasions for men—doctors, lawyers, judges, police, jury members—to gather together in a public place and affirm their right to govern women's bodies, to define women's rights, and to enforce women's vulnerability. Second, Ruth's trials (and the trials of more than fifty other women abortionists whose ordeals were matched against hers) were dramas that titillatingly pitted one woman against another—the alleged abortionist against her putative client—and milked the encounter. Finally, and not surprisingly given the first two governing elements, the whole event was drenched in sex. Wherever it occurred, the trial emerged day by day and in sum as a species of pornography, a cryptoporno show in which, *in the name of the law and public morality, men invoked women's naked bodies, their sex, and their vulnerability in a style that was both contemptuous and erotic.* It is shocking to put it this way, but there is really no other way to describe what happened when men dragged women into court to account for abortion.

Ruth Barnett's first trial, in the spring of 1952, was a fitting sequel to the lubricious extravaganza the press had dished out ten months before. In the courtroom, as was typical in these cases, the lawyers on both sides argued their cases by discrediting a female as being, paradoxically, both sexualized and not a woman. Throwing delicacy and gallantry to the winds, they relied on the principle that a female who could be sexually humiliated in public was, by definition, a useful tool, a slut, a criminal, or maybe all three.

Charles Raymond, the assistant district attorney assigned to prosecute Barnett in 1952, built his case on the back of a teenage girl, "Ann Kelly," who had been brutally raped by her cousin and brought by her distraught parents to the Stewart Clinic for an abortion in the winter of 1950. According to Ruth, the law heard about this young girl's ordeal as a result of her parents' attempt to get the rapist to help pay for the abortion.

"The cost of the operation had bitten deeply into the family's small savings," she said. It seemed only reasonable to them, therefore, that the cousin responsible should pay at least a part. They wrote to him. But when their letters brought no reply, they decided on another tack. Safe in another state, he might ignore their pleas, but they thought he would listen to the law. The Kellys went to see the district attorney of their downstate county, explaining they sought no publicity, did not want the cousin jailed but just frightened enough to pay his share. Would the D.A. write a letter using big, official words, they wanted to know? Would he throw a scare into the rapist? Enough of a scare so the offender would rush to the post office with a money order to cover the expenses of Ann's operation?

"The reaction to the Kellys' request was not exactly what they anticipated. Indeed, the D.A. was interested. But his office was not a collection agency. The Kellys would have to find another means of obtaining redress. Greater issues were at stake here. The D.A. was not speaking of rape, brutal and criminal though it had been. That apparently did not concern him. No prosecution against the cousin was planned, either then or later. But the operation—abortion—was against the law. He told the Kellys [erroneously, in fact] they would be compounding a felony if they refused to divulge the details. Confused, frightened by threats of arrest and prison, the Kellys talked freely."

What the Kellys said to the D.A. became the basis for the case against Ruth, and the ammunition Raymond carried into the courtroom, where Ann Kelly was put on the stand and made to describe, again and again in open court, the rape, the subsequent infection, the gynecological examinations ("Describe for us, Ann, how you were positioned on the doctor's table? Were your legs raised and your knees spread wide apart?), the abortion. When the prosecution was finished portraying Ann Kelly as a pathetic victim of Ruth's vicious abortion mill, Ruth's lawyer stood up and characterized the girl (to Ruth's horror) in the terms any defense lawyer on an abortion case might use in those days. Offering the jury a chance to see that the Kelly girl and not Ruth was the tainted female, he suggested the girl was "a fallen woman past redemption who should be exposed." The jurors and the newspapermen and the ordinary citizens who filled the courtroom gazed at the prim, frail girl on the stand whose legs had been spread apart now so many times over in their minds' eye, and they knew they had to settle on the essential identity of Ann Kelly. The identities they were to choose between were only two: the prosecutor's version or the defense attorney's. The way it worked, after the rape, Ann Kelly's dignity died first in the hands of a D.A., and then again on the courthouse steps. As for Ruth, ever since the headlines of the previous July, her claim to public dignity was fatally compromised as well.

A great many of the details of Ruth Barnett's 1952 trial have not been preserved, because although the abortionist initially appealed her conviction, she later withdrew the appeal as part of a plea bargain. As a result, no transcript of these proceedings has survived. What does remain, however, makes it clear that the Portland trial was in every way representative of other, similar proceedings of the time, and a great many transcripts of these trials have been preserved. In St. Louis, Los Angeles, Sacramento, Trenton, all over the country, such trials demonstrated a nationwide willingness to pump up the courtroom with the gaseous vapors of cryptoporno when women were on trial.

The available transcripts allow us to walk in and out of court-rooms in the 1950s and observe women abortionists on trial. What was common to all these courtrooms was an atmosphere dense with sex and smut, and with notions about women that could have stimulated misogyny in even the most generous-minded observer.

Before entering the halls of justice, it's important to understand the broad social consensus that encouraged men to speak so loud-ly and with such confidence there. The fact was, when politicians and police and journalists mounted a raid on an abortionist's chambers, they needed to arm themselves with more than the pres-sures of political exigency (and the often elusive search warrant). They needed a cultural sanction in the form of experts' ideas about women practitioners and their patients that unequivocally defined those females as fodder for the restraining hand of authority. Without the cultural assumptions that supported their presence in the courtroom, stained the lawyers' language, and shaped the entire proceedings, the trials might have played out differently indeed.

In the postwar years, the medical experts were never at a loss to describe the character of such "types" as Ruth, a naturopath and an abortionist (almost always referred to as "midwives," no matter the particulars), or their right to ply their trade, and none of what they had to say was good. The assessments followed a different trajecto-ry from the smear job that, for example, *The Oregonian* indulged in, but fit together with it nicely. Central to the assessment was the issue of "midwifery," a tag that had, in the relatively recent past, usually conferred a legitimate distinction on a woman who looked after the gynecological and obstetric needs of other women. But by the middle of the twentieth century, in every region of the country, that distinction had shriveled and died as doctors cornered the market on providing these services. Now midwives were all but fully degraded as members of a moribund profession, and their lingering association with abortion proved it. Fueled by a combination of popular prejudice and medical dicta, all women abortionists, whether they were naturopaths, public health nurses, or chiroprac-tors, were cast as a species of midwife and thus, by definition, as out-of-date charlatans and even sadists.

Doctors regularly complained at mid-century that midwife-abortionists were dirty and unskilled. They charged that if a midwife could show any credential at all, it was a contemptible *female* credential, no more than that. Obstetricians, psychiatrists, and other male experts made it fashionable and evocative to describe a midwife-abortionist as being tied to ancient, antiquated, even animistic traditions. One commentator described a woman typical of practitioners at mid-century. He said that Rachel was "a wrinkled, tottering Negro woman who was just a few months short of her ninetieth birthday. Rachel had lived in Fairfax County for more years than she knew. Her mother, once a slave, had been a midwife. Rachel had learned the art from her mother and had worked as a midwife all of her active life. By the time she had grown too old to keep up the work, she found that there was no longer much demand for midwives anyway except for an occasional request for her services as an abortionist. Rachel lived in a smoke-blackened grimy log cabin back in the woods . . . a surprisingly primitive little voodoo refuge."

It also became fashionable to cast midwife-abortionists as know-it-all harridans, isolated in crazy covens. A novel about the abortion scene in New York after the war includes a characteristic treatment of the woman abortionist as witch. "The only ones you could go to were the clannish group of midwives who earned extra money for their families by doing abortions. The midwives sometimes met to discuss their methods, babbling their systems to each other like witchdoctors in passionate search of the miracle solution. Over coffee or tea, they speculated about tissue-tearing mixtures or how to shape kitchen utensils so there was only a little pain."

Probably most fresh and convincing to a public steeped in the misogynistic psychiatry of the era, midwife-abortionists were described as emotionally distorted females. A court psychiatrist described one such woman as "without psychosis but an unethical type with a strong need to be punishing, domineering, and even sadistic toward members of her own sex. She feels inadequate as a woman and has some masculine traits both psychological and physical. Her most compulsive need to amass cash causes her to deprecate her very real financial holdings and she has an irrational fear of poverty which is deeply rooted on a neurotic basis." The psychiatrist determined that this unfortunate specimen was virtually a sideshow freak, as well. Drawing on the report of the extensive physical examination this woman underwent upon entering prison, he implied that her emotional distortions were mirrored by her repulsive physical anomalies: "There is an unusually large clitoris present which extends beyond the prepuce and the labia. The mammae are seen to be flat with undersized involuted nipples. Hirsutic growth is remarkable and somewhat masculine in distribution."

All this almost fully explained the woman's profession, but required one further observation to be complete. This was that women abortionists, as a class, were "reacting in large part, to an unconscious need to reject children or to deny them to others of their sex by reason of certain emotional deprivations in their own background."

Here was the unkindest cut of all: women abortionists were not women, not mothers, and were compelled by their own disabilities to destroy other women's potential as women and mothers. Psychiatrists had license to cast these aspersions as part of their general appraisal of "independent" women. Other doctors, the media, lawyers, and judges could pick up on the diagnoses, trade them back and forth, until, woven through the culture, they perforce became true. When Ruth Barnett sat in the courtroom with only her native aplomb and her furs to protect her, she was the personification of this freakish type, and a spectacle. People stared, and they were altogether prepared to believe the worst.

Defense attorneys had these pejorative images and the ugly stares to overcome when they tried to drum up respect, or at least some sort of sympathy, for their clients. But in the process of trying, they never failed to position their ace in the hole front and center. Inevitably, that ace was the cluster of associations with which the same group of experts who defined midwife-abortionists in those days defined girls and women who sought abortions. When the defense attorney shifted the jury's judgmental eye onto the witness for the prosecution, he was making an effort to convince them that it was she who was perverse, not his client.

In almost every way these females, too, were discredited before they stepped into the courthouse, mainly because so many physicians, psychiatrists, and other cultural arbiters regularly declared in the media and elsewhere that the only real woman was a happily pregnant, married woman or a mom. The experts expanded the picture by explaining that a woman who couldn't get pregnant was prevented by her own neuroses, and that any woman unhappily pregnant was likewise neurotic. It became self-evident, they said, that any woman who wanted, and especially any woman who obtained, an abortion was sick. Using colorful tropes, the experts insisted on these diagnoses. Alfred Kinsey, for one, reminded his colleagues, in the midst of a discussion about the neuroses of women who sought abortions, that during their medical training, all doctors encountered the old saw, "menstruation represents the red tears of a frustrated uterus."

Another doctor provided grist for a defense lawyer trying to undermine the credibility of his client's accuser when he identified a syndrome he called "willful exposure to unwanted pregnancy," or WEUP. The physician claimed that this condition was particularly common in women "who are immature, psychoneurotic, or under emotional stress." A prominent woman psychoanalyst went several steps further in cataloguing the disorders an abortion-seeking woman suffered. The psychoanalyst, Mary Romm, claimed in a 1954 volume on therapeutic abortion that "the very fact that a woman cannot tolerate a pregnancy is an indication that the pre-pregnant personality of this woman was immature and in that sense can be labeled as psychopathological. The problem centers around unresolved oedipal situations. Exaggerated narcissism is present in all cases. Since pregnancy and childbirth are the overt proofs of femininity, the exaggerated castrative factors become overwhelming and threatening. Identification with the mother is predominant and hostile. Receptivity in the feminine sexual role appears as debasing. Competition with the male is at all times at a high pitch. This, in turn, is an interfering factor with tender feelings toward their husbands. These maladjusted women cannot identify with the accomplishments of their husbands; they cannot enjoy the success of their mates. Envy and jealousy of men are rampant. Pregnancy as a challenge of femininity is unacceptable to them."

Doctors made overwhelming, devastating charges like these against unwillingly pregnant women over and over in these years, when abortion cases were more likely to be found in court than they had been. It is likely that, at the time, the doctors who crafted such theories were pleased to see their work popularized and used, if sometimes obliquely, at trial.

Sometimes the "diagnoses" showed doctors to be very angry at what they considered the childish willfulness of such women. An obstetrician in the early fifties, whose patient begged him and a psychiatrist to support her request to a hospital abortion committee, described the woman later to a colleague as "a spoiled brat badly in need of a spanking." He said he could see no reason why anyone should listen to her complaints. The psychiatrist agreed completely, saying the girl was "merely trying to put on a show, and would carry the child to term if no attention were paid to her."

Like the doctor who defined the WEUP syndrome, physicians in the fifties often took the position that an unwanted pregnancy was a woman's fault, or at least her doing (as in, "she got herself pregnant"). Dr. Iago Galdston believed that if a woman claimed later to regret the pregnancy, she had best first examine the manipulative impulses she'd indulged to get herself that way. As far as he was concerned, women too often were simply victims of their own stupidity. "Not uncommonly," he said, "a young lady who has been going around with a young man in her judgment all too long, might think that, if she becomes pregnant, it would hasten the marriage." Alternately, he pointed out, "a woman who is utterly frustrated in her relationship with a man may try to compensate for her frustrations by becoming pregnant, only to find that the unsatisfactory relationship is aggravated rather than made tolerable by the pregnancy."

Of course, not every lawyer or judge or juryman involved in abortion cases had encountered Dr. Galdston words or the other medical and psychiatric profiles common in that era of "abortion midwives" and "aborted women." But most had encountered popularized versions in magazines of all types, in novels, or in the dark, merely hinted-at corners of fifties movies. By the time larger numbers of women found themselves in court, forced to tell about their experiences in the dangerous arena of criminal abortion, just about everyone knew what they were supposed to think about these sorts of females. A woman like Ruth in the defendant's seat, or a girl like Ann Kelly in the witness stand, triggered some or all of these associations in the minds of those who entered the courtroom to size them up. And the assessments attached to these women *a priori* imparted a skepticism that rendered the promise of presumptive innocence absurd.

As the women abortionists and their clients filed into courtrooms in cities around the country in the late forties and fifties, they too were aware of the mounting reservoir of hostile sentiment against their kind. They were aware that the typologies meant to capture them were as threatening in a court of law as the indictment or the subpoena that had brought them inside to begin with. Indeed, the abortionist and her clients all had a great deal to fear.

The stories that women tell today about what it was like to sneak off into the so-called back alley almost always mingle shame with fear and determination. It is never easy to resist the law and go outside it to achieve an end. In those days, especially in the absence of a feminist community and a feminist argument for abortion, it was very difficult to hold one's head high and to counter the widely held characterizations of the women involved. The courtroom became a house of horrors for both the abortionist and her client who entered it. Feeling the weight of both legal and moral censure, they were robbed of both pride and dignity. Simone de Beauvoir, in another context but in the same era, described a piece of what the internal confusion must have been made of. She wrote, "Many women are intimidated by a morality that for them retains its prestige even though they are unable to conform to it in their behavior; they inwardly respect the law they transgress, and they suffer for their transgression."

These women entered the courtroom suffering the indignity of having been prepackaged and prejudged. Their just deserts were likewise predetermined, by judges like Walter Tooze in Portland, who said from the bench that "all good citizens condemn the abortion racket. It long has been a foul stench in the nostrils of the body politic and its complete eradication is demanded by every sense of morality and decency." There was a movement afoot to accomplish the eradication by, as one medical enthusiast put it, "taking militant action. It's up to us," he said. "Let's make pregnancy reportable." A lawyer suggested a different tactic to respond to women determined to control their own fertility: "In order to discourage women from seeking to have abortions performed, it is submitted that the women, too, should be penalized. After all, it is often she who initiates the commission of the crime."

It is a wonder that twenty women a day and sometimes more slunk into Laura Miner's office in San Diego and Ruth Barnett's in Portland, given what they risked and what a number of them actually came to suffer in the courtrooms of the time. The fact that so many girls and women made the trip speaks volumes about both the latitude fertile females had come to depend on and their determination to preserve the choice, even while choice remained illegal and had to be exercised in a poisonous context. Yet, many women desperate for a Ruth Barnett or a Florence Stallworth were indubitably scared off by the threat of the kind of exposure that hung over the practice of criminal abortionists.

It is very likely that as the public attack on abortion, abortionists, and "aborted women" grew fiercer in the forties and fifties than it had been since the end of the nineteenth century, more women than ever before felt compelled to protect themselves against public or legal exposure by resorting to the most dangerous possible solution to their dilemma: self-abortion. Abortion trials in the postwar years were littered, in fact, with evidence that women tried *everything* before they tried a "legitimate" criminal abortionist. As Ruth Barnett pointed out at the time, "The majority of women who came to me had already taken any of the thirty or forty different pills sold over the counter of drugstores." Into the fifties and beyond, pregnant women tried quinine pills, ergot tablets, soaps, hot mustard baths, tansy tea, turpentine capsules, douches, slippery elm (the "old maid's method"), and some tried throwing themselves from high places. A fourteen-year-old black girl in Texas drank a hot ginger tea and when that didn't work, she inserted a penknife up her vagina. Only then did she and her grandmother go looking for a woman who knew how to help a desperate girl.

In the largest sense, the abortion trials became arenas to address a culturally crucial question, that is, who is not a "real" woman? By defining female abortionists and their clients as perverse and unwomanly, the qualities of real womanhood were reaffirmed. The lawyers, the doctors, and the judges in command of these trials met no resistance as they defined the female transgressors before them. The political context made it easy to interpret an act of "exposing deviance" as an act of concern for the safety of the community. The social context sanctioned efforts to reinforce rigid gender roles in the aftermath of the war. The men who ran the show almost always adopted an offensive mode to promote these defensive ends, and the offensive mode was cryptoporno, a way of titillating the crowd while at the same time invoking shame and repugnance.

The show in the courtroom was rigidly formatted and rarely varied. First, both the abortionist and her client were either silenced in the court or severely constrained by both the rules of evidence and the representations of "her type" that made objections sound pitiful or like lies. (Ruth Barnett never testified in any of her trials after Reno, due to the fact, she said, that her lawyers knew she would speak out boldly and truthfully about her activities, thus killing all chances for acquittal.) Then, two men—the prosecutor and the defense attorney—slugged it out before an audience of citizens, for the purpose of proving which of the two women—the abortionist or her client—was more completely alienated from womanhood. They used arguments designed to prove that the "other" woman lived a life too close to sex and that she was alienated from maternity as well. On both sides these were powerful thrusts, since then (as now) it was so often membership in the cult of true motherhood that saved women from sexual degradation. And in an abortion trial, the core issue in those years was much more the charge of murdering motherhood than it was the charge of murdering the "unborn child."

Specifically, the prosecutor's job was to convince the jury that the woman abortionist was fundamentally a predator, a witch-like female who preyed on women's bodies without any feeling. The prosecutor needed to conjure up a creature who had power over others of her sex, helpless others whom she made lie down and spread their legs while she inserted instruments into their privates. A judge in Cincinnati listened carefully to the prosecutor and got the point. Mary Paige, a long-time, highly skilled abortionist in that city was arrested in 1954, and the judge imagined out loud what the abortionist used on her visitors. The instruments brought into court, he said, "have formed a macabre picture in my mind, reflecting the tortures of the medieval dungeons and the places of torture as we read of the practice in the olden days."

The prosecutor created this macabre picture of a predatory hag and then tied the interests of the creature he invoked through sex and torture to greed for money. The prosecutor in the St. Louis trial of Sophie Miller offered a related spectacle to the jury: "Any woman who would be in a business like this, can you imagine what kind of a character she has? Abortions! Taking advantage of the fact that girls get into trouble. You take a woman like Sophie Miller—who is not desperate like this little girl here—but who got into the business because she could make money that way. All she wanted to know was, 'Did you bring the money?'"

The "little girl" made to testify about her abortion might be, in fact, a young mother of four, a professional woman of thirty-two, or even a grandmother in her forties, but the prosecutor's opposite was bent on making this female small, and at the same time insidiously helpless. The defense lawyer's fundamental question was, Who could believe a woman like that? During the trial of May Ramsey in California, the defense lawyer posed the question particularly volubly and vividly, but still typically. The man stood up— one could see his lip curl—and he pointed at the unmarried woman known in the courtroom as the "prosecutrix." "They produce Miss Brown," he sneered, "to whom they have given immunity from prosecution. Miss Brown and girls of her type are not the type of girls who can be relied on and believed in this or any other type of situation. They are immoral, they are dishonest, they would do anything for their own welfare. There has been many a girl who has told her boyfriend that she needs $250 or $500, and then goes through some kind of a maneuver because she has missed one menstrual period and then pockets the rest of the money and then buys pretty clothes. And you saw how Miss Brown was dressed and her way and her style of appearance. Do you think she would be above it or beyond it? Are you going to take the testimony of that kind of girl?"

In other courtrooms it was not enough to discredit the prosecutrix (who was generally present under the harsh, coercive threats of the D.A.'s men, who told her they would publish her picture in the papers or take away her children if she didn't appear) by associating her with trickery and slatternly ways, and with being "that type of girl." In other courtrooms, defense attorneys accused women who admitted to having had abortions of being drunks (because they met the abortionist in a bar), trollops, stupid, not sufficiently embarrassed, immoral, unwed, and unfaithful, of being, in short, the sort of female who can be neither respected nor believed.

One defense attorney was very clear on what the proceedings were about. His opening argument drew the battle lines of perversity. "The prosecutor is going to paint this girl here to be a Simon Pure girl and say that this woman [the abortionist] here is a terrible woman. I am sorry this little girl here got herself messed up, but it's not the fault of my client. What did this girl do? She got herself in a desperate situation and Lord knows what these girls will testify to. She would have done anything to get rid of that fetus. The girl took sixteen ergot pills, day after day. Day after day she was taking hot baths, doing anything to get rid of that baby, and then she goes out looking for someone who is going to save her. It makes me angry how a girl like that gets up on the stand and wants to hurt somebody. Now," he concluded, "do you think a girl like that is on the square?"

Sometimes these women on trial spoke out for themselves, or tried otherwise to defend themselves against the vicious attacks. Most often a woman was direct and honest and tried earnestly to get the court to understand that she was a good person. A forty-year-old mother of two who had been crudely described in court as a "divorced woman who during the month of December 1953 had intercourse on two occasions with some man not her husband" was heart-wrenchingly straightforward on the stand. "Well, I didn't feel I was in a position to have a child. I was divorced and I had two children to take care of and I didn't feel I could take care of another child. It was not a matter of not wanting the child. It was a matter of not being able to support it and take care of it."

Other women were not so plaintive. But no matter how they tried to defend themselves, the gesture was swept aside or used against them in the abortion courtroom. In a 1948 trial in Sacramento, the defense attorney demonstrated a most effective way to discredit a woman who had tried, in her own way, to hold onto her dignity. The prosecutor should have "prevailed upon Mrs. Albert," he said contemptuously, "to either remove the gum from her mouth or at least not to chew it with such gusto. For some reason this woman was most antagonistic toward me. As the old saying goes, if looks could have killed, I would have been stretched out on the floor of this courtroom like the proverbial block of ice. Mrs. Albert is hard-boiled, she is unfemale."

At some point during the course of the trial, the defense attorney inevitably used still another strategy to discredit such women. He invited them to tell stories about the cruelty and coercion the police had used to get them into court. In another sort of case, in another cultural climate, stories like these might have created sympathy for the women; here they simply deepened the sense that a woman who got an abortion was sickeningly weak, vulnerable, *open,* and probably lying under pressure. *The Woman's Home Companion* reported in 1955 that when the law tracked down an abortionist's client, "in all probability the detectives will threaten to arrest her unless she tells who treated her," despite the fact that an arrest was counter to abortion statutes. The women involved, however, were usually terrified and shamed when cops showed up at their homes or offices with photos showing them entering an abortionist's office. They were not familiar with the letter of the law. And now in the courtroom, they were forced to relive the degradation of the police interrogation.

At Laura Miner's trial in California, for example, Jackie Temple, who was shaking in the witness box, was grilled by the defense lawyer: "Did they tell you that they would drag your name through the mud in the newspapers unless you came here and testified?" Jackie whispered, "Yes. They said it would be a lot of unpleasant publicity for my little boy. They just kept hammering and beating questions at me and I had to answer them." The lawyer did not take a chance that the jury missed the point of all this. He said, "They told her they would prosecute her if she didn't come down and they would throw her into jail and take her little boy away." Don't forget all that, he insisted, when you evaluate this woman's veracity.

Another woman who testified at Miner's trial told how she had sought an abortion because, during the first weeks of her pregnancy, she had contracted German measles. She was aware that if she carried the pregnancy to term, the baby would likely be born deeply damaged. She told how a policewoman posing as the receptionist in Miner's office suddenly grabbed her arm. Then, she said, "Two men rushed in and grabbed me by the other arm. And I was so scared. I tried to call my husband but they wouldn't let me. They said they were taking me to the County Hospital for an examination. But they took me to the D.A.'s office. I was there about an hour, being hounded over all the questions." Again, the defense attorney tried to show the jury that a woman who had been treated brutally was a female who could not be believed. She was, instead, a pitiful dame who was coughing up the story some legal tough wanted her to tell. In this case, the woman told an effective tale of the police coercion she'd endured in Laura Miner's office. It was, she said, "a feeling like you see in the moving picture shows of two Nazi agents. I was being kidnapped, and I was completely paralyzed at the time."

Sadly, it was not unusual for the prosecutrix to feel paralyzed when confronted by the police, by the typically aggressive defense lawyer, by the courtroom setting. A seventeen-year-old Oakland girl named Marlene, whose parents took her to Sacramento for an abortion in 1950, found herself being grilled several months later in court by her abortionist's lawyer. The man was trying to establish, in the usual fashion, that the girl had implicated his client merely because she had been threatened with prosecution herself if she refused to do so. Here the defense lawyer began his job of reducing Marlene to the status of an unbelievable and pitiable fool by badgering her about her use of words like "erect," which he implied a "good girl" would not know. He needled her about how she came to use such a highly technical term as "fetus" in her testimony ("Who fed you this word? Who have you been listening to?"). And then the lawyer hammered away at the role that shame played in bringing her, finally, into court. "You and your mother and father determined that your pregnancy would expose you and your family to a disgraceful situation, is that true? And you determined that you would quietly attempt to eliminate such a thing transpiring, is that so? You were cognizant of the embarrassment that it would bring upon you and your family? Your father was very concerned about it and wanted the condition eliminated and the family saved from disgrace? Likewise your mother? You were fully alert to the fact that it meant disgrace and embarrassment to you and your family, is that correct?" To each question, Marlene whispered, "Yes," and by the end of the session, the lawyer felt quite sure he had made his rather odd case that a young girl and her family facing the disgrace of illegitimate pregnancy would do *anything*, including lie about his client, in an effort to protect themselves.

The defense lawyer's perverse sensitivity to the shame that haunted a girl or woman who'd gone for an abortion hardly stopped him from pushing the shame into full-blown public humiliation if it would help to further discredit his client's accuser. One surefire way to do this was publicly to shred a woman's claim to sexual modesty and propriety. A popular tactic was to get the girl to admit that she had slept with a man not her husband, or that she was just plain promiscuous. In the trial of Ida Steadman, for example, the defense attorney's trajectory was typical. "You have been pregnant before?" he asked Polly Smith, the girl who had gone to Steadman for help. "And you were not married? You have never been married, have you? Who is the father of *this* child, if you care to tell, or would you care to tell us if the same man was the father both times?" At this point, the prosecutor objected. (Polly, of course, had no lawyer of her own, despite her obvious need for a champion; she was merely a witness for the prosecution.) But the judge found none of the foregoing questions objectionable. Not surprisingly, Polly did. "Well, I'd rather not answer these questions," she said, but the judge made her respond.

In all of these trials, girls and women were pressed in the same way. In California, a young woman was asked, "Do you remember telling Mrs. Garcia [the abortionist] that it was not your regular boyfriend who had caused your pregnancy, but another man? And that at that time you didn't want your regular boyfriend to know this?" In St. Louis, a defense attorney who established the unmarried status of the prosecutrix as soon as she took the stand remarked, "You should have thought of marriage before you got whatever you got."

In a variation on this strategy, some defense attorneys believed they could help their case by shredding a woman's integrity because she had been willing to disassociate sex and maternity. In a 1956 trial the lawyer addressed Vera Black: "You are the girl who said you and your husband could not afford a child, is that right? I believe you own a 1957 hardtop automatic, don't you?" When the attorney was asked to justify his question, he said, "If she can afford a new car and not a baby, it certainly casts doubt on her credibility as a witness." A bit later, the lawyer added, "It is easy for me, as a lawyer to swing into a girl like Vera Black. I have no malice toward her. My position is to be a lawyer. Her business is to be a mother which if she would be, she would be a very good one, probably."

Unfortunately, it was all too common for the defense lawyer to claim he was only doing his job and to assure the woman, "I'm not trying to embarrass you, you understand." Nor was it uncommon for the woman on the stand to experience her appearance in the courtroom as a kind of living death. A young woman in San Francisco tried hard to participate in the proceedings as she had been instructed, even though it was much, much worse to be on the stand than anyone had told her it would be. Her attempt to explain herself makes that clear. "Well," she said, "I had—had an abortion. I mean, you know, they. . . . I mean I don't know how to explain it—Let's see. She said something—I can't remember. I'm so nervous I can't think."

Quite often, prosecuting lawyers seemed to act on the theory that the more sexual references and sexual innuendo they could spread around in the courtroom, the more perverse the case and the more perverted and culpable the accused. So, in the name of cleansing the community of the foul stench associated with abortion, the prosecutor did spread sex around quite thickly. Over and over and in every trial, women were forced to describe how they undressed in the abortionist's office. They were made to respond to questions like this: "Miss Smith, when Dr. Jowers examined you— I don't like to be unpleasant about the thing—but I just want to know if he inserted his hand or finger into your vagina?" And then, "Miss Polly, maybe somebody may not know what you mean when you say your 'privates.' Which of your privates was it that she injected her instruments into? Did she insert it into your rectum?" To which Miss Polly answered weakly, "I know where she put it, but I don't know how to tell you."

As in Suzanne Tyler's trial near the end of the pre-*Roe v. Wade* years, girls and women in many of these postwar trials had pictures of their "privates" drawn on courtroom chalkboards ("to a pretty large scale, please") for the edification (or delectation) of the audience. They sat in the witness box as the abortion table was wheeled into the courtroom and placed in front of them. They were told to speak up and describe exactly how they were placed on the table ("How far apart would you say your legs were spread?"). They were made to identify the "macabre" tools of the trade, also brought into the courtroom, and tell which ones were placed inside of which of their orifices.

Even after all this, the lawyers did not stop. Perhaps their own libidos were uncontrollably loosened by the eroticized atmosphere they had strategically pumped up. In many courtrooms, men began to play with sex and sexual references as if to make sure that the parties in attendance personally felt the erotic charge. In a California trial, for example, the judge noted "in all fairness" (in a setting, incidentally, where all the jurors were female) "You can get a person up on a table for a large number of things. I take it most of these women jurors have also been examined, most of them have been on a table." A moment later, after everyone had gotten a chance to imagine the ladies of the jury with their legs spread, the defense attorney gazed at the abortion table thoughtfully and remarked, "Ah, but I don't think I could get Mr. Macomber [the prosecutor] on that table, to tell you the truth."

Sometimes the cryptoporno atmosphere was brutal. In a 1950 Georgia trial, a glass jar was brought into the courtroom. It contained a tiny fetus and, much more prominently, the vagina of a woman who had died at the hands of a real back-alley butcher. In the name of public morality and the need to display "the nature and the kind of injuries inflicted on this woman's female organs," the judge justified the presence of the jar in the courtroom, no matter that for some, the contents of the jar evoked the darkest, most violently perverse associations imaginable, and its contents were hardly necessary to prove the pregnancy or the death of the woman.

The fact was, the lawyers and the judges running these trials, along with the journalists covering them and the doctors and politicians who testified, and even the interested citizens who filled up the courtrooms, did not seem to find the eroticization of the court inappropriate or unseemly. In Portland, when women's bodies were the subject of rough discussion during Ruth Barnett's trials in 1952 and throughout the decade, the men in the room, at least, did not squirm, because such displays were not out of line with the tone of other public hearings in town. Many of them must have known, for example, what was going on down the street in the City Council chambers where their professional colleagues, their brothers-in-law and country-club bridge partners, could sometimes be found indulging in a bit of cryptoporno themselves. This was in the fifties, when Ruth often felt that every time she turned around, she was arrested again. At that time, the City Council was, as usual, avoiding the topic of abortion in chambers but having a pretty good time looking into the matter of the Star Theater, a downtown burlesque house that some council members believed should be shut down for "presentation of lewd, indecent performances on stage" involving nude women. The City Council members called a hearing on the subject, they said, because such performances tended "to create a public nuisance and a menace to the peace and general welfare of the city."

Here again, in the name of public morality and decency, upstanding men in the community had—and took—the chance to share with each other their visions of women's naked bodies. In the City Council meeting devoted to the goings-on in the Star Theater, things got hot quickly, and they stayed that way. A number of men who had attended the burlesque show were invited into the august chamber on the evening of November 19, 1955, to tell the council members what they had seen. Apparently, the members did not feel that one or two reports would suffice. They wanted to hear a lot of versions. The string of men who appeared before the council members described "a pretty animal type show." They described girls who "showed everything they had" in as "good a solo orgy you will ever find presented." After reviewing the stripping and the bumps and grinds of performers dancing completely in the nude, one added that there had been "no attempt at hiding from the audience any portion of their private parts, but on the contrary," he said, "there was nothing left undisclosed, and the act was just plain raw." Each witness provided the same details, almost verbatim, as the man who came before him. Indeed, the City Council members urged each one to leave nothing out. In the end, all the reports were explicit, appreciative, and censorious in the way that cryptoporno always is.

The authorities directing the cryptoporno shows in the council chambers, just like the men in charge at the courthouse, shared a dreadful sense in the postwar decades that the gender roles and gender relations they'd depended on were threatening to give way. The fact that they and their peers around the country conducted such proceedings so brutally is an indication of how sharply the authorities perceived the emergence of a cultural shift and how sharply they felt the threat it represented. In these public venues where women were on trial, the script called for degraded, humiliated, thoroughly vulnerable females, divided against each other and exposed. The most private facts of their lives were publicly revealed and reviled: their bodies, their sexuality, their wombs, the intimate sources of their personal dignity. At the same time, the script allowed for men—doctors, lawyers, judges, journalists, and myriad expert witnesses—to stand up, one by one, and reaffirm their prerogatives over women's bodies and their lives.

These scenarios were enacted against a backdrop of postwar demands for the domestication of women after a generation of Depression and war and the economic and social responsibilities women had shouldered then outside of their homes. Cultural arbiters of every sort—teachers, clergymen, magazine editors, fashion designers, novelists, as well as obstetricians, psychiatrists, and other medical men—ordered women to go back home, to be proper wives and mothers, to be content. The incidence of abortion after the war provided distressing evidence that many women were resisting some parts—or all—of this prescription. The trials provided the opportunity to humiliate resisters, to drive the injunction home once again, and to underscore an important source of cultural as well as legal authority.

The politicians and the law enforcement officers who cancelled the old arrangement that had tolerated abortion as a "needed necessity" in town as long as nobody got hurt, and the courthouse men in charge of naming women's guilt and setting their punishment, were together resisting the spectre of a community in which women could decide when and whether to associate sex and marriage, sex and maternity, marriage and maternity. In the 1950s, these men had the institutional power they required to resist this spectre by targeting individual women. But their leverage extended even farther because the displays in the morning paper after an abortion bust and the scenarios played out in the courtroom where abortion trials were heard carried powerful cultural messages to the general citizenry in the decades after World War II. These spectacles announced the danger and the just deserts that any woman associated with abortion could encounter. They also announced that the law was predicated on a willingness to place women in danger and also on a contempt for women's self-determination. Anyone could see that enforcing anti-abortion laws involved the degradation of women. In this way, the mid-century prosecution of women associated with abortion embodied the message that every woman, whether or not she ever had or ever would climb up on the abortionist's table, was endangered by the statutes that criminalized abortion.

Chapter Nine

PERSISTENCE

What remains of Ruth Barnett's 1952 trial record makes it clear that the courtroom proceedings were every bit as raw as the other abortion trials of the era. "Raw" was the way such things were in the fifties, in the absence of a politics or a movement to constrain these uses of women's bodies in public arenas. And so it was, after an eleven-day trial, that Ruth Barnett was found guilty, not of performing abortions, exactly, but of a misdemeanor: "maintaining an establishment injurious to public morals." It was a decision Ruth called a subterfuge and a foregone conclusion. The judge sentenced the abortionist to six months in the county jail and six months probation. Ruth, who had not stopped performing abortions during the time between her July 1951 arrest and her May 1952 conviction ("Week after week the importuning of women made me more and more distraught. I could not ignore their pleas for help. Despite the case pending against me, I reopened my clinic."), was able to use her considerable resources to appeal the conviction.

Even after the conviction, while the appeal was in the works, Ruth could not bring herself to padlock the Stewart Clinic or put down the tools of her trade. Maggie remembers that time. "If a woman was waiting at her door when we got home from a movie, crying, broke, why she just had to do that case. She had to. She just couldn't turn someone down. She'd cry on the phone with them. She said, 'I can't do it, don't you understand, I'm in jeopardy. If I do it, it's terrible. But what are *you* going to do if I don't?' If she couldn't find someone to take care of them, she'd take another chance." In this behavior, Ruth was strikingly similar to her colleagues around the country who continued to practice through all their travails with the law.

As the appeals process dragged on through the rest of 1952 and into 1953, Ruth took on a growing number of cases. In time, the

Stewart Clinic was as bustling an office as it had been before the big bust in 1951. Ruth's persistence was not a matter of judgment or calculation, though her financial obligations in the early fifties were considerable. Nor was it even a matter of what today we would call "politics." Going ahead with her work was simply what Ruth felt she had to do, and she did it. Her heart continued to respond to unhappily pregnant women. By any rational standard, however, it was not a good idea for her to follow her heart in Portland, a city that remained in a crime-busting mode throughout the fifties. Soon enough, Ruth encountered the consequences of her refusal to quit.

Years later, Ruth remembered the details. "One day, early in 1953, we were visited by a woman posing as a wronged girl in need of an abortion. With her was a male newspaper reporter posing as her brother. After the reporter handed some marked bills to the receptionist, the 'patient' was escorted to a dressing room. The receptionist entered my office with the money. As she placed it on my desk, the phone rang. I had difficulty placing the excited voice, that of a deputy sheriff whose wife I had once befriended. 'Get everyone out of there, Ruth,' he said. 'The district attorney's going to raid you again today.'

"I relayed the message to the receptionist, who picked up the bills and handed them to the masquerading 'patient.' 'Take them back,' said my receptionist. 'And get out, quickly. There may be some trouble and we don't want you involved.' The woman refused the money, pretending not to understand. 'I won't take it,' she insisted. 'I came here to be helped! I must be helped! Please hurry and take care of me.'

"'There's going to be a raid,' the receptionist explained, 'and we're trying to protect you. You don't want your name dragged through the courts, do you? You've got to leave quickly.' The 'patient' laughed, reached inside her brassiere, and pulled out a handful of crumbled papers. 'I'm a policeman,' she announced, 'and here are the warrants for everyone's arrest.' Then she ran to a side door, opened it, and a squad of arresting officers trooped in. Once again I went to the county jail, marched up the steps to be booked and released on bail."

Ruth always remembered the details of her ordeals, and most often she cast them philosophically. Maggie, on the other hand, is angry to this day. From Maggie's point of view, her mother's second arrest was just like all the others. "It was always a setup," she maintains. "Mother was never arrested or never sentenced because of her operations, or because of a hazard to someone's life. Each time it was because someone said, 'Well, it's time we raided the abortionist's office again.'"

In those days, Maggie was still busy juggling husbands, babies, and nursemaids, and waiting for Ruth to come by each week to pay the bills. But when Rolla Crick and his "little sister" hit on her mother this time, Maggie was fit to be tied. She was so angry, in fact, that even though by the early fifties her life looked more ordered and middle class than it ever had (at least on the surface), she reached back to the old days, to the ways of wild Maggie, to address the situation. "I had a bootlegger friend," she said, "from many years back when I played with the racket boys. Curly White. Curly ran a little after-hours spot in northwest Portland, and I used to wind up there when I couldn't go home. Curly arranged it so for three hundred dollars—which I paid—Rolla Baby would be beaten to a pulp. Not killed, mind you, but for the same price I could have had that done. But the arrangement was to nab him in the dark leaving the Journal Building with his little portable typewriter. Then fingers and typewriter were going to be smashed together. I wanted that little jerk off's hands smashed so badly he would never type again. But Dorothy Taylor made me cancel Rolla's appointment because she said it would be blamed on Mama."

Indeed, Ruth had enough on her shoulders in 1953. She had been sentenced to six months in jail on the 1951 misdemeanor charge; she was on probation for a second charge in the '52 trial; and after "little sister's" visit, she was certainly likely to be found in violation of the terms of probation. Plus, she faced a series of new charges stemming from the raid in 1953. As she put it, it was time for her to take "a long, hard look at the future." Most especially, she felt, she had to deal with the problem that doctors kept sending her patients and desperate women would not stop seeking her out on their own. To deal with the situation, she decided to make a public statement announcing her retirement. Then, she figured, people would start believing that she was out of circulation for real. The vehicle for her public statement, Ruth decided, would be *The Oregonian*, via that paper's star reporter, Wally Turner.

Till the day she died, Ruth believed that Turner was the white-hatted newsman and his competitor, Crick, the black-hatted. She enjoyed the idea of using the paper (that had, to such sensational effect, used her two years before) for her own purposes. And she could give Wally a boost over Rolla at the same time. It is worth noting that Turner's paper considered Ruth's "retirement notice" important enough to give it prominent front-page space on March 25, 1953.

The reporter's lead was dramatic, yet presented the abortionist with her dignity fully intact. "Dr. Ruth Barnett Tuesday announced closure of her Stewart Clinic and began vacating her eleven-room suite on the eighth floor of the Broadway Building. 'I have closed that Stewart Clinic,' the naturopath said. 'I have completely discontinued all my practice. I am retiring from my lifelong work, not from choice. Everyone who reads the newspaper knows why I am retiring.'"

Turner alerted his readers that Barnett "pulled no punches" during the interview, that is, she did not shrink from the facts as they were. "I have been proud to own and run this clinic for many years," she said. "It is about sixty years old now, and I bought it from Dr. Ed Stewart. The clinic units have always been as good as the best anywhere else in Portland. We've always treated women's diseases generally," she explained, "but much of the work we have done has been the performance of abortions. About 75% of the abortion cases have been referred to the clinic from physicians and surgeons in Oregon and other states." Ruth carefully explained that doctors accepted her and referred patients to her "because of the skills, techniques, and standards we've had here at the clinic," and she complained that the newspapers never mentioned the fact that doctors considered many medical conditions to justify an abortion. Finally, Turner gave Ruth a chance to tell the public one more thing about herself: "I've spent a lot of hours talking young women into going ahead and having their babies," she insisted. "Lots of times I've bought layettes for them in order to get them to agree that they wouldn't leave my office and go someplace else."

Ruth declined in the interview to discuss the legal matters in which she was embroiled, and Turner did not press her. The reporter had always appreciated the woman's elegance and professionalism, and now he allowed her to craft her own exit from the public eye. It would be a very temporary exit. Turner knew that, and he did not choose to interfere with her dignity.

It was only a matter of months before Ruth's next appearance in public, back in the courtroom to face the charges associated with the 1953 "little sister" raid. This time the trial itself was aborted as Ruth and her lawyers decided the abortionist didn't have a chance to prevail. Instead of sitting through a humiliating trial, Ruth changed her plea to "guilty" just after the jury was impanelled (a process the newspapers called "laborious" because so many prospective jurors felt that the sensational publicity about Barnett had colored the way they felt about the woman). At the same time, Ruth withdrew her appeal of the 1952 conviction. The result was less than she hoped. As she put it, after agreeing to so much, "the blow finally came and it left me stunned. True, I had expected some sort of sentence, but not the two consecutive six-month jail sentences handed me by Circuit Judge James R. Bain."

Ruth may have been stunned, but even so, she remained pointedly sensitive to one salient effect of the truncated trial. "It seemed to me that both the jury and the gallery were a disappointed bunch of people. No chance to see my client, frightened, cowering, twisting her handkerchief on the witness stand. No testimony from expert witnesses about such gruesome things as blood clots, pathological tissue, and discharges. The morbidly curious had to content themselves with the afternoon newspaper's headlines: 'Ruth Barnett Pleads Guilty, Gets Year in Jail.'"

On March 17, 1954, Ruth Barnett became the first of the Portland abortionists arrested almost three years earlier to be incarcerated, an event the *Oregon Journal* hailed as marking "the end of the free and easy days" that had allowed an abortion racket of "amazing" proportions to flourish for so long in Portland. After thirty-six years as a practicing abortionist, Ruth entered the Rocky Butte jail. They put her in a cell alongside a young black woman whose common-law husband had told her he planned to cut her heart out, so she murdered him. Ruth's other neighbors were a woman convicted of using a knife on a girl in the midst of a drunken fight, a prostitute and narcotics addict, an eighteen-year-old shoplifter—all of whom she befriended and determined to cheer up, despite the atmosphere of despair that blanketed the place.

In jail Ruth tried hard to keep her spirit strong, though she was very bitter that the authorities saw fit to imprison her for what she called "a misdemeanor in the same category as spitting on the sidewalk." Besides, the regimentation of prison life made everything so deadly dull. "My days swiftly fell into the required pattern," she said. "Breakfast at 7:30. Luncheon at noon. Then rest. Exercise in the yard on clear days. Dinner at 4:00. A bath before bedtime. Lights out at 10:00."

Many people in Portland figured that the queen of abortionists, with her well-known charm and connections and her financial resources, would find a way to make the prison authorities work for her. But three days after Ruth's incarceration, Jack Matthews, the jail superintendent, was moved to issue a public statement addressing this issue. He said, "I don't care how much money a prisoner has or how prominent they are, they can expect no special privileges here. I'm not going to jeopardize my own career. All are treated fairly here. None is abused."

So Ruth Barnett joined the other women in the "housekeeping duties" that fell to women prisoners. "We mopped and scrubbed and polished. We sewed, mended, darned, and patched." On Tuesdays the women were assigned to mend the workshirts and jeans of the male prisoners. In Ruth's own account of her stint, she was a trooper: resourceful and cooperative, a woman used to finding herself among other women, especially women disturbed and dislocated by an unfair world. Instinctively, she knew how to step into the culture of jail and find solutions to living the daily grind. "Blessed with a sense of humor," she said, "I somehow managed. The matrons were, in the main, wonderful. The work, in the main, dismal. We did what had to be done. But sometimes we did it on our own terms. We exchanged chores. This probably sounds like a little thing to you," she said, "but it was a means of self-expression, a small display of personal decisions and individualism. I was able to keep my spirits up and my weight down with a rhythm system. When the dining room had to be cleaned, I had about twenty chairs to lift from the floor to the table tops. So, I hummed a song with a measured beat, using the chairs as weights. I did the same with mopping, dusting, any job that had repetitious movements which I could set to a musical pattern." Ruth also found ways to meet the needs and desires of the other women. She bought them ice cream sodas and home-permanent kits, and made them laugh.

She stewed about the range of injustice that had brought these female inmates together. The plight of the shoplifter she called "Dixie" particularly worried her. "Dixie was only eighteen. She was a docile girl who had given birth to five children by five different fathers. When she was caught shoplifting, she was stealing to feed her family. According to law, Dixie had committed a crime against society. But surely, society was not guiltless. What about the crime of enforced poverty in a land of affluence and plenty? What about the crime of inadequate education in a so-called age of enlightenment? What about the crime of society's indifference? If Dixie was solely responsible for her crime, then it can only be that the five fathers of her children are utterly irresponsible. And society, too, had shown a measure of irresponsibility. Why hadn't contraceptives and birth control information been made available to her? Why hadn't she been able to come to me—or another skilled abortionist—for our services?"

Ruth did not waste the time she spent in jail, and ironically, living with Dixie and the others deepened her intention to go on with her work because the experience had deepened her sense of the interconnectedness of injustices. And this was despite what she now knew about the full spectrum of the dangers involved. In the end, being in jail "nauseated" Ruth. She said, "I failed to see what it could accomplish," for herself, for Dixie, or for any of the women. "It cages the body and beats the human spirit." For all of them, she felt, "it had the overall effect of brutalizing and tearing down the dignity which man has tried so hard to develop."

In the end, Ruth did not have to endure the brutality of prison life for very long. Apparently, the combination of her "good behavior" and the indulgence of two circuit judges allowed Superintendent Matthews (who had himself become fond of Ruth) to usher her out of jail after one hundred and twenty days, or one-third of her sentence. The *Oregon Journal* was incensed by the brevity of her incarceration. Editorially, it invoked the hard work of the D.A. and its own reporter, Rolla Crick, that had gone into snaring the abortionist, "Dr. Barnett got off lucky. Too lucky, considering the nature of her crimes," the editorial concluded on July 21, 1954.

Now that Ruth, nearly sixty years old, was free again, it was not long before she was back at the old business, her "retirement" statement to Wally Turner and the public notwithstanding, and despite the fact that the Oregon State Board of Naturopathic Examiners had recently revoked her license. "Moreover," as she put it, "friends, lawyers, associates all hammered at me with the idea that I was under a probationary sentence and that if I were caught and convicted of another breach of Oregon's abortion laws I would face a much stiffer jail sentence. They reminded me that I was no longer a young woman and even I—one who had fibbed about her age for so long she wasn't sure just how old she was—was aware that I had reached the August of my life." Right before she died, an interviewer asked Ruth how she could have ignored such advice when she knew she stood such a likely chance of being arrested again. She answered, "That's right. You can't understand that, but I can."

For a woman like Ruth, it was all too easy to understand, once the stream of desperate girls and women had begun to find her again. This time, with the Stewart Clinic closed for good, Ruth was operating out of the weight-loss clinic she set up with a chiropractor, Dr. Jesse Helfrich, in early 1954. Helfrich had run the place with what Ruth called "amazing results" while she was in jail and now, after her release, the Slim-U Clinic slowly but surely became primarily an abortion office. The staff was more careful than ever. They screened every patient meticulously, knowing that the word around town was that Slim-U was a front.

Ruth herself was thrilled to be back in the saddle, helping girls and making a living. But still the abortionist's world was precarious. For Maggie and her increasingly complicated household, times had been hellish when Ruth was in jail. "When she went down, we all did," Maggie remembered painfully. "All the people who worked for her. The salaries stopped. The house payments stopped. The car payments stopped. That was part of the pressure she was under." Ruth's renewed earnings eased the pressure, but for the two years that she worked out of the weight-loss clinic, the abortionist spent a great deal of time looking over her shoulder in a way that today's abortion providers would recognize. "Periodically," she said, "while driving to an appointment or going shopping, I had the feeling of being followed. Several times while walking, I was certain that a man or woman was shadowing me. There were strange phone calls at odd hours from people whose stories didn't add up. And there were the occasional visits from candid reporters who would say, 'Come on now, give us the lowdown on what you're doing.'"

Not surprisingly, as it turned out, Ruth was not unreasonably paranoid. In November of 1956, she was arrested. Again, she and her lawyers fought the indictment at first, but in the end they bowed to the strength of the case against Ruth and her staff, and the abortionist pled guilty. Maggie remembers the character of her mother's fierce determination at this time. "She could have stopped any of this trial business before it ever started. All of it. If she would have made a few phone calls and said, 'Hey, fellas, get me off the hook or your name will be mentioned.' That wasn't her code of ethics, even after she'd tasted the slammer. She would not tell who sent her patients, or the names of her patients. She would not make anybody responsible for what she was doing. Her philosophy was that she knew it was against the law, and if she had to be punished for it, so be it. But, on the other hand, she believed in it and she was going to be doing it as long as she could."

This time Ruth was sentenced to Rocky Butte for a year. "Again," Ruth recalled, "there was the weary soul-destroying drudgery. This time, too, I tried hard to keep my spirits up by making a game of it." According to Maggie, "Mama was absolutely willing to give up her freedom because this was the right thing to do. She knew this—and mentioned it many times—yet people couldn't understand how she was so stoic when she went to jail. No one could believe that this woman who lived like a queen on the outside could go to jail with a stiff upper lip and never complain, never complain about anything."

Now that Ruth knew the ropes at Rocky Butte, this time she was even more ready than before to keep company with the women she called her "new friends and associates." She played pinochle and canasta with drug dealers and prostitutes. She instructed her visitors to bring goodies for all ("We shared everything"), and she used her extra cash to buy toothbrushes and toiletries as welcoming gifts for each new woman inmate who arrived. Whether or not Ruth felt that doing abortions made her a criminal, the fact was that her lifetime of standing by desperate women meant that in jail she did not need to alter her ways. Ruth's friends—JoAnn, who had murdered her tormenting husband, and Jean, who had stabbed a rival for her lover's attention—had much longer sentences by far than the abortionist found guilty of "manslaughter by abortion." So when Ruth was released, her poorer and apparently guiltier friends stayed behind, as before. She was not eager to join them inside again, but nor was she eager to change her ways. "You might think," she said, "that this time, for good and all, I would have given up my abortion practice. I had twice been to jail and had been stripped of my license to practice. I faced serious penalties if ever arrested again. I had no clinic and little chance of renting office space in Portland. But what did I do in 1959 when I was released a second time from that grim rock-walled prison at Rocky Butte? I went back to work helping women in trouble."

This was the era when Ruth's practice was reduced to what she called "a backstairs sort of clientele," a mere shadow of the grand days in the Broadway Building. First she set up an office in Maggie's house on Vista Avenue, in a maid's room and bath off the kitchen. According to Maggie, "We made a complete surgery out of it, white tileboard walls, examination table, recovery couch, deep sink, proper plumbing, and all under a Yale snap lock so my kids wouldn't know what was happening."

Business was quietly steady, and for the first time in years, Ruth felt safe. What had changed was that Charles Raymond, the former assistant district attorney in charge of prosecuting her in 1952, had since become her friend and sometimes attorney. And now he had been elected the Multnomah County district attorney. For the first time in nearly a decade, the abortionist felt that no one in particular was out to get her. Now Ruth was able to resume bankrolling Maggie—ten thousand dollars toward buying a nightclub, fifty thousand for redecorating it, money for a new house, trips to Hawaii, the works. It was the era when Charlie Marshall, the police captain, stopped by for a night or two at a time and Ruth, now in her late sixties, began to relax.

Except that Maggie, now approaching fifty, was entering a phase of renewed manic craziness, nagging Ruth for thousands for her Portland nightclub, then for one in Alaska, then for thousands more for a sybaritic reducing salon of her own, the Roman Weight Control Center, an establishment Maggie built (and then abandoned) to copy and update the old Stewart Clinic. "It looked," says Maggie, like a Cecil B. De Mille set with twelve rooms, private offices and consultation-rest rooms, and a small kitchenette. We put in bottle-glass cathedral windows and a huge revolving clock on the roof with "Time to Reduce" emblazoned across the face. The *Playboy* gremlin was my signature. We put over a hundred and fifty thousand dollars into it. Oriental carpets, music poured in, carved Chinese and teak desks, custom-made furniture, beautiful lights and pictures." Maggie was marrying again, as well. More lowlifes ("With my lifestyle, I never met a gentleman"), pimps and gamblers who stole from Ruth and hoods with long rap sheets.

Ruth's relaxation was also compromised by the fact that she was getting old, and now she found out that she was seriously ill with melanoma. The disease was enervating and sometimes painful. But most of the time it did not stop her from picking up her phone when the girls called and driving down to Henry Thiele's Diner, where the base of the Southwest Hills met Burnside and Twenty-third, to pick up a client. It didn't stop her from taking a girl back to Maggie's house, and later, when she felt more confident that no one was watching, back to her own basement laundry room, to perform abortions.

Ruth's condition should have slowed her down. She should have quit responding to girls and women in trouble. She felt sick as often as not in the mid-sixties, but still her commitment and the money pressures pushed her on. And her addiction to glamour, intact after all these years, pushed her on as well. Earl Bush was long gone by this time, replaced by a succession of hard-drinking, sometimes violent men, barely more respectable than Maggie's stable. But Ruth still believed that stepping out with a man on her arm was the way to go, despite the fact that the abortionist almost never had a good thing to say about men, and in her line of work, she'd amassed quite a damning natural history of the species. Nevertheless, nearly seventy, she was still on the prowl. The man Maggie calls her mother's "last sweetie and her final lover" was a new type for her: quiet, bashful, younger, and wealthy. Maggie claims that Ruth still knew what she was doing in this department. "In her late sixties, she was still beautiful and giving lush, wet parties. She really knew how to kiss a man's ass. Hung on every word, fixed all kinds of goodies, tidbits, and champagne and encouraged him to have his business associates up to her house to play cards and get smashed. In exchange, this guy bought her a white mink coat for Christmas."

Nearly a decade and a half had passed since Ruth's first arrest. She had spent endless hours during that time with lawyers, weeks at a time in and out of courtrooms, and months in jail. In some ways, however, the harshest blow was yet to come, even though in the middle 1960s, some aspects of the criminal era were beginning to seem passé. Many people—doctors included—were now speaking out in public about the need to legalize abortion and a few state legislatures were actually taking steps to ease the laws. Ruth had begun to fantasize that she would live long enough to practice again in the light of day. On some days, in fact, the *politics* of the abortion issue loomed even larger in her mind than her own mortality. "My cancer," she said at this time, "is nothing. It doesn't worry me a particle compared to the agony I suffered as a young girl when I was pregnant. The point is, they must change the law. They *will* change the law."

When the blow came, it came once again in the form of a politician, the young Multnomah County district attorney, elected in the mid-sixties and determined to make his mark, in part by resurrecting a tried-and-true strategy: crack down on the abortionists. In retrospect, Ruth said she doubted that she would have stopped doing abortions even if she had paid closer attention to the intentions of the newly elected D.A. By that time, she simply couldn't stop. When her troubles began again in 1965, Ruth sometimes spoke about how the people who knew her well in those years understood that. Her lawyer, for one, knew her well. "My attorney has often remarked that I am a rational woman in all other matters of life, but he questions my sanity on the subject of my chosen vocation." Ruth said soon before she died. "He has even suggested, more than half seriously, that he could plead me 'insane' on this one subject because he says even though I know of the existence of the law, have been arrested, convicted, and incarcerated because of the law, I continue to defy it."

And defy it she did. Between the end of 1965, when Suzanne Tyler had the extreme bad fortune to visit Ruth while the police were watching, and 1967, the abortionist was arrested five times. It seems today like a pitiful irony: when the law came after Ruth Barnett one more time, the 1854 statute still packed enough force to push the old abortionist, dying herself, behind bars.

Like Suzanne Tyler, Dolores Lesser had a pile of bad luck in this final season of criminal abortion. Dolores was thirty-nine in March 1966 when her married boyfriend took her to Ruth because the circumstances of Dolores's life were such that she had no conflict about ending her accidental pregnancy. As she put it, "I was living alone and near the end of the completion of my divorce. I had the four children to take care of. I didn't see any other solution to my problem. It was a desperate situation for me because I had no money. I had no relatives."

Several days following Dolores's abortion, she developed peritonitis, an abdominal inflammation associated with inexpertly performed abortions. The infection was serious enough to catch the attention of one doctor at St. Vincent's Hospital, then of the police, and finally of the district attorney. Seven months later, in October, Dolores spent two days in a particularly poisonous courtroom, her life revealed and judged in the most humiliating terms imaginable.

To a considerable extent, it was the same old story: the prosecutor reviling Ruth, the defense attorney discrediting Dolores, the abortionist's accuser. Even in 1966, it was still easy and natural to pit the two women against each other and drive it home for the jury that this was a contest to determine which one was the less adequate woman. In the case of Dolores Lesser, it did not seem difficult at all to make this argument. And Ruth's attorney dove into the task with enthusiasm. Revitalizing, once again, the tired old insults, he began disingenuously: "I don't like to comment too much on Mrs. Lesser. I'm sorry for her. She is an unfortunate person, and we heard from the doctor as to the fact that she is a person we could easily call a nymphomaniac. I think," the lawyer went on, "the evidence justifies the appellation. I am not going to condemn her because she didn't want to divulge the fact that she had unusual sexual demands. I am going to skip over it. She was desperate. Do I have to tell you what a desperate woman does?" Even the prosecutor conceded Dolores's taint, apologizing to the jurors that he could not provide them with a "young, airy, loveable, virginal witness," the sort who convinces juries.

Most of the trial followed the conventional scenario. But then, during his summation, Ruth's lawyer, Leo Levenson, struck out into new territory. He gazed solemnly at the jury, composed, as it happened, of twelve mature women, and admitted quite seriously, "It isn't up to me to tell you how a woman suffers with these things." He was pleading for all the women jurors to identify with the mess before them. "There isn't a person on this jury," he said, "either themselves or some member of their family, hasn't had a problem like that." So Dolores Lesser wasn't such a lowlife after all. This problem of accidental, unwanted pregnancy, he suggested, could happen to anyone. Then he fixed his gaze even more sharply on the women of the jury and added, "I might say that there is no doubt about the fact that there is a lot of hypocrisy about this matter of abortion, but you are women of understanding and intelligence, and I ask you to use plain common sense in this case." Here Levenson didn't deny that Ruth Barnett had performed an abortion on Dolores Lesser; rather, he appealed to the jury to be honest about what any woman, even themselves, would have done in Dolores's situation. Let's face it, he intimated, this is what women want, and what women today do, and Ruth Barnett must be there to help them. This was a new approach.

But Levenson did not stop there, with intimations and appeals to common sense. He felt, indeed, that the time had come to unfurl the fundamental argument and see if it would fly. The lawyer read, for the jury's benefit, the text of the Oregon anti-abortion statute. He read slowly and carefully and gave special stress to the crucial phrase that lay at the heart of the matter: *"unless the same is necessary to preserve the mother's life."* Then Mr. Levenson dropped his voice and spoke slowly into the faces of all the jurors. "To me I think that a woman is more than a breeding animal," he said deliberately. "I think that a woman should have as much freedom in this world as a man, and that is the freedom of life, and I say that life under this law means the right to be free of her child, or not to have a child."

It is not surprising that Levenson's evocation of the women's rights argument did not move the twelve female jurors; in 1966, *Roe v. Wade* was still a very long seven years down the road. For another thing, even though by now everyone knew that countless women regularly defied the law to control their fertility, a great many people still made a sharp distinction between a desperate necessity and a right. Besides, the jurors felt that the law was still the law, and Ruth Barnett was a flagrant, chronic violator. The jurors stuck with the prosecutor, who warned them that the Oregon abortion statute "doesn't get in to those esoteric phrases about the role of women in our society." He said, "That is the sort of argument which can be made to the legislature, to the PTA groups, and to others concerned—social groups—but it most certainly is not appropriate here."

Still, Dolores Lesser's trial marked a significant milestone on the road to legalized abortion. The old stereotypes of the greedy abortionist—"There is only one reason that she performed this abortion and that is $500," the prosecutor insisted to the jury—and her nymphomaniac client persisted and ultimately won out one more time. But Ruth's lawyer was one of the first to bring the notion of abortion rights directly into the courtroom, and demand that the prosecutor and the jurors consider this angle. And the "rights" notion, no matter how battered it has become, has proved impossible to drive out of that venue to this day.

Ruth was proud that Leo Levenson spoke out as he had, even though his words did not save her from being convicted of manslaughter by abortion. She believed in Levenson and had high hopes that, despite the unending round of arrests and convictions she'd lately suffered, the lawyer would find a way to keep her from serving the eighteen-month sentence she had been handed in Suzanne Tyler's case, or the new two-year sentence. Levenson tried hard. At Ruth's final appearance in court, when Judge Robert Jones pronounced her sentence in the matter of Dolores Lesser, the lawyer argued for leniency not only because the old abortionist was suffering from terminal cancer. He reiterated and defended the arguments he had used at the trial, this time adding that abortion was merely the surgical means of achieving the same goal that women regularly achieved by taking birth control pills, available to women since 1960. He drew on an extremely popular notion of the day by insisting that abortion was a boon to society, since it protected the resources of taxpayers who would otherwise foot the bill for the care of unwanted babies born to "women caught in a treadmill of endless childbearing." And finally, Levenson made the point that the *laws* against abortion—not an abortionist like Ruth Barnett—caused women to suffer degradation, pain, and death.

Judge Jones listened attentively to Mr. Levenson's presentation and then he turned to Ruth Barnett, standing before him in the courtroom, leaning on the cane that was her constant support in her final days. It had been tough, the judge said, to know what to do in this case. In fact, he admitted that the decision about whether to send the abortionist to prison had caused him "mental anguish." He was aware that many of Mr. Levenson's arguments made good sense. He was aware, as well, that a great many people had submitted personal references to the court in Ruth's behalf that spoke of her fine qualities. Yet, the judge went on, he could not overlook her "constant performance of abortions," or her mistaken conviction that she could take the law into her own hands. Moreover, he pointed out, the courtroom was not the place for setting public policy. On these grounds, Judge Jones resolved his anguish and sentenced Ruth Barnett to a two-year stint, this time in the Oregon State Penitentiary.

Leo Levenson managed the appeal of both the Tyler and the Lesser cases and was turned down both times by the appeals court. On February 5, 1968, in her seventy-fourth year, Ruth Barnett entered the penitentiary as the oldest woman ever incarcerated by the state of Oregon.

In the interim between Ruth's final trial and her incarceration, the Greater Portland Council of Churches voted to support the Hoyt Bill, a measure liberalizing the state's abortion laws then before the Oregon legislature. Soon after that, the Westminster Presbyterian Church in Portland held a public forum at which a minister, a doctor, and an academic leader strongly supported the proposition that what they called "therapeutic abortion" should be legal and accessible, not just to rich women, but to poor women as well. Both ordinary and prominent citizens began to write to their legislators in Salem, urging passage of Senate Bill 218. Most of the letter writers urged their representatives to support the bill for a reason that had little to do with women's rights. The letters reflect a citizenry that had become convinced that legal abortion was the only really effective means of saving the country from the wages of the population bomb. Or perhaps the letters show that a number of citizens identified this argument as the one most appealing to their legislators.

A woman in Eugene wrote, "My husband and I have become extremely concerned over the population problem in the world, and hope this bill might be the first step leading the way for other states and nations to follow, toward stemming the tide of too many people." A registered nurse in Portland sent a letter to the state capital expressing her concern about "our exploding population and rising illegitimacy rate." A woman in Corvallis whose sister, married to a Methodist minister, had been forced to seek out a criminal abortionist, had a somewhat broader view of the need to legalize abortion. She wrote, "It is high time we end the hypocrisy of the present situation which provides subterfuges for the rich and discriminates against the middle class and the poor. Women are forced to bear unplanned and unwanted children often at the sacrifice of the standard of living of the family. I do not see how this squares with a society facing a population crisis, a society where many are screaming about the cost of welfare."

Few citizens, even in the late sixties, were willing to speak in the terms that Ruth Barnett was using at the time and had used for almost fifty years, that abortion is a woman's right and must be a woman's choice. At the end of her life, Ruth wrote to a public she hoped was alert: "Millions of American women have had abortions. Millions more will seek such operations in the future. My sympathies will remain with them as long as I live because I have known their plight. And I have known also what it is to be helped in such a situation and to face life anew. So, while the laws against abortion remain, your duty is clear. If you believe as I do, that abortion is a matter of personal decision, then you must rise up and demand a change in the laws."

On July 1, 1968, after five months in prison, Ruth promised a panel of five "solemn men"—the Oregon Parole Board—that she would never again perform an abortion. As she put it, "I looked them right in the eye and I said, 'I will give you my sacred word as a lady, I'll never do another abortion.'" There is no evidence that this time she broke her word. Sixteen months later, in December 1969, Ruth Barnett died of melanoma in Good Samaritan Hospital.

Maggie says her mother's funeral was a sad affair. "She'd have been terribly disappointed. She was sure she was going to have a big turnout. It was just a scattering of people that came, just a few of the intimate people. The people she'd been drinking and playing cards with." Both Portland newspapers gave the abortionist a prominent and respectful obituary. The day after she died, her old nemesis the *Oregon Journal* printed an appreciative column on Ruth's life that indulgently noted her penchant for "a faultless perfection, a touch of drama, and a great glory-grabbing gusto for being center stage." More important, the column noted, "So much of what Ruth Barnett believed—and her convictions about the 'rightness' of a woman's right to abortion were genuine enough—is already coming to pass." By 1976, the *Journal* was calling Ruth "a woman ahead of her time." How times had changed.

But in one way, at least, history has enduringly consigned women like Ruth, who devoted her life to performing abortions in the illegal era, to the dark, sordid back alleys of the past. When her kind are remembered at all, they are invoked only as a warning. They are associated with the wretched dangers of the bad old days, before legalization. Practitioners like Ruth have been separated out from the real doctors, the physicians of conscience who performed illegal abortions, it's said, out of a sense of ethics and duty. Ruth and her sort are remembered and discussed as mercenaries, as a source of danger and death. They are held up as symbols of what we must struggle against in our efforts to preserve *Roe v. Wade*.

Ruth Barnett would not have been surprised to find her kind still being reviled twenty-five years after her death, but she would have snorted in contempt because she knew, as well as anyone ever did, where the source of danger lay, and it wasn't the abortionist. It was the law. It was the law that created the opportunity for a crook like Reg Rankin, and horror for young women like Diane McDermott and Shirley Packer, and even Dolores Lesser, denied access by law to a medically appropriate facility. And it was the law that placed Ruth Barnett, herself in some degree of danger every day for fifty years and locked her up, from time to time, even while she gave her life to providing a service that thousands of women were determined to get and few others would provide.

Ruth Barnett was, indeed, a woman ahead of her time, but her time has endured into our own in the sense that a great many people still believe that anti-abortion statutes can and will stop abortion. Ruth Barnett would have snorted at that one, too. For again, she knew—she lived her life as proof—that an unwillingly pregnant woman will find her own determination much more powerful than a coercive legislative prohibition. Nevertheless—and Ruth knew this, too—these statutes were devastatingly effective throughout her lifetime.

It is true that *Roe v. Wade* has had the effect of alleviating some of the contempt and danger that shaped women's lives before 1973. After more than twenty years of legal abortion women are safer in this terrain. They are, for example, less likely to find themselves the prey of operators like Reg Rankin and less likely to resort to self-abortion. Still some substantial dangers remain. Abortion continues to be difficult for poor women and those in rural areas to obtain, partly because the number of abortion providers has diminished percipitiously over the past decade. Some politicians continue to play with the abortion issue and with women's lives for political gain. Many states are placing one obstacle after another in the way of girls and women seeking to manage their own fertility. And thousands of anti-choice proponents have vowed to agitate until the final barriers against legal abortion have been resurrected.

It is a profound irony that nearly a quarter-century after Ruth Barnett's death and the legalization of abortion, the abortion practitioner is again reviled and endangered in the United States. As in Ruth's day, there are precious few women and men who can afford the psychic cost of performing abortions, never knowing if and when they will be targeted. And as in Ruth's day, the ones who continue to practice do so out of a deep and abiding commitment to women's choice. In a curiously telling twist, the practitioner is endangered today not so much by the spectre of the law, of course, or by the crackdowns and raids that shadowed abortionists in the past, as by the violence of anti-choice fanatics. But what is clear by now is that whatever the individuals or groups or public policies that threaten and endanger qualified abortion practitioners—in the United States or abroad—they also endanger the human dignity, the access to full citizenship, and the very lives of all girls and women determined to decide for themselves whether and when to become mothers.

Beyond these substantial dangers that continue to shape the abortion arena today is one more grave danger: our disregard for the past. The fact is, as the illegal era became history, it met the ignominious fate that history often suffers—denial, neglect, distortion.

Anti-choice proponents have denied the facts of the past as they press for the recriminalization of abortion, claiming both that new laws will eradicate abortion and that their campaign for anti-abortion statutes has nothing to do with a willingness to degrade and endanger women. Young people who did not live through the illegal era often neglect the past or forget its relevance when they assess what role the state should have in regulating female fertility. Even pro-choice advocates today are guilty of distorting the history of the illegal era when they propose that *Roe v. Wade* must be sustained to protect women from the vile back-alley practitioners who prevailed before legalization.

The story of Ruth Barnett and the criminal era challenges these re-readings of history. In Ruth's story, the law did not stop abortion. Nor did the law protect women. It most certainly did not safeguard the morality and the dignity of the community. And yet, in Ruth's day, anti-abortion statutes were fearsomely powerful, as the lives of all women were shaped by the contempt and danger embodied in the state's effort to coerce and control female fertility.

BIBLIOGRAPHIC NOTE

This book began as a study of women abortionists who were arrested, tried, convicted, and sent to the penitentiary in the decades immediately preceding the Supreme Court's 1973 decision legalizing abortion, *Roe v. Wade*. To begin with, I amassed more than fifty trial records and appeals court decisions that documented the circumstances of women practitioners in the 1940s, 1950s, and early 1960s.

In the process of locating tens of thousands of pages of court records, I had the very good fortune to locate Margaret St. James, the daughter of Ruth Barnett. Maggie provided me with her mother's privately published memoir, *They Weep on My Doorstep*, and with her own vivid memoir describing her life as an abortionist's daughter. She also generously lent me Ruth Barnett's photographs and diaries, graciously and enthusiastically allowed me to interview her for many hours about her mother's life and work, and urged Dorothy Taylor, Ruth Barnett's employee for many years, to speak to me as well. These materials, along with the newspaper accounts and extant transcripts of her mother's trials, made it possible for me to write this story of one woman's ordeal as an illegal practitioner in the twentieth century. Chapters 1 and 2, especially, draw heavily on the material that Maggie made available to me. The story of Suzanne Tyler's ordeal is a composite, constructed from several of Ruth Barnett's final trials.

The main source for the material in Chapters 3 and 4 is the 1936 Los Angeles trial of Reginald Rankin and the members of his West Coast abortion syndicate. The transcript of this trial comprises over two thousand pages. It is an extraordinary document of the illegal era; it is unlikely that a fuller account exists of an abortion syndicate in the 1930s. In Chapters 3 and 4, as elsewhere in the book, I have used the real names of abortion practitioners, but not of the clients of abortionists or other innocent bystanders. In several cases I have created composite portraits of clients and events in order to ensure anonymity. In one instance, when Laura Miner pays a call on William Byrne, the details of her visit are a composite of the account she gave of the event and several other accounts provided by women involved in illegal abortion elsewhere during the same era.

Chapter 5, which takes Ruth into Rankin's orbit and to Reno, Nevada, draws on the record of the preliminary examination conducted by Judge Harry Dunseath in the Justice's Court of Reno Township, County of Washoe, State of Nevada, on December 10, 1940. The material on Julia Ruuttila in this chapter was generously passed on to me by Sandy Polishuk, who is writing a biography of this heroic labor organizer and who interviewed Ruuttila extensively before her death. Chapters 6 and 7 benefitted from Ruth's and Maggie's memoirs, newspaper accounts, city vice investigations, and general scholarship concerning municipal affairs in Portland in the 1940s and 1950s. I am grateful to Joe Uris for providing me with a copy of his dissertation, "Trouble in River City: An Analysis of an Urban Vice Probe." This study explores attitudes and responses to crime in Portland in the mid-fifties.

While the entire book has been shaped by my reading of scores of abortion trial transcripts, Chapter 8 explicitly incorporates details of a number of trials conducted all over the country in the postwar decades. Chapter 9 again uses material from Ruth Barnett's memoir as well as her prison diaries. It draws on letters to the Oregon State Legislature from citizens eager for abortion reform, and most important, uses material from Ruth Barnett's final trial in 1966. The transcripts of Ruth's trials in 1966 exist because only following these did the abortionist appeal her convictions.

BIBLIOGRAPHY

BOOKS

Abbott, Carl. *Portland: Planning, Politics, and Growth in a Twentieth-Century City*. Lincoln: University of Nebraska Press, 1983.

Barnett, Ruth. *They Weep on My Doorstep*. Beaverton, OR: Halo Publishers, 1969.

Bates, Jerome E. and Edward S. Zawadski. *Criminal Abortion: A Study in Medical Sociology*. Springfield, IL: Charles Thomas Publishers, 1964.

Bishop, Leonard. *Creep Into Thy Narrow Bed*. New York: The Dial Press, 1954.

Blake, Nelson M. *The Road to Reno*. New York: MacMillan, 1962.

Bromberg, Walter. *Crime and the Mind: An Outline of Psychiatric Criminology*. New York: Lippincott, 1948.

Calderone, Mary S., ed. *Therapeutic Abortion in the United States*. New York: Harper and Brothers, 1958.

Chesler, Ellen. *A Woman of Valor: Margaret Sanger and the Birth Control Movement in America*. New York: Simon and Schuster, 1992.

Davis, Nanette. *From Crime to Choice: The Transformation of Abortion in America*. Westport, CT: Greenwood Press, 1985.

de Beauvoir, Simone. *The Second Sex*. New York: Knopf, 1953.

Donner, James. *Women in Trouble: The Truth About Abortion in America*. Derby, CT: Monarch Books, 1959.

Dr. X as told to Lucy Freeman. *The Abortionist*. Garden City, NY: Doubleday & Co., 1962.

Dunbar, Flanders. *Psychiatry in the Medical Specialities*. New York: McGraw Hill, 1959.

Gordon, Linda. *Women's Body, Women's Right: Birth Control in America*. New York: Grossman, 1976.

Hall, Robert E., ed. *Abortion in A Changing World*, Vol 1. New York: Columbia University Press, 1970.

Heilbrun, Carolyn G. *Writing a Woman's Life*. New York: Ballantine Books, 1988.

Kesselman, Amy. *Fleeting Opportunities: Women Shipyard Workers in Portland and Vancouver during World War II and Reconversion*. Albany, NY: SUNY Press, 1990.

Keve, Paul W. *Prison, Probation or Parole: A Probation Officer Reports*. Minneapolis: University of Minnesota Press, 1954.

Knudten, Richard D. *Crime in a Complex Society: An Introduction to Criminology*. Homewood, IL: The Dorsey Press, 1970.

Lacey, Robert. *Little Man: Meyer Lansky and the Gangster Life*. Boston: Little Brown, 1991.

Lader, Lawrence. *Abortion*. Indianapolis: Bobbs-Merrill, 1966.

Lait, Jack and Lee Mortimer. *U.S.A. Confidential*. New York: Crown, 1952.

Laxalt, Robert. *Nevada: A Bicentennial History*. New York: W.W. Norton, 1977.

Lee, Nancy Howell. *The Search for an Abortionist*. Chicago: University of Chicago Press, 1969.

Luker, Kristin. *Abortion and the Politics of Motherhood*. Berkeley: University of California Press, 1984.

Lundberg, Ferdinand and Marynia F. Farnham. *Modern Woman: The Lost Sex*. New York: Grosset and Dunlap, 1947.

MacColl, E. Kimbark. *The Growth of a City: Power and Politics in Portland, Oregon 1915–1950*. Portland, OR: The Georgian Press, 1976.

McLaren, Angus. *A Prescription for Murder: The Victorian Serial Killings of Dr. Thomas Neill Cream*. Chicago: The University of Chicago Press, 1993.

Miller, Patricia G. *The Worst of Times: Illegal Abortion—Survivors, Practitioners, Coroners, Cops, and Children of Women Who Died Talk About Its Horrors*. New York: HarperCollins Publishers, 1993.

Mohr, James C. *Abortion in America: The Origins and Evolution of National Policy*. New York: Oxford University Press, 1978.

Montgomery, David. *The Fall of the House of Labor: The Workplace, the State, and American Labor Activism, 1865–1925*. New York: Cambridge University Press, 1987.

Newman, Sidney H., Mildred B. Beck, and Sarah Lewit, eds. *Abortion Obtained and Denied: Research Perspectives*. New York: Population Council, 1971.

New York State Supreme Court, King's County. *A Presentment on the Suppression of Criminal Abortion by the Grand Jury for the Extraordinary Special and Trial Term*. New York: The Hamilton Press, 1941.

Olasky, Marvin. *The Press and Abortion, 1838–1988*. Hillsdale, NJ: Lawrence Erlbaum Associates Publishers, 1988.

Overstreet, Edmund W., ed. *Therapeutic Abortion and Sterilization*. New York: Harper and Row, 1964.

Petchesky, Rosalind Pollack. *Abortion and Women's Choice: The State, Sexuality, and Reproductive Freedom*. Boston: Northeastern University Press, 1990.

Reckless, Walter C. *The Crime Problem*. New York: Appleton-Century-Crofts, 1961.

Rosen, Harold. *Therapeutic Abortion*. New York: The Julian Press, 1954.

Schur, Edwin. *Crimes Without Victims: Deviant Behavior and Public Policy*. Englewood Cliffs, NJ: Prentice Hall, 1965.

Slovenko, Ralph, ed. *Sexual Behavior and the Law*. Springfield, IL: Charles Thomas Publishers, 1965.

Smith, David T., ed. *Abortion and the Law*. Cleveland, OH: The Press of Case Western Reserve University, 1967.

Solinger, Rickie. "Extreme Danger: Women Abortionists and Their Clients Before *Roe v. Wade*." In *Not June Cleaver: Women in Postwar America*, edited by Joanne Meyerowitz. Philadelphia: Temple University Press, 1994.

Solinger, Rickie. *Wake Up Little Susie: Single Pregnancy and Race Before Roe v. Wade*. New York: Routledge, 1992.

Susman, Warren I. *Culture as History: The Transformation of American Society in the Twentieth Century*. New York: Pantheon, 1984.

Taussig, Frederick. *Abortion, Spontaneous and Induced: Medical and Social Aspects*. St. Louis, MO: C.V. Mosby Co., 1936.

The Abortion Problem. Baltimore: Williams and Wilkins, 1944.

Wade, Carlson. *Butchers in Waiting: The Shocking Story of Abortion in the USA*. New York: Chariot, 1960.

West, Ray B., Jr. *Rocky Mountain Cities*. New York: W.W. Norton, 1949.

ARTICLES

Barno, Alex. "Criminal Abortion Deaths, Illegitimate Pregnancy Deaths, and Suicide in Pregnancy: Minnesota 1950–65." *American Journal of Obstetrics and Gynecology* 98 (June, 1967): 356–67.

Bolter, Sidney. "The Psychiatrists's Role in Therapeutic Abortion: The Unwitting Accomplice." *The American Journal of Psychiatry* 119 (September, 1962): 312–16.

Fisher, Russell S. "Criminal Abortion." *Journal of Criminal Law and Criminology* 42 (July-August, 1951): 242–49.

Friedman, Jacob H. "The Vagarity of Psychiatric Indications of Therapeutic Abortion." *American Journal of Psychotherapy* 16(April, 1962): 251–54.

Frost, Jack. "Abortion—Need for Legalized Abortion." *Journal of Criminal Law and Criminology* 29 (November, 1938): 596.

Gold, Edwin M., Carl L. Erhardt, Harold Jacobziner, and Frieda G. Nelson. "Therapeutic Abortions in New York City: A Twenty Year Review." *American Journal of Public Health* 55(July, 1965): 964–72.

Hall, Robert E. "The New York Abortion Survey." *American Journal of Obstetrics and Gynecology* 93(1965): 1182.

Hamlin, Anita. "Portland's New Mayor." *Independent Woman* 27 (August, 1948): 237–38.

Harrington, J.A. "Psychiatric Indications for the Termination of Pregnancy." *Practitioner* 185 (November, 1960): 654–58.

Heffernan, Roy J. and William A. Lynch. "What is the Status of Therapeutic Abortion in Medical Obstetrics?" *American Journal of Obstetrics and Gynecology* 66 (October, 1953): 335–45.

Henker, Fred O. III. "Abortion and Sterilization from Psychiatric and Medio-Legal Viewpoints." *Journal of the Arkansas Medical Society* (February, 1961): 368–73.

Ingram, James M., H.S.B. Treloar, G. Phillips Thomas, and Edward B. Rood. "Interruption of Pregnancy for Psychiatric Indications—A Suggested Method of Control." *Obstetrics and Gynecology* 29 (February, 1967): 251–55.

Israel, S. Leon. "Editorials: Therapeutic Abortion." *Postgraduate Medicine* 33 (June, 1963): 619–20.

Joffe, Carole. "Portraits of Three 'Physicians of Conscience': Abortion Before Legalization in the United States." *Journal of the History of Sexuality* 2 (July, 1991): 46–67.

Johnson, John. "Termination of Pregnancy on Psychiatric Grounds." *Medical Gynecology and Sociology* 1 (1966): 2–6.

Leavy, Zad and Jerome M. Kummer. "Criminal Abortion: Human Hardship and Unyielding Laws." *Southern California Law Review* 35(Winter, 1962): 123–48.

Leavy, Zad and Jerome M. Kummer. "Let's Talk About Abortions." *Police* (July-August, 1961): 15–16.

Lehfeldt, Hans. "Willfull Exposure to Unwanted Pregnancy: Psychological Explanations for Patient Failures in Contraception." *American Journal of Obstetrics and Gynecology* 78 (September, 1959): 661–65.

Levine, Arnold S. "The Problem of Psychiatric Disturbances in Relation to Therapeutic Abortion." *Journal of the Albert Einstein Medical Center* 6 (1958): 73–78.

Loth, Myrna and H. Close Hesseltine. "Therapeutic Abortion at the Chicago Lying-In Hospital." *American Journal of Obstetrics and Gynecology* 72 (August, 1956): 304–11.

Martin, John Bartlow. "Abortion." Parts 1–3. *Saturday Evening Post.* (May 20, 1961): 19ff; (May 27, 1961): 20ff; (June 3, 1961): 25ff.

"Maternal Mortality in Fifteen States." U.S. Children's Bureau, Publication No. 33, 1939.

May, Joseph. "Therapeutic Abortion in North Carolina." *North Carolina Medical Journal* 23 (December, 1962): 547–51.

Moore, J.G. and J.H. Randall. "Trends in Therapeutic Abortion: A Review of 137 Cases." *American Journal of Obstetrics and Gynecology* 63 (January, 1952): 28–40.

Neuberger, Maurine. "Portland's First Lady." *New York Times Magazine* (November 21, 1948): 33–34.

Packer, Herbert L. and Ralph J. Gampell. "Therapeutic Abortion: A Legal and Medical Problem." *Stanford Law Review* 11 (May, 1959): 417–55.

Pearse, Harry A. and Harold A. Ott. "Hospital Control of Sterilization and Therapeutic Abortion." *American Journal of Obstetrics and Gynecology* 60 (August, 1950): 285–301.

Pitzer, Paul. "Dorothy McCullough Lee: The Successes and Failures of 'Dottie-Do-Good'" *Oregon Historical Quarterly* (Spring, 1990): 5–44.

"Reflections of an Abortionist." *Family Planning* 16(1967): 51–55.

Rosenberg, Allan J. and Emmanuel Silver. "Suicide, Psychiatrists, and Therapeutic Abortion." *California Medicine* 102 (June, 1965): 407–11.

Russell, Keith P. "Changing Indications for Therapeutic Abortion: Twenty Years Experience at L.A. County Hospital." *Journal of the American Medical Association* (January 10, 1953): 108–11.

Savel, Lewis E. "Adjudication of Therapeutic Abortion and Sterilization." *Clinical Obstetrics and Gynecology* 7 (1964): 14–21.

Savel, Lewis E. and Irving K. Perlmutter. "Therapeutic Abortion and Sterilization Committee: A Three Year Experience." *American Journal of Obstetrics and Gynecology* 80 (December, 1960): 1192–99.

Scherman, Quinten. "Therapeutic Abortion." *Obstetrics and Gynecology* 11 (March, 1958): 325–35.

Solinger, Rickie. "A Complete Disaster: Abortion and the Politics of Hospital Abortion Committees, 1950–1970." *Feminist Studies* 19 (Summer, 1993): 241–68.

Southeimer, Morton. "Abortion in American Today." *Women's Home Companion* (October, 1955): 44ff.

Star, Jack. "One Million A Year: The Growing Tragedy of Abortion." *Look* (October 19, 1965): 151ff.

"The Abortion Menace." *Ebony* (January, 1951): 21ff.

"The Abortion Racket: What Should be Done?" *Newsweek* (August 15, 1960): 51.

Tietze, Christopher. "Abortion as a Cause of Death." *American Journal of Public Health* 38 (October, 1948): 1434–41.

Tulkoff, Myer S. "Legal and Social Control of Abortion." *Kentucky Law Review* 40 (May, 1952): 410–16.

"When a Lady Runs the Town." *The Ladies Home Journal* (January, 1952): 49ff.

Woodside, Moya. "Attitudes of Women Abortionists." *Howard Journal.* 11 (1962): 93–111.

PORTLAND DOCUMENTS

Portland City Council Minutes: June 28, 1951; July 5, 1951; July 10, 1951; November 17, 1955; June 2, 1966. Portland City Archives.

"City Club Report on Law Enforcement in Portland and Multnomah County" (1948). Copy on file at the City Club, Portland, Oregon.

The Vollmer Report (1948). Portland City Archives.

St. James, Margaret. "The Abortionist's Daughter." Unpublished manuscript.

The Conscience of a City: The City Club of Portland. Portland: City Club, 1966.

Papers of State Senator Victor Atiyeh, Oregon Historical Society, Portland, Oregon.

Uris, Joseph. "Trouble in River City: An Analysis of an Urban Vice Probe." Ph.D. thesis, Portland State University, 1981.

INTERVIEWS

Margaret St. James. Interview with author. Ocala, Florida, June 21–23, 1992; Portland, Oregon, Nov. 8–10, 1992.

Dorothy Taylor. Telephone conversation with author, July 12, 1992.

Rolla Crick. Interview by Judy Lewis, 1992. Transcript supplied by Judy Lewis; telephone conversation with author, Jan. 22, 1994.

NEWSPAPERS

The Oregonian, 1940–1970.

The Oregon Journal, 1940–1970.

The Los Angeles Times, 1936.

The Reno Evening Gazette, 1940.

The Wichita Beacon, 1952, 1954.

The New York Times, abortion- and birth control-related articles 1935–1975.

TRIAL TRANSCRIPTS

TRANSCRIPTS RELATED TO RUTH BARNETT AND REGINALD RANKIN

People of the State of California v. R.L Rankin et al. (1936). Transcript in California State Archives, Sacramento.

People of the State of California v. Laura K. Miner, Nedra Montana Cordon, and Josephine M. Page (1949). Transcript in California State Archives, Sacramento.

State of Nevada v. Cushing et al. (1940). Preliminary examination. Transcript in Reno Courthouse.

State of Oregon v. Ruth Barnett (1966) #15959. Transcript in Oregon State Archives, Salem.

State of Oregon v. Ruth Barnett (1966) #15870. Transcript in Oregon State Archives, Salem.

ADDITIONAL TRANSCRIPTS

People of the State of California v. Sophie Alvarez (1945). Transcript in California State Archives, Sacramento.

State of New Jersey v. Hazel King (1945). Transcripts in New Jersey State Library, Trenton.

State of New Jersey v. Boyd and Cawthan (1947). Transcript in New Jersey State Library, Trenton.

People of the State of California v. May Ramsey (1947). Transcript in California State Archives, Sacramento.

State of California v. Geraldine Rhoades (1948). Transcript in California State Archives, Sacramento.

State of California v. Virginia Macias Garcia (1948). Transcript in California State Archives, Sacramento.

People of the State of California v. Alta Anderson, Mae Rodley and Gertrude Jenkins (1948). Transcript in California State Archives, Sacramento.

State of South Carolina v. Ida Steadman (1948). Transcript in University of South Carolina Law Library, Columbia.

People of the State of California v. Alta Anderson et al. (1949). Transcript in California State Archives, Sacramento.

State of Missouri v. Sophie Celine Miller (1951). Transcript in Missouri Supreme Court Library, Jefferson City.

State of California v. Lena Califro and Andrew Mareck (1952). Transcript in California State Archives, Sacramento.

People of the State of California v. Mickey Vosburg and Marie Vosburg (1953). Transcript in California State Archives, Sacramento.

State of Missouri v. Ida Lillian Hacker (1954). Transcript in Missouri Supreme Court Library, Jefferson City.

State of Louisiana v. Electra Dore (1955). Transcript in New Iberia Courthouse.

State of North Carolina v. Lucille Roper Furley (1956). Transcript in North Carolina State Supreme Court Law Library, Raleigh.

State of New Jersey v. Eva Muzynska, Irene Musconsky, Walter Musconsky, and William Sudol (1956). Transcript in New Jersey State Library, Trenton.

People of the State of California v. Vera Odmann and Stanley Odmann (1957). Transcript in California State Archives, Sacramento.

State of Missouri v. Fraulein Scown (alias Judy Anderson) (1957). Transcript in Missouri Supreme Court Library, Jefferson City.

State of California v. Esther Clemons (1959). Transcript in California State Archives, Sacramento.

People of the State of California v. Petra Virgil (1959). Transcript in California State Archives, Sacramento.

People of the State of California v. Ruth Bawden (1960). Transcript in California State Archives, Sacramento

People of the State of California v. Ester Clemons (1960). Transcript in California State Archives, Sacramento.

State of North Carolina v. Geneva Phifer Hoover and Florence Stallworth (1960). Transcript in North Carolina State Supreme Court Law Library, Raleigh.

Faye Wasserman, Probation hearing, March 27, 1962. Transcript in New Jersey State Library, Trenton.

ADDITIONAL TRIALS

Griffrida v. the State of Georgia, 7 SE 34 (1940).

State of North Carolina v. Forte, 23 SE 2d 842 (1943).

Smith v. the State of Oklahoma, 175 P 2d 348 (1946).

State of North Carolina v. Jordon, 42 SE 2d 674 (1947).

State of Missouri v. Seddon, 208 SW 2d 212 (1948).

State of New Jersey v. Lillian Del Gobbo Vince, 67 A 2d 141 (1949).

Beigun v. the State of Georgia, 58 SE 2d 149 (1950).

Roberta Jarquin v. the State of Texas, 232 SW 2d 736 (1950).

Eva Hodges Housman v. the State of Texas, 230 SW 2d 541 (1950).

Soldaat v. the State of Georgia, 57 SE 2d 705 (1950).

People of Louisiana v. Allen, 231 P 2d 896 (1951).

People of the State of Illinois v. Helen Stanko, 95 NE 2d 861 (1951).

Adams et al. v. the State of Maryland, 88 A 2d 566 (1952).

Ruth Hutson et al. v. the State of Maryland, 96 A 2d 593 (1953).

State of Ohio v. Mary Paige, 120 NE 2d 504 (1954).

Emma Cortez v. the State of Texas, 275 SW 2d 123 (1954).

People of Illinois v. Mary Murawski, 117 NE 2d 88 (1954).

Clara Mayberry v. the State of Texas, 271 SW 2d 635 (1954).

Commonwealth of Pennsylvania v. Dorothea G. Willard, 116 A 2d 751 (1955).

Maria Wasy v. the State of Indiana, 123 NE 2d 462 (1955).

State of Missouri v. Ida Lillian Hacker, 291 SW 2d 155 (1956).

People of the State of Illinois v. Catherine Heidman, 144 NE 2d 580 (1957).

State of Texas v. Mary Martinez Romero, 308 SW 2d 49 (1957).

L.D. Parnell v. the State of Texas, 312 SW 2d 506 (1958).

State of Kentucky v. Anna Danzell, 312 SW 2d 354 (1958).

Carrie Bell Phillips v. the State of Mississippi, 123 So. 2d 499 (1960).

People of the State of California v. John L. Flynn, 217 Cal. Reptr. 2d 289 (1961).

People v. Florita Gomez, 194 NE 2d 299 (Illinois, 1963).

Jesse Catching v. the State of Texas, 364 SW 2d 691 (1963).

People of New York State v. Nan Lovell, 242 NYS 2d 958 (1963).

State of Minnesota v. Josephine Delores Zecher, 128 NW 2d 83 (1964).

Rodriguez et al. v. the State of Florida, 183 So. 2d 656 (1966).

Minnie Lee Webster v. the State of Tennessee, 425 SW 2d 799 (1968).

ACKNOWLEDGMENTS

It is difficult for me to understand how I could have had a good time working on a book about injustice and danger. But the fact is, writing this book was fascinating and completely engaging from start to finish. This was partly due to the relatives, friends, and colleagues who helped in various ways.

First I'd like to thank my mother, Janet Solinger, and my sister, Martha Solinger, each of whom assisted me in developing resources and contacts that were very important as I began work on this project. My sister, Dorie Solinger, was, as always, a scholarly inspiration.

As an independent scholar, my contact with other historians is much sparser than I'd like, but a number of far-flung colleagues were kind and helpful while I worked on this book. Elaine Tyler May, Joanne Meyerowitz, Amy Kesselman, Rayna Rapp, Erika Doss, and Carole Joffe all responded to my work with interest and either raised or answered important questions about the fifties, abortion, politics, culture, and medicine. Amy and Carole both gave me information about Ruth Barnett at a defining moment in this project, and Erika helped me look more carefully at the Portland newspapers.

I was very lucky to get top-quality research assistance where it was important. Hannah Fox in Eugene was terrific at finding what I needed in various Oregon repositories. Rick Pillar in Portland and Kristin Iverson in Denver were likewise very helpful. Victoria Johnson in California was organized, timely, and sent me just what I was hoping for. I was most fortunate to find Jackie Ruffin in Reno; her assistance in locating evidence of a brief event in that city more than half a century ago was invaluable.

My friends, who are also far-flung, offered a variety of riches. Marty Karlow allowed me long-distance access to his superb reference library. Sight unseen, Sandy Polishuk agreed to take me in when I went to Portland, and she proved to be a perfect host, a friend, and a source. For years, Jonathan Birnbaum has kept me supplied with relevant news clippings, for which I am very grateful. Elizabeth Baker, Lee Bell, and Amy Kesselman offered support on a regular basis. Closer to home, Patti and Sylvie Gassaway are by now my dear, old friends. I believe Patti knows how much I appreciate her willingness to listen while I read pages of my manuscript to her over the phone. I deeply appreciate Kay Obering's respect for this material and her artistic reconception of Ruth's world. Jennifer Heath's warm enthusiasm, Naomi Harris's sisterly affection, and David Barsamian's friendship as I worked on this book were all important to me.

The Rockefeller Foundation and the American Council of Learned Societies both supported this project as I was beginning it. I was, therefore, able to buy all the trial transcripts my heart desired, go on the trips I needed to take, and pay people in other cities to help me when I needed to stay home.

I would not have been able to write the book I have if I had not found Maggie St. James, the daughter of Ruth Barnett. (I have Carole Joffe to thank for providing the clue to her whereabouts.) Maggie, in her late seventies when I first went to see her in Ocala, Florida, is a woman of enormous spirit and generosity. She also has the ability to trust a stranger and to tell a visitor an almost endless string of excellent stories. I am deeply grateful to Maggie for allowing me into her life and sharing her mixed bag of treasures with me.

I am very glad that Dorothy Taylor decided to tell me about her work in the Stewart Clinic with Ruth Barnett; the conversation was extremely helpful. Judy Lewis's willingness to share resources was especially welcome; I admire her sleuthing and enterprising spirit. I was absolutely thrilled to speak to Rolla Crick, the Portland newspaperman. My stack of forty-year-old clippings under his byline had become sanctified sources; I could hardly believe my ears when he called me to talk about Ruth Barnett.

Over the years I've lived in Boulder, I have gotten to know Dr. Warren Hern, a valiant, rock-willed abortion provider. Warren and his colleagues—brave, determined practitioners—are heroic as they stick to their work despite the threats, because they believe that women must have the right to determine their own lives. I appreciate the fact that Warren recognizes me as a comrade, and I sometimes imagine how much he and Ruth Barnett would have to talk about.

Joyce Seltzer and Cherie Weitzner at the Free Press did magnificent editorial work on this book. I am enormously impressed by the number of infelicities they expunged. It was a pleasure to work with both of them.

My family, Zachary Leeds, Nell Geiser, and especially Jim Geiser (who encouraged me to use our dawn treks up Mt. Sanitas to go on about Ruth Barnett) have often let me know that they believe in my work. I thank them here for that. It is a wonderful thing to live with justice-loving feminists.